"It is better to light one candle than to curse the darkness"

This book has been prepared for the average citizen: the man in the street, the housewife in her home, the farmer, the stenographer, the plumber, the doctor, the lawyer, the student, the truck driver, the actor, the writer, the corner grocer. It shows over and over what one person can do to protect the God-given rights of all citizens.

You can find in it stories of what other people, like you, have done to strengthen the greatest government in the world.

The story boils down to this: *"Either you run your government or government will run you."* It can be as good or as bad as you, individually, permit it to be. Government is your responsibility, a direct and personal responsibility. You cannot delegate that obligation or pass it on to others.

The future holds great hope if enough individuals like you, who believe in your own power for good, under God, make it your business to see that government on every level is your servant . . . and not your master.

BY JAMES KELLER

Government Is Your Business
Careers That Change Your World
One Moment Please!
Three Minutes a Day
You Can Change the World
Men of Maryknoll

Government Is
Your Business

BY JAMES KELLER, M.M.

Permabooks
A Division of Doubleday & Company, Inc.
Garden City, New York

FOREWORD

This book is not intended for the experts. Nor will it make anyone an expert on government. It has been respectfully prepared for the average citizen; the man in the street, the housewife in her home, the farmer, the stenographer, the plumber, the doctor, the lawyer, the student, the truck driver, the actor, the writer, and the corner grocer. All of these, with all of the rest of us, constitute the government of the United States. Primarily, his book was written to remind each citizen of his own personal, individual responsibility toward his government.

All government receives its authority from God through the people, or, as Jefferson put it, "through the consent of the governed." Therefore the responsibility of government resides first in the citizen: it comes from him and it should be directed toward him. It is his job to see that it does.

Those who chance to read this work will soon discover that it emphasizes and re-emphasizes elementary ideas and suggestions that are neither new nor breath-taking. They are as old as the hills; yet they have done much to bring "peace on earth to men of good will." Coupled with an abiding faith in the goodness of God, these ideas have proved down through the ages that they belong in the formula for successful living.

To You in Particular

This book is not addressed to people in general. It is addressed to you in particular. Its purpose is to re-awaken your sense of importance as an individual and to stress the importance of the role that you personally can play in changing the world for the better. If you begin with these understandings, you will develop your imagination and resourcefulness in tackling even the worst situation.

Almighty God has endowed you individually with a certain power that has been given to no other person. He has also given you a mission in life to perform, a mission assigned to no one but you. If you neglect to fulfill the responsibility that He has placed in your hands for the peace of the world, everyone else will suffer by it. In like manner, you will suffer by the failure of a friend or neighbor to discharge his obligation toward God and his country.

In choosing "Government Is Your Business" as a title, we propose to focus attention on the need for a universal sense of personal responsibility and individual initiative in order to preserve and develop our nation. Our belief is as simple as this: If most Americans can be made to feel individually responsible for their government, the general improvement of government is more likely to result.

You Decide for Yourself

We have endeavored to limit the scope of this volume to emphasis on basic moral principles and suggestions on how those principles may be applied in everyday life. It is not our business to take sides on political issues. We believe it best that each individual discover for himself how, where, and when he should make his influence felt. In keeping with the Christopher thesis, we stress positive constructive action by the individual. Negative criticism is usually a waste of time and effort.

So we leave it to you to stand on your own two feet; to make your own decisions; to join or support any political party you like; to vote as you see fit; to take whatever stand you consider best; and to decide yourself which organizations you will join to add your voice to that of others. It is between you and God.

A World in Turmoil

Since 1914, when World War I began, most of the world has
been in constant turmoil. The gigantic forces of war, of
pestilence, of hunger and uprooting, have driven mankind
into a state of mental and emotional upheaval which has not
yet settled. Only the older Americans can remember a prewar world that was stable, where values were fixed—right was
right, and wrong was wrong. Under the battering of huge
forces, the individual tended to question his values and to
forget his code of living. For most Americans living today, it
seems that the world has always been either at war, in an inflation, or in a depression. Living on an even keel has become
for many but a dim memory in the past.

Before the American invasion of North Africa an American
diplomat went ashore by submarine to get the latest information on political conditions as an essential part of the invasion. In conversation with a French political leader in Algiers,
the American asked what the general political climate of
North Africa was. With a sad smile the Frenchman replied,
quoting a famous American: "Most of us here lead lives of
quiet desperation."

Much of that desperation can be blamed on the weakness
or corruption of governments the world over. But more of it
can be blamed on the failure of the average good citizen to
meet his responsibilities toward government. The greatest
strength of those dedicated to evil lies in the indifference of
those dedicated to good. Many times it has been said: "While
the good people have been taking care of themselves, the
wrongdoers have been taking care of everyone else."

While the good people have been slackening their grip on
government, the evildoers have been tightening theirs. As a
result, those who are morally corrupt and subversive have
advanced while the great body of Americans have tended to
retreat. Wherever moral breakdown has occurred in public
administration the world over, its roots will be found in the
breakdown of the individual's life.

If we judge it correctly, this is the present state of the world; an advance by evil and a simultaneous retreat by good forces. This is but one phase, the current phase, of a war between good and bad that has been going on down through the ages. It is by no means the whole story of that war, and should not be mistaken for the whole story just because it is currently with us.

Hopeful Outlook

Already we see hopeful signs in this seemingly depressing picture. On all sides in America, voices are raised for a higher standard of morality in government. They come from the leaders of all political parties; from high-level and low-level officials in government; from the homes, the churches, and the schools. This is a rising tide, and a tide that can eventually push back the forces of evil. Our purpose in this book is to point out to the individual some ways in which he might contribute to that rising tide.

First, let us say at once that conditions in America are much better than most Americans think they are. While all levels of government show some defects, these defects are not so serious that they cannot be cured. Secondly, the individual citizen still has the God-given rights guaranteed by our Constitution. The power to better our present situation lies in the exercise of those rights. By exercising his functions as a citizen, any American can strengthen public administration. He can also restore vigor and vitality to those sections of government which seem to need new force.

The Uses of Criticism

If you are a worker in government, you may have experienced the feeling that your work is often neither understood nor appreciated. You know all too well the hackneyed unfair greeting; "Well, still feeding at the public trough, I see."

If you work outside government, you may have uttered such a remark to a friend or relative in government service.

At best, it is a senseless complaint—false, hurtful, and by no means the rounded criticism you might mean it to be. Within the bounds of reason, criticism can be beneficial. To be helpful, it is not prudent to say: "Don't do it that way!"

If you want to help, try saying: "Why not try it this way, instead of the way you have been doing it?"

At least the latter way shows, first, that you appreciate the problem; secondly, that you have devoted some thought to solving it; and thirdly, that your suggestion is meant to be helpful. Too many are pointing out what is wrong with America, and too few are emphasizing what is right with it. Negative criticism generates much heat but little light. If we devoted more time to improving and less to disapproving, we would be well on the road to peace.

"Let George Do It"

Our chief fault as individual citizens is that many of us have put aside our duty. "Let George do it" seems to be the general attitude. It has become habitual and perhaps fashionable to disdain government as something beneath us. Today the chief obstacle to good government is the widespread belief that it is a job for someone else, not for us. Many of us have dropped into the dangerous belief that others should make the sacrifices for good government while we do nothing more than sit on the side lines and complain about how the doers are doing.

Jack Johnson, the great Negro heavyweight boxing champion, nailed the flaw in this attitude during his championship fight with Jess Willard way back in 1915. As the bout was fought under Havana's blazing summer sun, a spectator at the ringside kept up a running fire of abuse at Johnson. He criticized Johnson's style, his ancestry, his color, and finally his courage in the ring. Between rounds Johnson leaned over the ropes, smiled, and said: "Man, you're down there talking. I'm up here fighting."

For Democracy to Survive

Under a democracy each citizen forms a component part of his government. The democracy can survive only by the active participation of its citizens. To be "down there talking" is not enough. All of us have to be "up here fighting" at least part of the time.

Active citizenship involves minor inconveniences such as registering and voting in elections. No good citizen would recommend that his vote be abolished. Yet he abolishes it himself if he fails to register and vote. Close to half of the eligible voters in this country did not vote in the last presidential election. By their neglect, they might have abandoned their form of government to those who would exploit it. They leave the voting to others, and thus play into the hands of the enemy. By their sin of omission, the non-voters may do the country more harm than a carload of Communists. The only cure for apathy and indifference is activity and interest. The very survival of democracy depends on your activity and the activity of every other person like you.

Another source of our present trouble lies in our forgetting the fundamental spiritual principles on which this country was founded. Without them, our country cannot reach its ultimate peak of development.

Today the biggest battle centers on the worth of the individual. The tradition that every human being is made in God's image is neglected by many Americans, even though it has come down to us through centuries of Christianity and Judaism. In religion, as well as in government, many erroneously believe that their small voices count for nothing. This belief leads readily to the armchair philosophy of the man who does nothing because he thinks his efforts do not count. As a last step, he uses comfort to stifle conscience.

Of one hundred and fifty million Americans approximately one hundred million either belong to no church or have forsaken any formal practice of religion. That amounts roughly to two thirds of the population. While deriving all the benefits of Christianity, they do little to perpetuate it. Few of them have any clear idea of where they came from, why they are here, or where they are going. Lacking knowledge, they also lack the courage that knowledge gives. They think in terms of the body and not of the spirit. The net result is that they become more and more confused, more and more afraid.

The Need to Relearn

Someone once said: "Courage is fear that has gone to school." What does that mean, when we analyze it? It means simply that fear can be largely overcome by knowledge.

Knowledge and experience do much to dissipate fear. Then courage and faith may enter. As soldiers of the Lord, Christ-bearers face a thrilling challenge to carry their faith, hope, and charity into the market place and help those who know not the Way, the Truth, and the Life. As apostles of good, they can far outdo the apostles of evil. By blending and integrating the divine into the human, they can go far in preserving the soul of democracy for those who come after them.

Religion and Liberty Go Together

More than a century ago the scholar De Tocqueville said: *"The Americans combine the notions of Christianity and liberty so intimately in their minds that it is impossible to make them conceive the one without the other."*

Freedom in our nation began on this principle. If America loses sight of the Divine Source of its strength, it will risk the loss of the liberty we all cherish so dearly. Enemies of decent government the world over know that the more quickly and completely they remove the idea of God from the hearts and minds of men, the more easily they can enslave free peoples. That fact in itself should inspire every decent American who believes in God to see that His spirit and truth are maintained in all human activity, especially in government.

The home, the church, and the school should join in convincing Americans that government is an honorable calling, entitled to respect rather than derision and abuse. The times call for a rededication to godliness and decency in public life. If these qualities are absent, it is the home, the church, and the school that suffer most by their absence. For a government which fails to protect people and families in their relation with God tends to impair proper functioning of the home, the church, and the school.

The story boils down to this: *Either you run your own government or it will run you.* It can be as good or as bad as you, individually, permit it to be. Government is your responsibility, a direct and personal responsibility. You cannot delegate that obligation or pass it on to others.

The future holds great hope if enough individuals like you, who believe in your own power for good, under God, make it your business to see that government on every level is your servant . . . and not your master.

Whatever merit this book may have is due in no small measure to countless competent people who have given us the benefit of their experience and advice, and who in many other ways, large and small, generously assisted in its preparation. Like each of you, these people are individuals. Each gave of himself what he could toward a goal aimed at the common good. This book, therefore, reflects their individual interest in it, their sense of purpose channeled toward it, and their combined desire for improvement. To each and all of them we are deeply grateful.

James Keller

THE CHRISTOPHERS
FATHER JAMES KELLER, M.M., DIRECTOR
18 EAST 48TH ST., NEW YORK 17, N.Y.

EXPLAINING THE CHRISTOPHERS

The word "Christopher" is derived from the Greek word *"Christophoros,"* meaning "Christ-bearer." Individually and personally, the Christopher carries Christ into the market place. By prayer and work he strives to bring Christian principles especially into the vital fields that touch the lives of all people: (1) education, (2) government, (3) writing, and production end of television, movies, and radio, as well as newspapers, books, and magazines, (4) labor, (5) social service, and (6) library work. Much of the tragedy of our times is due to the fact that godless elements have swarmed into these same spheres, while the followers of Christ have too often remained on the side lines, doing little more than saving themselves. Complaining, criticizing, negative analyzing will accomplish little. Positive, constructive action is needed.

Features of the Christopher Approach

1. NO ORGANIZATION. There are no memberships, no meetings, no dues—no organization beyond Christopher headquarters at 18 East 48th St., New York 17, N.Y.
2. LIMITATIONS. The Christopher movement confines itself to one phase of a big problem. It is merely an attempt to supplement, not replace, basic and essential organization. It restricts itself to emphasis on primary truths while recognizing the importance of all the truths that flow from them.
3. THE DISTINGUISHING MARK. Love of all people for the love of God should be the distinguishing characteristic of anyone who would play the role of a Christopher. In no case should there be a return of hate for hatred. Those who would be bearers of Christ must be ready for all the ingratitude, suffering, rebuffs, and countless disappointments which the Master encountered. Each must strive to be kind while still remaining firm, to be able to disagree without becoming disagreeable. *"Love your enemies: do good to them that hate you: and pray for them that persecute and calumniate you"* (Matthew 5:44). With this motivation, the most difficult task can become a labor of love.
4. EMPHASIS ON THE INDIVIDUAL. Because God has im-

planted in every human being a desire to be creative, to make a certain contribution to the peace of the world that no one else can make, the Christopher approach stresses individual initiative. Our policy is to point out elementary principles and then leave it to each person to work out his own method of incarnating the divine into the human. This allows for greater freedom, within reasonable limits, and encourages that element of originality, imagination, and enterprise which is possible only when the individual feels a personal responsibility in changing the world for the better.

5. NO PLACEMENT BUREAU. Despite repeated requests, we have purposely refrained from setting up any placement bureau. We feel that it is better for each to go into a job of his own choosing, when and where he likes. Furthermore, we are convinced that it is frequently necessary, in the missionary approach of the Christopher movement, for such a person to go through the difficult and often discouraging ordeal of finding an opening in a career that counts. God blesses the very effort of trying.

6. DEPENDENCE ON GOD. By the very nature of our work, a deep conviction of dependence on God, of being an instrument, however unworthy, in the hands of God, is absolutely essential. The closer one is to Christ, the more he is bound to accomplish. Competence is needed, to be sure. But ability without godliness can be a great danger even for those who have dedicated themselves to a good cause.

7. OUR ONLY CONTACT. At present several million people throughout America are at least acquainted with the Christopher idea. Our aim is merely to suggest and encourage. We leave it to each individual to find out for himself whatever special formation or training is needed. Our only contact with all of them is through Christopher talks, literature, books, and moving pictures. Christopher books (*You Can Change the World, Three Minutes a*

Day, One Moment Please!, Careers That Change Your World, as well as *Government Is Your Business*) have already had a total circulation of nearly a million copies. The first Christopher movie, *You Can Change the World,* has been seen by nearly three million people. Plans are under way to produce twenty-nine other movies.

8. CAREER GUIDANCE SCHOOLS. Any group may start a Career Guidance School, even on a small scale, and use a Christopher book as a basic text. However, entire responsibility for and control of each school rests with those who undertake its establishment. All that we can authorize is the material that we publish in our Christopher books or literature.

9. NO CHRISTOPHER CLUBS. Because we restrict ourselves to developing individual initiative and personal responsibility, *we do not authorize Christopher clubs or groups of any kind,* or the use of the Christopher name in connection with any project that has resulted from the Christopher idea. We leave it to each to decide whether he will work alone or join any one of hundreds of excellent organizations. Each individual speaks and acts for himself, not for the Christopher movement.

10. FINANCIAL SUPPORT. In keeping with our policy of no memberships, no subscriptions, no dues, we merely announce our needs, while soliciting funds from no one. We depend entirely on God to provide, through voluntary contributions, the five hundred thousand dollars a year now needed for our various Christopher projects.

11. THE CHRISTOPHER POSITION. The purpose of the Christophers is to restore the love and truth of Christ to the market place. Begun under Catholic inspiration, the Christopher movement has the voluntary support of hundreds of thousands of Americans of all faiths and in all walks of life. Nearly a half million of such people have individually requested that they be sent our monthly *Christopher News Notes,* which are available to all, free of charge.

Inasmuch as the movement has no memberships and no meetings, each person participates in the work of the Christophers as far as he can and will.

An outstanding example of the widespread interest in the Christopher movement was seen in the spontaneous support given by well-known movie stars and personalities in producing the first Christopher movie, *You Can Change the World,* which tells the story of the movement. The following gave their services freely: Eddie "Rochester" Anderson, Jack Benny, Ann Blyth, Bing Crosby, Paul Douglas, Irene Dunne, William Holden, Bob Hope, and Loretta Young, as well as Leo McCarey, director, and William Perlberg, producer.

I. IT'S YOUR COUNTRY TOO!

I. IT'S YOUR COUNTRY TOO!

1 WHAT ARE YOU DOING ABOUT IT?

Either you run your government—or government runs you!
This is one country where you still have a free choice. When
things are in a bad way, it's partly your fault. When things are
right and decent, it's to your credit.

Here in America every two or four years we can elect
new officials when we think a change is needed. Long before
candidates' names are nominated we can find out from our
district clubs who is being considered and whether the best
men are being brought forward. We can praise when the
choice is right, protest when it is wrong.

The country you live in is the greatest successful experiment
in government by the people that the world has known. Whose
business is it? It's yours!

Curiously enough, people from abroad often show keener
appreciation of its benefits than those born here.

Early on a September morning a few years ago a group
of us stood on the deck of the *Queen Elizabeth* as she moved
slowly up the Hudson River toward her berth in New York
Harbor. Near by was a well-educated German woman of middle age who seemed more eager than any other passenger to
set foot on American soil. Excited over her first visit to this
country, her beaming smile told the world how glad she was
that she had been given permission to remain here for the
rest of her days. So eager was she to join in her small way in
the peace and security with which the United States is blessed

that she was up long before dawn to catch her first glimpse
of the coast line. While the chugging tugs hooted and whis-
tled, she could hardly contain her enthusiasm. At first most
of her fellow passengers viewed her eagerness with mild
amusement. They tried to convey the impression that arriving
in this country was an old story to them. But her excitement
was so contagious that even the most reserved caught something of it.

There was one exception. A college student returning to
this country after a summer of study abroad took a cynical
view of her enthusiasm about the United States. He proceeded
to throw a little cold water on her eager spirit. In conversation
with the German-born woman, he emphasized certain defects
of the American system of government. Not once did he say
anything good about it.

This woman, thrilled with the prospect of a new home in
America, listened patiently to the student's detailed account
of what he thought was wrong with America. Most of what
he said was not new to her. Before sailing she had studied
conditions here and had discussed them with her friends. She
had also talked to Americans in Europe about the strength and
weakness of the American system. Long ago she had decided
that the country's advantages far outweighed its disadvantages.
When the student finally finished his cynical tirade, the new
arrival gave him a smile that was both pleasant and patient.

"Thank you very much," she said. "But I honestly feel that
if America is twice as bad as you say it is, it is still twice
as good as any country I have ever heard of!"

More Appreciative

Perhaps all would not agree with her high estimate of the
United States. But she had a point, and that point was that
the privileges and advantages of America were far more striking to her than to the native-born Americans who surrounded
her on the ship's deck. Because of her attitude, every fellow
passenger who saw her was impressed with her appreciation.
Some had to admit that they had been somewhat blind to the

true merits of this country. One or two critics discovered that they had been selling America short in their own personal contacts, without quite meaning to do so.

Any country may be easily undermined if a majority of its people adopt the lazy attitude of exaggerating its faults and minimizing its virtues. This attitude leads in turn to a pessimistic outlook on the country and perhaps despair about its future.

In any country it is true that the evildoers are the flamboyant ones who are featured in most of the newspaper headlines. Since these are so spectacular in the public mind, we tend to forget the vastly larger number who serve the best interests of their country in creditable fashion. Citizens should remember that while the evildoer makes the headlines, the good citizen seldom does. This may be an injustice in life, but it is nevertheless a fact.

No Takers

Why is it that so few of those who denounce the United States night and day really want to leave this country when opportunity offers? That circumstance in itself is an illuminating tribute to American life.

One man we know became so disgusted with the hypocrisy of those who glorify Communism and condemn the American way that he offered to furnish a free one-way passage to Russia for anyone who believed the Russian way was better. His offer stood for quite a while, but he had no takers.

When Robert A. Vogeler, an American businessman, was released by the Communists after seventeen months in a Budapest prison, one of his first statements to American reporters was: "You never know what freedom means—until you lose it!"

Mr. Vogeler was quite ill from his long imprisonment, and the sudden shock of unexpected freedom was an added burden to his nervous system. Doctors forbade him to give interviews to newsmen, fearing that the pain of reliving his prison experiences would harm him. Friends counseled him to seek seclusion and rest until he got back on his feet. But he would not, could not rest until he had said what was uppermost in his thoughts.

"I have a message for my fellow Americans," he declared in a press interview. "I feel that every individual American should realize that what happened to me can happen to him. We must get busy and defend the right of a person to go where he wants to go and say what he wants to say; without hindrance by authorities or police. He should be able to go to bed at night with an easy feeling, not fearing that perhaps in the middle of the night he will be taken away from his family to prison.

"I think that is our mission now," Mr. Vogeler concluded forcefully. "That is the mission that God has given us to perform, so that we can live in peace, freedom and happiness."

Coming This Way

If we ever doubt the unparalleled advantages of life in the United States, we need only look at the millions trying desperately to gain entrance to the United States. Quota admissions from practically every country are filled for years to come. Most of these desperate people would gladly exchange their present existence for the life of the poorest American.

"America is the land of opportunity for all," they will tell you. "The air is free—a man can breathe."

Recently we read of a family that embarked from Estonia—behind the Iron Curtain—braving the dangers of an Atlantic crossing in an open sailboat to reach the freedom of these shores. If immigration restrictions should by some miracle vanish overnight, and those behind the Iron Curtain in Europe and Asia could pick the country of their choice, millions would set out like the Estonian family. They would flock to the United States from every corner of the globe. They would walk, run, swim, and use every conceivable means of transportation. They would come as stowaways, on rafts, in open boats, or any other way they could manage.

Because of the Past and the Future

If this book does nothing more than open the eyes of a few Americans to the precious heritage given them by a bountiful Providence, it will serve its purpose. We owe much to those who suffered and sacrificed to bring this country into being. Unlike us, they had to endure hostile savages, the killing cold in dead of winter, the ever-present dread of disease and wounds. We have the privilege of protecting America's God-given freedom, even for those among us who least appreciate it.

"The grass always looks greener in the other fellow's back yard" is an old saying. But America's back yard looks greener to most of the world. The real appreciation of this country comes from immigrants who have lived part of their lives elsewhere. They appreciate the contrast between their native countries and this country. We who live here know comparatively little about oppression, fear, or intimidation. We therefore tend to take our numerous benefits for granted. But not the immigrant—*he knows the difference!*

On our shoulders rests the great responsibility of preserving our precious heritage against enemies for the generations of Americans yet to be born. They have a future right to our inheritance, just as we have a present right to it.

The more this sense of responsibility is awakened in each individual, the more hope we can have for the future. By a curious paradox, the larger and more complex government becomes, the less responsibility does the average person feel toward it. In turn, that establishes a public apathy toward government that paves the way for mediocre or poor government.

A Big Difference

On April 1, 1950, the United States Census placed the population of the United States at 150,697,361 individuals. A short 160 years before, in 1790, this country consisted of 3,929,214 souls, living chiefly in rural areas and supported almost entirely by the soil.

Under the concept of democracy laid down by Thomas Jefferson almost everyone was a landowner. Jefferson believed that since most Americans owned land, ownership would give them an interest in the workings of their government. In his time it was easy for everyone, young and old, rich and poor, to feel that he could have a hand in shaping the destiny of the new country. Government was more personal, and closer to the people.

As the country's population increased, however, industrial development in great cities also grew. When the American became separated from a direct interest in the soil, his interest in government likewise suffered. Today we see hundreds of thousands so interested in making a living in the city that they have little time for their friends, let alone for their government.

Despite this, millions of Americans are buoyed up by their underlying conviction that as they are faithful to God, so will they be loyal to their country and their fellow men. With the Hebrew psalmist of old they could agree that:

"Unless the Lord build the house, they labour in vain that build it" (Ps. 126:1).

Conflicting Interests

As expanding America tended to force individuals into economic groups, these groups developed selfish interests. The dairy farmer wanted to produce his milk cheaply and sell it to the city dweller at a good price. The city dweller complained that milk was too high and blamed the farmer.

Pressure groups of all types today bedevil government on all levels. Each seeks its own good to the exclusion of all the others. People generally begin to display a selfish attitude toward government and concentrate on what they can get out of it. At the same time the voices of those who want to protect and improve their country tend to be drowned out in the babel of demands for special interests.

Sometimes those in high position become so overconcerned with the care of self that they dodge responsibilities in which they could render great service to the well-being of all.

An important corporation vice-president who really had something constructive to offer government "ducked" when he was asked to fill a high-level post in Washington. His only thought was fear that he might be misunderstood and mistreated if he became a federal official. He summed up his own attitude by saying: "I wouldn't take that abuse for anything."

Anyone can readily understand why men and women of good reputation hesitate to risk the unfair criticism that so often is the price of public service. But if a few should make up their minds to chance possible misunderstanding for the good of all, they might prevent the greater misery that is bound to come if our free institutions go by default.

Those already in government service need courage to go about their daily tasks while storms of criticism rage around them. Perhaps it is as a combat officer told his troops in the last World War:

"You will acquire combat maturity when you decide that not all of the enemy artillery shells are aimed at you personally."

Whether the criticism is general or direct, there is a growing feeling that there is too much criticism and not enough commendation for jobs well done. If this attitude persists, it can discourage able people who might otherwise enter government service.

One Person Taking a Stand

It refreshes and encourages us to see examples of how one person, by taking a firm stand, can turn the tide. Only fifty-five individuals took on the task of drafting the Constitution of the United States.[1] They assembled at Philadelphia in May 1787. When a few delegates showed desires to favor their

---

[1] The complete text of the Declaration of Independence, Constitution, and Bill of Rights is printed in the Appendix, page 332.

own sections of the country in preference to the national welfare, George Washington, president of the convention and delegate from Virginia, made a short, forceful speech. In it he took a challenging stand that should make all of us pause and reflect upon his words.

"If to please the people," he said, "we offer what we ourselves disapprove, how can we afterward defend our work? Let us raise a standard to which the wise and honest can repair. The event is in the hands of God."

He Woke Up

Only recently in San Francisco the simple courage of one young lady swung a man[2] from a lucrative career in business to a post in the State Department.

The two first met at dinner. The young man, a native of Boston, quickly got on the subject of "What's wrong with the government." He had nothing but criticism and faultfinding for those in government employ. His dinner companion let him talk himself out. Then, when he had wound up all his critical remarks about his own government, she smiled sweetly and said: "And what are *you* doing about it? It's your country too!"

Taken aback, he was at a loss for a reply. Her question made him realize that for years he had been complaining about bad government and exerting no effort for good government. For several months he tried to forget the question, but he could not rid his mind of it. "What are *you* doing about it?" kept coming back to him. Finally he realized that government was just as much his business as any American's. He saw that he had no right to ask others to devote their lives to it while he did nothing but complain. He forsook a promising business opening and took the State Department job to make what contribution he could. With his new attitude of service to his

[2]Personal names are used in relating incidents whenever the information has already been made public. In all other instances names have been withheld, usually at the request of the individuals concerned.

government, we can believe that his contribution will be substantial.

Whether you are a housewife, a farmer, a butcher, or a baker, the more you feel government is your business the more you will do to improve it. All of us can say:

"It is my country. And when my life ends, this country will be a little the better or a little the worse for my having lived in it."

Deep Conviction Needed

Faith is the important ingredient here. Faith in the country will keep you from feeling hopeless about it. Faith in God and in yourself will show the way. But you must decide for yourself what you will do and how you will do it. Oftentimes in performing your duties as a citizen you may feel frustrated and forsaken by all but Him. Abraham Lincoln once said:

"I have been driven many times to my knees by the overwhelming conviction that I had no place else to go."

But Lincoln did not stay on his knees. He got up, his faith fortified by prayer, and went on to perform faithfully the tasks set before him.

Faith in your Creator and loyalty to your country go hand in hand. A Presbyterian minister, the Reverend Benjamin F. Farber, noted this relationship recently when he said:

"No people has ever been known to endure long without a faith in God . . . With no vision or understanding of the moral and spiritual teaching that lie at the heart of a religious faith, there is bound to be a disregard for truth, honor, and justice . . . We cannot neglect and disobey God and His commandments without paying the price of a decadent nation."

You Are Important

Each individual is important in a democracy. Each has a mission to perform. Each can make an individual personal contribution to proper government which no one else can make. Those who fail, by omission, to do their bit may be more reprehensible in the sight of God than those actually working to destroy the nation. In order to survive, democracy needs the active participation of all who live under its benefits.

Pope Pius XII has repeatedly stressed that every citizen has a moral obligation to share in the responsibility of government. In his Christmas message of 1944 he said:

"Considering the extent and nature of the sacrifices demanded of all citizens, especially in our day when the activity of the State is so vast and decisive, the democratic form of government appears to many a postulate of nature imposed by reason itself."

In the average American there is a tremendous reservoir of good will waiting to be tapped. Sometimes only an encouraging word is required to start the flow of goodness. In daily life we see how much further a constructive suggestion carries us than complaint and criticism.

We can face the future with hope. With God's help, the world our children see will be a better world than the one we live in. Countries all over the globe look with hope to America. It is only logical that we should feel in ourselves the same confidence that they place in us. Our faith and hope in this country are the cornerstones of its foundation. Unless the foundation is kept strong, we cannot preserve and build America for the future.

2 ONE PERSON CAN DO MUCH

The Raritan River in New Jersey drains an area of approximately one thousand square miles in three counties and passes many villages, towns, and cities. Because of neglect, filth of all kinds was allowed to drift into this beautiful river. It became a disgrace to the countryside. For years a relentless effort was made by a group of citizens who organized to promote interest in cleaning up the Raritan. Many arguments were used to stir the public out of its apathy toward the problem. People were bombarded with reminders of what would happen if they didn't take steps to free the river of its impurities. They were warned that it was a menace to public health and that its present state of pollution would have an adverse effect on property values. Despite every effort over a long period of time, little progress was made in ridding the Raritan of its sewage.

One day a man walked into the office of General Robert Wood Johnson in New Brunswick, New Jersey, who headed the group which had inaugurated the valley-wide program to restore the Raritan River. This visitor said that he had heard of their attempts. He felt that he had one positive idea that would catch the interest of practically everybody and get more action out of them than a dozen negative warnings.

His one and only proposal was that if the people of the Raritan valley would clean up the river the frostfish would return. The frostfish is small but very tasty and formerly swam up the Raritan in the springtime. Most of the people in the towns and villages would feast on the delicacy of frostfish for the short season of ten days to two weeks.

This man said he was the president of the Izaak Walton League for New Jersey, a group devoted to the art of fishing. General Johnson, somewhat skeptical about the frostfish angle, became even more so when he found that in those years the entire New Jersey branch of the Izaak Walton League totaled only forty-six members and that only the three who made up the Middlesex County Chapter could be counted on to undertake the campaign for the return of the frostfish. It did not seem that three men could make much of a dent in a project to which hundreds had given their time and energy over a period of several years. Still, there was no harm in trying.

The committee of three got on the job immediately. After their first meeting they visited newspaper offices up and down the valley and sent letters to the mayors of the various communities. Only one point was stressed: the frostfish would return if the river were cleaned up.

To the amazement of everyone, public opinion changed almost overnight. People would stop in the street and say to one another: "Say, this new valley project is wonderful, isn't it? I just read in the paper that if we clean up the river we'll have frostfish again. Be sure to get as many people as you can on the job."

Enthusiastic interest in the campaign flashed from person to person. More was accomplished in a few months by three men with little or no assistance than had been achieved by hundreds working arduously year in and year out for nearly a quarter of a century.

Positive and Hopeful

The whole experience was an eye opener to everybody concerned. It taught a powerful lesson. The public was quick to comprehend and respond to a simple positive proposal, while all appeals to clean up a mess that promised vague advantages in the distant future left them cold. It was the old story: it is always much easier and far more constructive to rouse interest in working "for" a goal that is affirmative and hopeful than merely to be "against" a bad situation.

This balance, or sense of proportion, is too seldom applied to the problems that usually beset government. But every time the positive approach is employed, even by a few, the results are more than gratifying. In short, it is "better to light one candle than to curse the darkness."

Perhaps the greatest handicap to good government today is the fact that too many people talk about what is wrong with the government and too few emphasize the good or take the time and trouble to build that good up until it automatically takes care of the weaknesses.

When a person is deathly sick the doctor doesn't come into his room and tell him he is 99 per cent dead. Instead he takes the attitude that there is still life, and where there is life there is hope. He does his best to inspire the patient with courage and determination. He keeps his sense of proportion. Even though disease has practically taken over, there is that small element of vitality left. He feels it is his responsibility to concentrate on the spark of life still remaining in the body and build it up until full recovery is a certainty.

A young marine veteran, wounded at Iwo Jima, heard a lot of people complaining about bad politics in their district, but nobody appeared to be doing anything about it. He plans to run for district leader. He says that he expects it to be a "tough fight" but that he is encouraged by a growing number of people who are surprised and delighted that someone like himself is taking a stand.

She Took a Chance

A young lady who was a stenographer for an insurance company wrote us that she felt she could do more to better government by getting into it. When her friends learned of her decision they made every effort to discourage her. Even though they had been overemphasizing the number of disloyal workers in government, they were endeavoring to make a bad situation worse by doing everything possible to prevent one whose integrity they respected from taking up a career in government. To top it off, they reminded her that if she ever got into government work "some Communist will probably have you fired and then you'll be of no use whatever." The young lady gave a short, sensible, and courageous reply to this. She said: "I'm willing to take my chances and leave the rest to God."

A subway conductor also displayed the power for good that even one individual can exert. He took it upon himself to run for Democratic leader of a district in New York City, said to be one of the most closely held sections for a political beginner to tackle. He chose for his campaign manager a subway motorman. Between them they had very little money to spend on campaigning. But they figured that designating petitions (on which they hoped to get nine hundred signatures qualifying the conductor to run in the primaries) would cost about eighty dollars. Leaflets, which they expected friends to pass out for them, were to be mimeographed to save money.

The subway conductor, a naval veteran of World War II,

knew that he had a difficult job on his hands, but he felt that
it was even more important to suffer this way than it was to
face any danger of war. His optimism was deep and realistic.
It was well expressed in his statement: "We know there are
a lot of people, particularly young people, who are fed up.
All we've got to do is get them to the polls."

In a talk not long ago in Washington, a newly elected member of the U. S. Congress from the South told us that it was
a twenty-five-cent pocket-size edition of the Christopher book,
You Can Change the World, which he picked up at a news-
stand, that sparked him to make a try. The going was not
easy for him. But he kept fighting, and to his surprise, he was
elected.

Purpose Makes the Difference

From Louisiana we received another sample of how the Christopher idea reaches out and touches people far beyond our
immediate scope. A young businessman wrote us: "It may interest you to know that the Christophers did much to influence
my decision to run for State Representative."

In his campaign he pointed out that "the most important
thing confronting local, state, and national government today
is the necessity for active citizen participation in order that
we may have a good efficient government." In his case it was
more than campaign oratory when he declared: "I'm an independent candidate seeking election for only one purpose,
that purpose being to carry out the wishes of the people of
——, to protect their interest at Baton Rouge, and to further
the interest of good government in every respect."

The future of America will probably be determined—for
better or for worse—by a small handful of people who are
dedicated to a cause bigger than themselves. A comparative
few, fired with the love of God and country, would have a
much easier task and certainly a more inspiring one than the
small number who are bent on wrecking this nation.

One of the most important requirements to enable such
people to persevere is a sense of proportion. While recognizing

difficulties for what they are, they do not exaggerate them into being insurmountable obstacles. In a very practical way they follow the wise admonition of Paul the Apostle when he said: "Be not overcome by evil, but overcome evil by good" (Romans 12:21).

Judge Medina Did It

An outstanding example of the power of one person for good is that of Judge Harold Medina in his superb handling of the trial of the eleven top leaders of the Communist party in the United States. That trial ended on October 14, 1949, with the conviction of all eleven defendants. Judge Medina was fortified and stimulated by a conviction that a single individual, fighting for good against great odds, is blessed by God in a special way and more often than not triumphs over evil. All through the nine grueling months of the longest criminal trial in our history, his extraordinary devotion to duty was put to the test day after weary day. The defense made every conceivable attempt to "sabotage" the proceedings. By endless maneuvering, ridicule, and sneering outbursts they sought to bring about complete confusion and cause a mistrial.

Difficult as all this was to endure, it must have been even more trying for Judge Medina to observe the apathy of a large section of the general public toward the trial. Few average good citizens attended the sessions. Yet day after day Communist sympathizers crowded the spectators' benches to give moral support to their leaders on trial. Typical of the indifference of the public was this remark by a New York businessman when a friend happened to refer to the trial as it reached its seventh month. "Is that thing still going on?" he grunted.

Here are a few points about Judge Medina that speak for themselves: He was sixty-one years old at the time of the trial. He had given up a $100,000-a-year law practice two years previous to the trial in order to become a federal judge at less than one sixth that income. At a time when most men are withdrawing more and more into their own little worlds, he had the daring to get into the mainstream and fight for the common good of all, regardless of the cost to himself.

If he had not been motivated by high purpose—a sense of responsibility to God and country—he would not have endured for nine days, much less nine months, the steady stream of abuse and insult that was directed at him without letup.

The example of Judge Medina is living proof of the Christopher thesis: once enough God-fearing individuals, both old and young, make it their business to follow careers where they can and will champion the sacred rights of all, then and only then will there be hope for the future.

Countless Ways

In striking contrast to the increasing number of those who are looking for government to help them is the story of one woman who had just finished a long tour of duty as a federal worker and still felt it was her business and privilege to continue to do all she could for her country. Instead of seeking any special privilege on retirement from government service—a retirement, incidentally, brought about by illness—Miss Margaret E. Gruver, aged fifty-three, deeded her ten-thousand-dollar home and lot in a Washington suburb to the United States Government.

In the deed Miss Gruver specified that she made this gift "for the purpose of creating a living memorial to justice" and because she appreciated "the privilege of being a citizen of the United States."

There are countless ways in which a solitary individual can make important contribution to the betterment of government, if he sets his goal high and is willing to take the time and trouble—and often the punishment—that is the price of doing anything worth while.

Great gains in this direction can be achieved by organizations of all kinds. But no matter what the group effort may be, more often than not it stems from the initiative and aggressiveness of a few individuals who are stimulated by a sense of personal responsibility to the greater good of all.

All through history there are numerous instances which prove the great power for good that can be exerted by one single individual.

Suggestions to Consider

The following suggestions may be found helpful in aiding the average person to play a constructive role in strengthening his government.

1. Recognize the weak spots in government but scrupulously avoid overemphasizing them.
2. Spend every bit of time and energy building up, not tearing down. Every precious moment and effort devoted to needless complaining and criticizing is just that much less that can be devoted to the big job of renewing the life and vigor upon which the nation depends.
3. Get as many people as possible to think more in terms of what they owe their country and less about what it owes them. There is an increasing tendency to talk too much about rights and too little about the obligations that are part and parcel of those rights.
4. Bear in mind that democratic government will be good or bad in proportion to the interest of its citizenry. When there is a slump in performance, it is not the fault of the democratic system but rather the failure of the rank and file to put it to proper use.
5. Be wary of oversimplifying. Running a government as vast as ours presents many complicated problems. Jumping to conclusions without a close and impartial study of the facts may hinder much more than it will help the situation.
6. If you see defects in government, make an attempt to do something about them. God blesses anyone who tries. The worse they are, the more your help is needed. Pray and work for a solution, regardless of how impossible it may

seem. Remember that belittling your own government does nothing but make it worse.

7. Encourage rather than discourage those who are considering a career in government. A passing word that you utter, one way or the other, may be the deciding factor. Far-reaching harm may result from such careless remarks as "You'll never get anywhere in government," "They are all a bunch of bureaucrats," "A man has to be a crook to get ahead in politics." Such statements not only are untrue but are grossly unfair to countless people who are now faithfully serving in the ranks of government or politics, trying to bring about the high type of public administration that everybody desires.

8. Remind as many as you can that there is something everyone can do to improve government. Many miss the forest for the trees by overlooking the numerous little duties that insure the big success. Show them the part that they can play in keeping politics clean and in getting many others not only to exercise their privilege of voting but, even more important, to register, for it has been said that most elections are won or lost on registration day. Also influence everybody you can to vote in primaries, for they determine even more than the general elections who your public officials will be.

9. Expect difficulties and disappointments. There is no royal road for those who would serve the cause of good government. Far from being easy, you should expect the way to be hard. The more you are ready to serve the common good of all, at any cost, the more you will be blessed by God and the greater the service you will render your country.

10. Do your bit, even at the risk of being criticized because of lack of ability or experience. As John Henry Newman said: "Nothing would be done at all if a man waited till he could do it so well that no one could find fault with it."

11. Make every legitimate effort possible to keep the cost of government on an efficient, businesslike basis. Extremes

should be cautiously avoided, however, lest shortsighted economies result in bigger bills later or in crippling necessary functions of government.

12. Keep constantly in mind that your interest in government should be a never-ending job. The very nature of democracy requires unremitting vigilance. Much like maintaining the health of the body, it demands continuing attention and therefore continuing responsibility. Few permanent gains result from a hit-and-miss interest.

13. Be ever conscious of the latent talent and great good will with which most Americans are blessed. With a little friendly prodding and frequent reminders of what one person can do, much of this great potential can be translated into action.

14. Try to see the advantages that can come from discussion and debate. Those who look with alarm on the airing of differences and controversy, and regard them as a sign of weakness in a democratic society, fail to see the many beneficial effects that follow from the presentation of various opinions. Out of disagreements that are conducted on a high plane often comes a clarification of issues that could be obtained in no other way.

15. Keep it clear that the basic source of government authority is God Himself and that our basic rights flow from Him. The Founding Fathers recognized this when they wrote: "All men . . . are endowed by their Creator with certain unalienable Rights." Note well that the builders of our nation spelled out, in no uncertain terms

    1. that men get their rights directly from their Creator;
    2. that the authority of all government comes from God by way of the people;
    3. the function of government, therefore, is to act as the agent of the people in securing these rights and promoting the public welfare.

Since individual citizens are unable by themselves to preserve their rights and procure the common good, they delegate this power to certain persons to administer public affairs for them. In this way the authority of power comes from God through "the consent of the governed." This has always been the fundamental Christian and American theory of government. It should be kept clearly in mind today.

3   RESTORE A SENSE OF INTEGRITY

When Frank S. Hogan, District Attorney of New York, completed the investigation of the college basketball players implicated in the fixing of certain games, he made this significant comment: "I wish any person so tempted could have seen, as we did, these stupid and dishonest young men when they admitted their guilt. Tears of remorse, self-repentance, scalding thoughts of the perpetual heartaches their disgrace will cause parents and loved ones—all of these came too late."

The public in general is beginning to realize rather late that an increasing disregard for ordinary honesty in nearly every phase of American life has now reached dangerous proportions.

It was bad enough for basketball players to take bribes to fix games for the benefit of gamblers. But it was far more serious and shocking to find that student bodies were backing them in their dishonesty, as happened in one well-publicized case.

While government suffers in a particular way from a lack of integrity, yet it is not often recognized that more or less the same measure of morality will exist there as prevails in most other phases of American life. In other words, it is next to impossible to expect honesty in government while a lack of respect for it is shown in the home, in school, in business, and in other walks of life.

Double Standard

One big job for you, a ceaseless day-and-night job, whether you are seven or seventy, is to restore the pride of the ordinary, honest American citizen. Whatever the elements that brought snide dealings and lowered standards into our midst it is high time that a change for the better take place. Restore the pride of honesty. Before God, each can search his conscience with, for example, the following questions:

1. Is what I'm doing decent enough to stand a blast of publicity?
2. Is it all right to cheat Internal Revenue but not to cheat Jane? Is it all right to lie to the Customs Office but not to Charlie? Okay to trick or steal from Amalgamated Fudge but not from Sis?
3. Isn't it stealing to charge twice as much as I should? Or is it "smart," and if so, is stealing "smart" and dishonesty "clever"?
4. Is it okay to take a two-cent stamp but not a twenty-dollar bill? If it's okay for me to take a stamp, is it all right for two hundred others to take a stamp? If I take a two-cent stamp each day, don't I steal the twenty-dollar bill in time?
5. Isn't buying far beyond what I can afford *really* dishonest —if only stealing from myself?
6. If I'm tricking the government, and tricking my country, am I also tricking the boss, my mate, my children, my loved ones, even my God? Is there anyone I *won't* trick? Just where does it end—and how did it start?
7. Is it right because "everybody's doing it"? Isn't a sin always a sin, no matter how many people commit it?

A few such sharp questions put to yourself and impressed upon your associates can shock a lot of decent but easygoing habit-blind Americans into a refreshened set of values.

It starts somewhere—the turnabout to honesty. It can start with you. If it does, it may seep into every corner and contact any person in your world.

Not long ago, for instance, in a gathering of businessmen, one man expressed horror at the increase of graft and corruption in government. There was a certain self-righteousness about his attitude that was further emphasized by a comment he happened to make when the conversation shifted to another subject. Within a few moments after expressing shock at undue influence in government, he quietly observed that he had a man in his employ "who could fix any traffic ticket"!

A double standard of morality in public affairs as well as in private affairs can prove disastrous.

For a long time in educational circles, especially on the college level, there has been an increasing tendency to impress upon the students that Christian morality is a thing of the past. A student in one of New England's outstanding institutions of learning said not long ago that over and over again in the classroom she and the other students are being specifically reminded that "there is no such thing as right or wrong." Students in many parts of the country say that this belittling of even the natural sense of honor and integrity is gradually becoming the rule rather than the exception.

In the home, too, which should be the nursery of all the fine qualities that made America strong, there has been a slow but steady decline in basic honesty. In proportion as religion disappears from the home, this condition continues to grow worse.

Again and again the home, the school, business, and other spheres of influence have so encouraged the attitude that anything goes so long as you don't get caught that in the minds of most "being caught" is getting to be the only crime.

It seems important for all of us to be reminded again and again, therefore, that those who administer public affairs will ordinarily be no better or no worse than the average citizen.

A Pointed Reminder

In the fall of 1945, just after the Christopher movement had been launched, a Spanish ex-Communist who had spent fourteen years working for the party both in and out of Moscow called at Christopher headquarters in New York City and told us a story that has stimulated us ever since. He recounted how in Moscow he helped train workers whose mission it was to infiltrate the United States and do all in their power to wreck it from within.

Their plan of attack was a most deceptive yet very effective one. As a result of study, the Communist high command had recognized that for a couple of decades a moral disintegration had been taking place within the United States. They saw that slowly but surely it was debasing America. They figured all that was necessary to complete the downfall of the country was to step up this internal deterioration. The particular objective of these missioners of Communism was to promote disregard for religion and morality. In its wake would follow dishonesty and indifference toward government, disrespect for authority, confusion about vital issues, and breakup of the home.

Last, but not least, they strove to bring about a penetration of all phases of government by (1) those unswervingly dedicated to undermine it, and (2) the incompetent and confused who so often unknowingly give aid and comfort to those who are downright treasonable.

This visitor from afar told us that he had broken with Communism when he finally realized that far from achieving any relief for humanity, under the guise of helping mankind it was using every means to enslave the entire globe. The Communists were shrewd enough, he said, to see that a breakdown within America would hurry the collapse of the entire world. And so they were concentrating in a particular manner on this country.

Upon getting away from Moscow, this ex-Communist came directly to America in a frantic effort to correct some of the damage that he himself had helped to inflict upon this country. Since he had actually trained emissaries of evil to wreck the United States from within, he felt that he had an obligation to risk his very life to warn Americans of the impending danger.

Although he was threatened with death by the Communists for exposing their plan, he made his way around our country trying to alert everyone possible to what was taking place. He was frightened and disheartened by the fact that few would believe such a diabolical plot could make any headway in this country.

He told us that he had heard of the start of the Christopher movement. And he added that he was impressed by its positive approach of encouraging as many people as possible to get into key fields and strive as hard for good as others work for evil. He warned us, however, that the Christopher movement would have to develop fast and on a much larger scale if it is to help save the day.

Much Yet to Be Done

During the intervening six years this former Communist's warning has been an impelling force in the development of the Christopher idea. God has blessed the movement with unusual growth. But still our great fear is that we are not expanding fast enough. Hence this book. Your help is needed. It is your government too!

If we compare conditions as they existed six years ago to those of today, we must admit that, however much or little the Communists are responsible, a trend toward a moral breakdown is on the increase. If measures are not soon taken to change the trend, it could eventually bring about the collapse of our country. There is great hope of averting this, however. It lies in finding enough persons who, fired with love of God and country, are willing to make every sacrifice to work for the best interests of the nation. The alternative is very clear, as Abraham Lincoln once warned: *"If this nation is ever destroyed, it will not be from without but from within."*

Is it the beginning of the end for our country? Is America, like Rome, being afflicted at the height of its might by a fatal disease from within from which it may never recover? There is undeniable evidence that this deadly cancer is still spreading in the body of our society. But something can be done about it, thank God.

Blaming it on Communism is to oversimplify the problem.

As we constantly repeat, if all Communists disappeared overnight, *the big task would still remain.*

A First Step

To get at the roots of the problem, Step Number One should be to restore a sense of godliness and decency to the foundations of society. That is a big task, but the sooner we tackle it, the sooner will that high sense of honor again take its rightful place in all spheres of activity which touch and determine the lives of all of us.

You citizens who make it a matter of conscience to be honest in thought, word, and action, in all that affects your private lives, could make a contribution to the betterment of government that would arrest the decay that is eating at its vitals. Even better, you could restore that condition of elementary justice that is absolutely essential if we are to survive as a free nation.

Once enough Americans who believe in God and country realize that the one big hope of the future is to carry into the market place the respect for honesty that dominates their own lives, then a change for the better can take place.

To be merely aroused and shocked by criminal investigations accomplishes little if the shock is not followed by positive action. Something must be done about it.

One of the most important measures to be taken is to get more individuals who are dedicated to honesty to take up career work in all phases of government. The best way to get better cooking is to get better cooks in the kitchen.

A Typist's Point of View

And, of course, the reverse holds true too. *One of the best ways to wreck a country is to allow bad cooks in the governmental kitchen.* One girl who took a temporary position as a typist with the State Department got this impression the very first day she was on the job. "I wasn't there one day," she said, "before I realized what even one typist could do to make or break America just by being honest or dishonest, loyal or disloyal, economical or wasteful." If you don't believe her, ask any of the thousands of government typists—or get in there yourself and you'll see.

It isn't any one big villain that wrecks a country. Rather it is usually a multitude of dishonest attitudes and practices on the part of many that cripple and often destroy that intangible vitality which is the only effective obstacle against the inroads of corruption and subversion.

Yet there is great hope on the American scene because a large number of those now employed by the public as their representatives in the running of government are fundamentally honest. But many more are needed to save the country!

Better to Face It

Tendencies toward graft and corruption have always existed and probably always will. They are a human weakness. But when the voice of conscience becomes weak or still, the way is left wide open for endless abuses of honesty.

One example of the lengths to which this abuse may go is seen in a situation uncovered in one city by postal inspectors. In one checkup they found that twenty-eight timecards had been punched for workers who had not even appeared on the the job that day. Many employees made it a practice to put in only one or two days each week at their government jobs, while others didn't bother to work at all because it would interfere with the full-time jobs they had elsewhere. Friends of theirs on the inside made a business of punching cards for absentees, charging from three dollars a day to ten dollars a week for this service. For those who checked in for work but left early, the fee was only one dollar.

Those whose moral sense has been dulled often argue that dishonesty is not very harmful, that, after all, the government spends so many billions that " nobody will miss the little that I take." It is this lack of integrity on a small scale that probably does more than anything else to promote the wave of corruption that can threaten the very foundations of government.

A Sense of Dependence on God

Shortly after the spy trials, the basketball scandal, the Senate investigations, and the exposure of graft in government contacts, a leading advertising firm ran a stirring full-page advertisement in several newspapers. It was a fervent plea for the average citizen to live up to his responsibilities. A portion blazed forth in bold type:

—what's happened to our ideals of right and wrong?
—what's happened to our principles of honesty in government?
—what's happened to public and private standards of morality?

Upon reading this advertisement a vice-president of one of the top automobile companies made an interesting comment: "Isn't that typical of most of us today. Not once in the whole 'ad' do they mention the name of God. Why does everybody avoid putting back the one thing that is missing? It's like complaining that an engine won't run while refusing to put gasoline in the tank!"

George Washington's Warning

The first President of the United States, George Washington, made a powerful comment on this very point in his Farewell Address in 1796 when he said: "Let us indulge with caution the supposition that morality can be maintained without religion. Whatever may be conceded to the influence of refined education on minds of peculiar structure, history and experience forbid us to expect that national morality can prevail in exclusion of religious principle."

Several months ago Senator J. William Fulbright made a ringing speech calling for a moral revival in government if we are to avoid the destruction of our free democratic system. He underlined the chief cause of the threatened breakdown when he said: "Too many people in our nation do not believe anything with conviction. They question the precepts of God or of man indiscriminately. The values of life which were clear to the Pilgrims and the Founding Fathers have grown dim."

If we are to restore to public as well as private life those qualities that are at the heart of any greatness that America can claim, the one above all that is absolutely essential is that of dependence on Almighty God. For the daring men of early America it was the one source of strength above all others. Because they felt a deep sense of responsibility to God and their fellow men, they displayed a loyalty and devotion to a cause that has seldom been equaled in history. They knew that it was practically impossible to expect men to avoid dishonesty and graft if they had no sense of accountability, if they forgot for one moment that they would one day have to render an account of their stewardship at the Judgment Seat of God.

In the very first Congress of the United States the assembled members seemed particularly anxious to anticipate the very temptation that we face today. They made only two additions to the original draft of the Declaration of Independence, and both of them were references to God.

In the next to the last sentence they inserted these words: *"appealing to the Supreme Judge of the world,"* showing clearly that they were ever conscious that they and everybody else who would follow them in government would one day answer at the high tribunal of Heaven for the manner in which they lived up to the responsibility entrusted to them.

In the very last sentence of the Declaration they strengthened their affirmation of our dependence upon God by adding the words: *"with a firm reliance on the protection of divine Providence."*

Many Are Loyal and Faithful

Thank God many in government service are faithful public servants, giving their best for the common good, or we would have been wrecked by now. They labor hard and conscientiously at their tasks because they are people of high purpose.

Their sense of duty and dedication to the role that involves the destiny of everybody removes a note of drudgery from even the hardest tasks and makes each one instead a labor of love.

Those who believe that honesty and integrity are indispensable factors in American government must follow the example of these devoted public servants. They must do more than bemoan the shocking disregard for truth and justice that they observe so often. If their love for God and country is deep and genuine, they will take action. They will engage as best they can in local, state, and national affairs.

And even if they themselves are not in a position to do so, they will do all in their power to see that men of principle and competence are stimulated to run for public office and that those already in government are encouraged, not berated. They will study the background of the candidates and the issues at stake. They will take the trouble to register and vote. Finally, they will take pains to see that all their representatives, whether in high position or low, observe the same high standards of honesty and efficiency that government must have if it is to function properly.

If we are to bequeath to future generations of Americans the precious advantage of God-given liberty that it is our privilege to possess, more of us will have to roll up our sleeves and put in the hard work that will guarantee continuance of that freedom for ourselves and for those who look to us to protect it for them.

Reflect on This

When an American citizen applies for a passport he is required to take and sign the following oath of allegiance before the application is even considered:

"I do solemnly swear that I will support and defend the Constitution of the United States against all enemies, foreign and domestic; that I will bear true faith and allegiance to the same; and that I take this obligation freely, without any mental reservation, or purpose of evasion: So help me God."

When the President of the United States takes office, he repeats these same words.

Every American would do well to read them over and over again and reflect on their deep meaning. They sum up succinctly what is expected of everyone who claims to be an American. They apply with even greater force to one who has the privilege of representing others as a public servant. He has a definite role to play, a challenging responsibility to fulfill. Merely to work "at" government falls short of the minimum that is expected of him. To use government "to feather his own nest" or as a steppingstone to personal advancement is to betray his trust. To do anything harmful to the best interests of all could be treason.

Of all qualities that have made America, loyalty stands at the top of the list. Devotion to our cause is a requisite. Only the loyal "will support and defend" the heart and soul of our country "against all enemies, foreign and domestic."

The final words of the oath, *so help me God,* are a constant reminder that loyalty should be rooted in the Author of all liberty, Who will supply us with the strength we need for the fulfillment of our duties and to Whom we must one day render an account for the integrity of our performance.

4 THE DIFFERENCE BETWEEN PUBLIC ADMINISTRATION AND POLITICS

The fact that we find several definitions of "politics" in Webster's New International Dictionary shows in itself that public understanding of this word is confused.

In its primary definition, politics is: "The science and art of government; the science dealing with the organization, regulation, and administration of a state, in both its internal and external affairs."

For a secondary definition, the dictionary gives us: "In a

bad sense, artful or dishonest management to secure the success of political candidates or parties."

The first definition states flatly what politics should be. The second definition is one that too many accept as defining the present-day practice of politics.

"Politics," as now generally accepted, often means "party politics," with party loyalty as its guiding principle, rather than the common good.

It is essential to understand the difference between "public administration" and "politics." The aim here is to eliminate the confusion in comprehending these terms. Unless a sharp distinction is drawn between them at the outset, the individual will have difficulty in knowing what he should do in the field of public affairs.

A Recent Development

Public administration is an essential part of American life. Literally, it means the art of government conducted for the common good, and not for partisan advantage. Many who are leaders in political circles are also excellent public administrators or appoint those who are fully qualified.

When the mayor of one of our cities made six appointments to top jobs recently, he insisted that political considerations be either minor or nonexistent. He selected them, he claimed, because each was qualified as a public administrator. He first consulted several civic groups for advice before reaching his final decision.

Colleges and universities offer courses in Public Administration. These institutions recognize that the field of government has become so complex that skilled training is required to administer it. Students who enter this field get a thorough grounding in the basic principles of public administration. They become familiar with various types of popular government. Finally, as advanced students, they acquire familiarity with government on the local, state, and national levels.

By contrast to this academic approach, old-time "politics" is still picked up from the professional politician. In many instances he is deeply interested in the public good. At other times he is not, except insofar as he can use it to win votes for his party.

At election time it is common for one party to proclaim that it has all the saints while the other has all the thieves and grafters. Both major parties have made a practice of it.

Most reasonable men and women are aware that neither party has a monopoly on goodness, that neither is exclusively bad. Our approach to the field of public affairs, therefore, is not based upon partisan political considerations. We recognize that there is good and bad in each. Our purpose is to encourage the good. By so doing, it may be possible, God willing, to raise the general level of decency in American public life. That is the sole purpose of this book.

When We Abdicate Our Rights

It is difficult to overemphasize the idea that "public administration" and "politics" are not one and the same thing. The single factor that makes them differ is the factor of partisan loyalty to a particular party and its candidates. Yet it must not be forgotten that a good politician can be a good public administrator if he consistently places the public good above party interests. Public administration employs the skilled techniques based on loyalty and honesty needed for government without the "artful or dishonest management" sometimes found in purely partisan activity.

Once we understand this distinction, the road opens clear before us. We know that our rights in a free democracy come to each of us from Almighty God. It is only when we abdicate these rights—by failing to register and vote, for example—that the government can become the prey of those who neglect or betray the public interests. No one should let his vote go by default by failing to register and to exercise his franchise.

Getting Personal

You ask: "Well, what can I as a single, small individual do about it?"

Just consider that the United States is made up of individuals like you, 150,000,000 of them. Of these, an esitmated 87,-000,000 are over twenty-one and therefore presumably qualified to vote either by birth or by naturalization. Some of this number may not pass literacy tests, and others may not pay the poll taxes required in some states. But for a round figure we will take the 87,000,000 qualified voters as a working basis.

How many "stay-at-home voters" are there in this group? Let's take the last national election in 1948, when the Truman-Barkley ticket ran against the Dewey-Warren ticket. In that election 48,402,070 Americans went to the polls and cast their ballots. The vote was: Truman, 24,105,812; Dewey, 21,970,-065; Wallace (Progressive), 1,157,172; Thurmond (States' Rights), 1,169,021.

Figures are dull? Surely. But it's worth a moment of time to analyze these. Remember, this was in a national election with four candidates running for President. Our domestic policies and our international policies depended upon the result. This election occurred at a time when America was counted upon for world leadership. The Communist threat was growing. We were only a few years away from the outbreak of hostilities in Korea. In all respects the 1948 national election was one of the most important in the history of this nation.

With these considerations at stake, we may assume that every voter qualified to cast a ballot in this country actually would cast one. But what do the figures show?

Of the 87,000,000 presumably qualified to vote, almost 40,000,000 chose not to vote. What was the margin of victory for the successful candidates? The actual difference in votes between winners and losers was 2,135,747. Divide the difference in half. Now we see that 1,067,873 votes actually meant the margin between victory and defeat. That number of votes plus one, applied to either of the two major tickets, could have spelled "Win" or "Lose."

So we come down to the net result of the apathy and indifference of a good segment of American voters. For a nation of 150,000,000 souls, a vote slightly over 1,000,000 decided the policies, foreign and domestic, which will rule them for four years. Is this the democratic principle in practice? By no means; the democratic principle depends for its survival on *voting by the majority*.

Here's an Example

By taking the 1948 national election as an example, we mean to do nothing more than use the most recent example. Perhaps if the stay-at-homes had voted, they would have given the winners a resounding margin. Or again, perhaps they might have changed the result. But all this is water under the bridge; the striking fact is that almost as many did not vote as the number who did, and of those who did, slightly more than one million were the crucial few who decided the leadership of a great nation.

As we indicated, the 1948 national campaign was not unique. For years past, the number of persons who actually vote has been far less than the number qualified to vote. The point here is that if the voters do turn out, the results of their voting represent a real exercise of the democratic franchise. If they fail to turn out, they may abdicate their God-given privilege to some politician who would be just as happy to keep an independent voter at home as he is to get a party voter to the voting booth. Either way, it helps the politician.

If half the voters stay away from the polls, the successful politician will not be responsible to any great force of public opinion. Those who voted in the election are not numerous enough to demand a high standard of conduct for the office-holder to meet. Whose fault is it, then, if we have inferior government? The responsibility must fall upon the American public which tolerates it.

Reason for Hope

Dark as the picture may seem at times, it has many hopeful aspects. Most noteworthy of these is the gradual public acceptance of the fact that good government requires workers of integrity and ability. As we see this trend increasing in public

consciousness, we see a parallel decrease in the power of purely political machines. In many states the once all-powerful
machine politicians have had their wings clipped by the public.

In addition, more citizens are becoming convinced that the
individual must make his voice heard in behalf of the general
good. The one tie that should bind all together is a common interest in honest and efficient government on all levels.

On the practical basis, let us consider what a family does before it moves into a new community. The father will very likely look first at his taxes and, second, at what he gets for them.
Both the father and mother want to be sure that a good education is available for their children, that the water supply is
safe, and that public health measures will protect them against
disease. All these considerations are part of wise family life.
But all of them are part of government too—local government
in this case.

Going further, we realize that government influences our
daily lives not only as local residents but as residents of a county, a state, and a nation as well. Try as we may, we cannot
separate ourselves from government. Our best course, then, is
to adopt a sense of personal obligation toward it which will
produce the best government at the least expense.

Your Newspaper Can Help

In the United States we have the blessing of constitutional
guarantee of a free press. Despite some exceptions and certain
defects of exaggerating or slanting the news for a favorite party
or interest, the American press is conscious of its responsibility
toward the people and aims at a sense of trusteeship toward
the reading public.

The press has countless opportunities to uphold morality in
public life. They do this by frequently pointing out deviations
from proper conduct in public affairs. The deed need not necessarily be criminal; if it departs from ordinary decency it may
get into print. *Many politicians who have little fear of criminal prosecution have a great fear of public exposure through*

the press. This factor alone helps to maintain a higher standard of government probity than could possibly exist without a free press.

How can you encourage the press in this respect? First, by doing your utmost to keep it free and by opposing any attempts to stifle it. Most of us have some idea of what happens in totalitarian countries with a controlled press. Away from the light of day, those in power can commit the most shameless acts without fear of public exposure. So it is to the interest of all to keep the press free.

Secondly, when you see a newspaper story dealing with government or public affairs, don't pass over it as something that does not concern you. Your newspaper may have taken considerable time and effort to get the facts and put them in your hands at a cost of a few pennies.

Thirdly, write to the editor, particularly in a positive way, to commend a well-written editorial, a well-conceived feature article, or a good job of factual reporting. Letters like these do much to keep a newspaper serving up the best in good journalism.

Getting at the Facts

No government can function well without an informed public opinion. How else could we single out the faithful public servant for commendation, spot the evildoer, or eliminate graft and corruption? First we must have the facts. The newspaper exists to give us the facts. With radio and television as additional means of information, we have little or no excuse for failing to know at least something about what goes on in public life. In addition, we should use every legitimate means to ascertain the facts regarding the conduct of government. But knowing the facts is step one. Voicing your praise, your disgust, your urgent plea and demand is necessary. A three-cent stamp, postcard, or a telegram is your best investment.

At present Americans show too much inclination to take their rights and privileges for granted. In local affairs we tend to go about our own business and leave it to others to serve up good government for us. And we are inclined to extend this tendency to our national life.

Always on the Job

But let's look at the other side of the picture. Our national enemies are more alive to the benefits of American democracy than we are. Hard to find is the Communist who does not know the Bill of Rights, the Constitution of the United States, his rights under the law, and the process of registering and voting.

These individuals influence American life because they do something about it. They try mightily to elect their own candidates, or candidates sympathetic to their cause. *They* organize campaigns, *they* picket, *they* wire to Washington, *they* write letters, and *they* collect funds. Though they are a small minority, they are effective because they are individually articulate. Each and every one makes his voice heard, his influence felt.

Remember the nation's first atomic-spy trial held in New York in the spring of 1951? Two defendants who later got the death penalty for transmitting the atom-bomb secret to Russia refused to answer all questions at the trial dealing with their Communist party membership or activities.

"I refuse to answer under the privilege granted to me by the Fifth Amendment to the Constitution" became their stock answer.

How many of us know what the Fifth Amendment provides? Most of us, no doubt, would have to go look it up. Briefly, it provides that no witness in a criminal prosecution can be forced to incriminate himself by his own testimony. When the defendants raised this point, the Court felt obliged to sustain their refusal to answer. Furthermore, the Court warned the jury in its charge that no inference harmful to the defendants was to be drawn from their refusal to answer.

Here, in capsule form, we have the contrast between patriotic Americans and subversives who seek to destroy our country. The loyal American takes his fundamental rights for granted. The subversive studies the Constitution and the law to take advantage of every loophole in his undermining mission. Our enemies take advantage of the law to accomplish destructive purposes. Our friends neglect the practice of rights which could help them in improving government.

With these broad statements in mind, the individual's relation to his local, state, and national governments will be developed in succeeding chapters. Government, in the last analysis, is conducted by individuals. We hope to be able to show that each person can play a constructive part in his government.

II. EVERYONE CAN DO SOMETHING

II. EVERYONE CAN DO SOMETHING

1 IT'S YOUR RESPONSIBILITY

During the recent Senate Crime Investigating Committee sessions, Senator Charles W. Tobey questioned underworld figure Frank Costello on what he had done to show his appreciation to the United States for all the advantages he had enjoyed as an immigrant to this country. At one point the senator asked:

"Mr. Costello, bearing in mind all that you have gained and received in wealth, what have you done for your country as a good citizen?"

"Well, I don't know what you mean by that," the witness squirmed. His tortured fingers locked and unlocked on millions of television screens.

"Look back over the years," the senator explained, "to the time when you became a citizen. Now—twenty years after that —you must have in mind some things you have done that you can speak of to your credit as an American citizen. If so, what are they?"

An anguished pause ensued. Costello seemed to be racking his brain for some evidence, no matter how slight, which would identify him as a good citizen. Finally, in his laryngitis-ridden voice, he spoke up.

"I paid my taxes," he rasped.

When the laughter in the courtroom subsided, Costello was asked if he had ever aided any American war effort.

"No," he mumbled in embarrassment.

Under further questioning Costello testified that he had

never voted. He justified this omission by saying that there were millions of other Americans who never went to the polls either.

A Lesson for All

Few members of the thirty million television audience could be classed with Costello as former bootleggers, slot-machine manufacturers, or gamblers. But the vast majority of viewers were probably grateful that they were not under the public spotlight, testifying under oath on what they individually had done for America in return for all America had done for them. Many would have had to admit that they had done little more than "pay their taxes" and that they seldom or never voted.

Strange but unfortunately true, it often happens that the more a person is benefited by his country the less he believes he should contribute to it. His thoughts get into the channel where he thinks more and more of what his country can do for him, not what he can do for it. He can be compared to the lady who heard they were making loyalty checks in Washington. She quickly dashed off a letter to Washington saying:

"When you pass out those loyalty checks, don't forget to send one to me."

Happily, this dangerously selfish attitude is the product of oversight rather than of malice. We are therefore convinced that it can be changed. Americans need to be reminded that they still possess an enormous potential of good will even if they are not making much use of it at the moment. A slight reminder frequently stirs them to action. They are the hope of the future.

Essential to Know

Before we expect much action, it is necessary for Americans to refresh themselves on the origins of this country; what makes it operates as it does; and the part that each individual must play if the American heritage is to survive and increase.

First, we must know what it's all about. It is an old truth that before one will serve God, he must love Him. But before anyone can love God, he must first know Him. In short, to know God is to love Him, and to love Him is to serve Him.

The same principle applies to one's country. To love the United States, one must know it. Love of country springs from knowledge, never from ignorance. Loyalty means a love of country. But devotion to a sound system of government is practically impossible unless we know its origin, its basic philosophy, the means required to sustain and perpetuate it. Above all, we should realize that no form of government can be any better than the individuals who administer it.

To know America is to love it, and to love it is to serve it. In our short history of one hundred and seventy-five years we have come from an untamed wilderness to the greatest productive country in the world. Yet, at the present peak of material power, all classes of Americans show signs of an inner feeling of insecurity. They seem beset by doubts, misgivings, fear of the present and concern for the future.

Effects Rather Than Causes

Is this inner weakness besetting us because today we tend to think in terms of things rather than of people? Do we pride ourselves on material power and productive genius, rather than on the causes which brought about this wonderful effect? Isn't our standard of American success measured not so much by high ideals but rather by our material achievements?

The underworld operates on that basis. Years ago its members found they could avoid the stigma of gangster activity by assuming an air of respectability. They "went legit." They got "a front." They mingled with businessmen on terms of equality. After all, didn't the mobsters have membership fees for the golf club too?

"Don't pay the government" became the watchword. "Pay a lawyer to tell you how you don't have to pay the government."

The magazine *Newsweek* offered a significant comment on this point. It said:

"It had become almost impossible to tell a gangster from a pillar of society without a Congressional investigation. Gangsters weren't hoodlums any more. They lived sedately—comfortably, of course, but not ostentatiously—in quiet suburbs. And they dressed sedately, too; nor did their tailors have to worry about the unsightly bulges that shoulder holsters made.

"They called themselves business men, and they had safe-deposit boxes crammed with stock certificates to prove it. They owned real estate and restaurants; traction companies and automobile agencies; breweries and clothing factories; oil wells and hotels. True, some of their interests were a bit illegal, but that's what lawyers were for. They had the best lawyers money could buy.

"Sometimes they also had the best Police Commissioners money could buy, and the best District Attorneys, the best state legislators, and even the best Governors. They were powers in politics who could fix a parking ticket or a trial for murder with equal ease.

"Nearly all the laws they violated were local laws. Yet, to many a Mayor trying desperately to put down crime in his community, it seemed they must be organized on a national scale."

And, indeed, they were, and still are. They operate on the simple theory that money is power. If you have enough money you can buy your way into anything, or out of anything. Why boggle at a $10,000 campaign contribution if you could put the successful candidate into your pocket the day after election? After that he was working for you, wasn't he? Certainly not for the "chumps" who voted for him, the gangsters said.

In contrast to this cynical, materialistic attitude, early America was distinguished for its *people*. People, not money, ran the country. People were the country.

The pioneers who blazed the trails thought not only of themselves but of the many whose footsteps would follow theirs. Building for the generations to come was a prime consideration with them. The God-given liberty which they established, through much suffering, into a form of government was the dominating force of their lives.

Learning from the Past

The more we know of their personal sacrifices in founding this nation, the more we will appreciate the rich heritage they bequeathed to us. The more we understand their noble outlook, the more we will do as individuals to follow their high sense of purpose and service. For them it probably meant no more than saying: "I had it hard, but my son will have it easier, and my grandson easier still."

But in that homely remark is one germ of a nation's development, because the remark encompassed the future as well as the present. How few of us today are inclined to believe that our own lives are building for the future of America. It is more common to hear the remark: "Why should I worry about you? I've got myself to take care of."

The first Pilgrims who landed on the Massachusetts coast in 1620 got a foothold there despite disease, privation, and death. As their modern counterparts, we too can gain a foothold in the struggle to bring this country back to its original concepts. We need their qualities of vision, daring, patience, fortitude, and a readiness for hard work.

Willingness to sacrifice for what they believed right was characteristic of the early Americans.

Lewis Morris, one of the signers of the Declaration of Independence, risked his personal possessions for what he believed was the public good. As a wealthy man, Morris well knew what it might cost him to sign the Declaration. He owned a beautiful family manor, a thousand-acre stand of trees, considerable money, and enjoyed a large measure of happiness which he shared with his family of six sons and four daughters.

The price he paid for his devotion to the cause of American liberty was high. The enemy burned his woodland, despoiled his mansion, scattered his livestock, smashed his fences, and drove his family and tenants off their land. For seven years thereafter the Morris family lived a hand-to-mouth existence.

As soldiers in the Continental Army, the three older sons tasted the hardships of the bitterly fought Revolution.

A Rich Heritage

Those who would make a better America today would profit by study and reflection on what our forefathers did at their own great cost to leave such a rich heritage for all of us.

President Woodrow Wilson, in addressing the cadets of the United States Military Academy at West Point, New York, said:

"America came into existence for a particular reason. It was as if in the Providence of God a continent had been kept unused and waiting for a peaceful people who loved liberty and the rights of man more than they loved anything else, to come and set up an unselfish commonwealth. . . .

"There is none like it in the whole annals of mankind—men gathering out of every civilized nation in the world on the unused continent and building up a policy exactly to suit themselves, not under the domination of any ruling dynasty, or of the ambitions of any royal family, doing what they pleased with their own life on a free space of land which God had made rich with every resource which was necessary for the civilization they meant to build up. There is nothing like it!"

These are words to keep ever before you, to pray over and above all to keep alive.

Everyone So Important

The American Government has gone far beyond the pioneer stage. Perhaps because it has grown so large, it tends to dwarf the individual. Fewer and fewer show any personal, individual interest in it. The average man is inclined to say:

"Government is too big. Anything I might do won't have any effect anyhow. So why bother?"

This defeatist attitude comes very close to the attitude of the Germans in Hitler's Third Reich. From them, American army officers on postwar occupation duty heard the same refrain many times over. It went like this:

"But what could we do? We were only the little people. We couldn't do anything in politics."

Isn't this the same attitude of too many in America?

The concept of personal responsibility for government is one that cannot be too often stressed. It is typically an American concept. It was the concept on which this nation was founded. The ties between the individual and his government are too numerous and too strong to be broken by either. If the individual disdains a voice in his government affairs, the government will certainly exercise a greater voice in the individual's affairs.

Purpose Makes the Difference

One influential and well-meaning gentleman is doing a harm that he certainly does not intend to do. He habitually repeats that one individual trying to improve government has about as much chance of succeeding as a drop of fresh water has of sweetening a salty ocean.

Ironically, while he discounts the effectiveness of the individual, he himself is doing a very effective job of discouraging everyone he talks to. By constant harping on the same negative theme, he disheartens those who might try to do something. After hearing his theme song, their ambition gives way to a weary "What's the use?"

On the brighter side we have the heartening example of an eighty-one-year-old Detroit grandmother who still feels she can strike a blow for better government. A friend found her reading the Christopher book *Careers That Change Your World*. Asked how she happened to be reading that book, the grandmother said:

"I have reached the conclusion that most of our trouble today results from the fact that the wrong people are in the right jobs."

With a smile, she acknowledged that it was pretty late for her at eighty-one to embark upon a new career in any vital sphere. Then, more seriously, she said:

"I feel that I ought to know about these careers because I

have fifteen grandchildren. If I can get them started thinking about the possibility for good in worthwhile careers, I feel that I will have done something for my God and for my country."

An Awakening

Again on the hopeful side, we recall the tens of millions of Americans who dropped their daily chores to look and listen on television to the Kefauver Committee hearings. It was the greatest cops-and-robbers spectacle in modern history, with the actors brought into the family living room on the TV screen. At the same time, it was government in action. For many of the viewers it was their first example of how government can exercise its powers of investigation.

The Kefauver telecasts gave the viewers a new sense of personal interest in government which they had never before experienced. The moral breakdown and the alliance between crime and politics which was depicted on the screens came home to the watchers.

Never before the televised Kefauver hearings had the criminal-political alliance been exposed so effectively to public view. Radio columnist John Crosby said:

"Public hearings have been held in this country since earliest times, and in the nation's infancy were held in a meetinghouse where the whole community could crowd in and watch. In a city of 7,500,000, that's no longer possible. But television has taken us a long way toward making it so."

The Senate committee show provided top-notch entertainment. The circus, opening in New York, felt the competition. Movie theaters were empty. Department stores complained of sagging sales. Housework was neglected. Bars and taverns with television sets did a stand-up business.

The TV watchers were entertained, but they were shocked too at the outright graft and the political power exercised by underworld leaders. When the shock wore off a bit, the individuals began to ask themselves if they did not bear some measure of responsibility for permitting such a sordid situation to develop. Once more, public apathy and indifference was the answer. They began to realize that with an alert and informed citizenry such a situation could never have developed.

We are all interested in good government, because good government *benefits* us. By the same token we want to eliminate bad government because it does us all harm. The more knowledge the public acquires about what is going on, the better the results will be. An informed public is the first weapon in the fight against bad government.

The Power of Public Opinion

In an entirely different direction, but just as effectively, the force of a united public opinion has been shown in the matter of government reorganization and economy. In July 1947, Congress, by unanimous vote, with full approval of the President, passed an Act (Public Law 162) which contained a provision for the creation of a Commission, commonly known as the Hoover Commission. Former President Herbert Hoover was selected to head it.

This Commission in its report frankly recognized that the entire project was in response to widespread public demand. It reads:

"This concern of Congress for economy and efficiency reflects the overwhelming interest of every thoughtful citizen and taxpayer in the land." (P. XIV.)

How It Came About

In a very few years our federal government has become the most gigantic human enterprise in the world. In less than twenty years the astounding growth of the scope of our government almost defies description. A few simple facts will give us a small idea of it.

In the last twenty years:

1. The number of federal employees has increased from 570,-000 to 2,100,000.
2. The number of bureaus, sections, services, et cetera, has multiplied four times.

3. Annual expenditures have increased from about $3,600,-
000,000 to over $70,000,000,000.

4. The national debt per average family has increased from
500 to $7,500.

This last item, perhaps more than the others, caused John Q.
Public to take another look at his government. His taxes are
more than ten times what they were in the twenties.

From this came a swelling interest on the part of the average
taxpayer in government and expenditures, efficiency and economy. Result: action in Congress to investigate the entire matter.

Act of Congress

The provisions of the Act of Congress creating the Hoover
Commission spell out in incisive terms the job to be done.
They read:

"It is hereby declared to be the policy of Congress to promote
economy, efficiency, and improved service in the transac-
tion of the public business in the departments, bureaus,
agencies, boards, commissions, offices, independent estab-
lishments, and instrumentalities of the executive branch of
the Government by—

1. Limiting expenditures to the lowest amount consistent with
the efficient performance of essential services, activities,
and functions;

2. Eliminating duplication and overlapping of services, activities, and functions;

3. Consolidating services, activities, and functions of a similar
nature;

4. Abolishing services, activities, and functions not necessary
to the efficient conduct of Government;

5. Defining and limiting executive functions, services, and activities."

Report and Findings

Under Chairman Hoover some three hundred outstanding men and women, experts in their fields, worked for sixteen months in twenty-four "task forces," and finally, in February 1949, submitted their report, known as "The Hoover Commission Report."

The findings showed that the concern of the people and the Congress was justified. The Commission found that "The U. S. is paying heavily for (a) a lack of order, (b) a lack of clear lines of authority and responsibility, (c) a lack of effective organization in the executive branch."

It also pointed out that "great improvements can be made in the effectiveness with which the Government can serve the people if its organization and administration are overhauled."

Unfinished Business

Thus far about half of the proposals for governmental reorganition have been adopted. It is estimated that this will mean an eventual saving of two billion dollars annually.

The remaining half of the recommendations are yet to be adopted. It is claimed that another two billion dollars could be cut from the expense of running federal government.

Only recently the New York *Times* editorialized on the need for eliminating "waste, duplication, and slovenliness in government" and pointed out that there is still much to be done in this way in such departments as the Post Office. Then the editorial continued: "Congress has it in its power, by adopting the Hoover proposals, to cure much of what's wrong there. The Veterans Administration is another administrative horror. So is the Agriculture Department.

"Federal medical and hospital services ought long ago to have been unified. And perhaps the most costly, wasteful, and needless duplication in all governmental history is that between the civil functions of the Army Corps of Engineers and those of the Bureau of Reclamation in the broad field of the control and use of water.

"In each of these cases there are powerful voices in favor of the status quo, but the public interest demands that changes shall be made. The previous Congress had to its credit a good beginning on the Hoover plan. It is up to the present Congress, backed by the Administration, to finish this unfinished business."

You Can Do It Again

Unfortunately, the strong surge of public opinion that brought action by Congress in 1947 in setting up the Hoover Commission is lacking today.

Congressmen say that most people don't bother to write them these days, that letters are too few and too scattered to be representative of American public opinion.

Necessary as investigations and commissions are, they cannot of themselves insure honest and efficient government. That depends on the influence and participation of the majority of the citizenry.

You have a sacred duty to make your voice heard. Whether you are a farmer, a stockbroker, a housewife, a college professor, a salesgirl, or even a government employee, that is your responsibility.

2   YOUR VOTE MAKES A BIG DIFFERENCE

Mr. Charles Edison, former governor of New Jersey, once said: *"Citizens will die for democracy, pay taxes for it, and give their blood for its soldiers. But vote? Work at democracy? It takes a revolution or a miracle to arouse them."*

What has happened throughout the world in the last thirty or forty years seems to verify that. But unfortunately, when revolutions take place in our day, they are fomented by those who are intent upon enslaving the people rather than on freeing them. Furthermore, they are playing for keeps and usually succeed in preventing those interested in freedom from ever getting a second chance.

As far as miracles are concerned, welcome them, to be sure. But don't count on them. The loving Providence which has blessed our land so bountifully does favor with an occasional miracle those who are trying their best. But even a miracle is usually a rewarding encouragement to those who are on the job, working day and night, to do everything in their power to make the best of the ordinary means that the Lord has put at their disposal.

Bringing a sense of personal responsibility in voting to Americans who fail to go to the polls is no easy task, and we would do well to face it. Most likely all eligible voters in our country will never present themselves at the polls on any one election day. Laziness, indifference, downright cynicism, and numerous other human defects are major obstacles to the fulfillment of this ideal. But that doesn't mean we should lay down on the job and be satisfied with fewer than half of the voters going to the polls.

It Can Be Improved

Something can be done to improve this dangerous situation. If a reasonable goal of achievement were set and ordinary sound practical methods used to attain it, a change for the better that could safeguard American freedom for generations to come might be effected.

Suppose, for instance, a million regular voters over the country should take it upon themselves, individually and personally, to seek out twenty non-voters each. That is easier said than done, of course. Actually it would raise the total of forty-eight million to sixty-eight million. If this could ever be achieved it would give an assurance that two thirds of all who could vote had exercised the privilege of making their voice heard in the running of their government. While this would be still short of the ideal, it would probably be sufficient to protect the God-given liberties of all 150,697,361 Americans.

It would seem that the Number One job to be done, then, is to get across to the average American citizen that he is important—that what he does as an individual can have a de-

cisive effect in changing for the better not only his country but
his world.

If John Q. Citizen could ever be made to realize that those
who elect anyone, from dogcatcher to President, are people
like himself and that the total of any vote is nothing more than
his voice over and over again, he would be much more disposed to play his role, insignificant though it might seem to be.

Remember, too, voting only in presidential elections doesn't
make you a top-notch citizen. Your voice is important in every
election—primary, bond issue, school board, or for the local
supervisor.

The prevailing attitude that "my vote doesn't count" is a
snare and a delusion that plays right into the hands of those
who are dedicated to corruption and subversion. It paves the
way for despotism in one form or another. Moreover, a single
vote has sometimes determined the course of history.

One Vote Makes a Difference

Two of our most famous Presidents, Thomas Jefferson and
John Quincy Adams, were each elected to office by a single
vote in the Electoral College. Another President Rutherford B.
Hayes, was elected by a single vote. When his election was
contested the matter was referred to an electoral commission.

Again, Hayes was the winner by a single vote. The man who
cast the deciding vote for him was a congressman from Indiana, a lawyer who had been elected to Congress by a single
vote. And that one vote had been cast for him by a client who,
though seriously ill, insisted that he be taken to the polls for
the balloting.

The National Institute of Social Relations pointed out that
"in 1924 . . . one Missouri Congressman got in by a margin
of 300 votes with 63,000 qualified voters in his district staying
away from the polls. A Pennsylvania Congressman nosed in
by a margin of 500 votes in the same election, with 40,000
voters not bothering to say 'yes' or 'no' to him. Each one was
probably thinking. 'What does my vote matter?' In the usual
city or county election, only a handful of the voters decide

who is going to run local affairs, and how. One vote counts for an awful lot in these elections."

There are numerous creditable methods of overcoming the apathy that characterizes too many elections. Simple positive means can accomplish much in seeing to it that the turnout at the polls is a representative one. Worthwhile organizations are in a position to stir up a patriotic sense of duty in voting. They can help instill in each individual a deep conviction that the best way to efficient government is through an informed and active interest in government.

The deeper this conviction on the part of the individual, the more effective he will be in any group or organization that has been set up to promote better government. And the less likelihood there is of such an organization being dominated by those who wish to use it for special interests.

For Forty-four Years

An encouraging example of what one person can do in this way is seen in the case of a young man who came to realize, through a chance conversation with a friend while he was in college, that only the people can make a democracy succeed or fail. This one brief discussion left a lasting impression on him. He appreciated as never before that the fight for good government never ends—that, like the human body, it requires constant attention to keep it in a healthy condition and prevent it from being overtaken by disease.

A new sense of responsibility to God and country started to develop within him. From that day forward he took a deep and growing interest in public affairs. He became a student of government while pursuing his regular college course. Any extra spending money he used to prepare leaflets and pamphlets to arouse the interest of other students in better government.

When he was twenty-one he was thrilled with the prospect of his first vote. He had studied the merits of each major candidate and had a fairly good knowledge of their backgrounds and what they stood for. It happened that he went to the voting booth with his father, and on the way home he asked him for whom he had voted. His father told him the names of the governor and a few others. But when it came to answering his son's specific inquiry as to whom he had voted for in the lesser offices, he replied: *"Well, I don't know. The party candidate, I suppose."*

The fact that he and his father, both conscientious voters, knew scarcely anything about the candidates for minor offices bothered him so much that it opened a new chapter in his life. He decided to devote as much time and money as he could spare to helping the ordinary citizen reach an intelligent appreciation of the merits of all the candidates and issues with which they were confronted on election day.

He persevered in his devotion, and thus far forty-four years of his life have been dedicated to this important work. Recently he retired from the vice-presidency of a large corporation at the age of sixty-five. But he did not withdraw into seclusion and spend the rest of his life in leisure. He immediately offered his services at no salary to a group whose high objective was to give aid to communities which are endeavoring to find ways and means of bettering their local government.

A Housewife Leads the Way

Another instance of the role that one individual can play was brought out by an energetic housewife who devised a little plan of her own to get people out to the polls. She had heard so many people complaining and doing nothing about it. Others claimed they could have no hand in the selection of candidates. Concluding that too many who do not assume responsibility themselves often take great glee in finding fault with those who do, she set about a course of action.

She contacted about a dozen other housewives whom she felt would be interested in "improving rather than merely disapproving." In her own way she pointed out how people are taking all phases of government too much for granted these days, with the result that it is failing more and more to measure up to the ever-increasing demands of the times.

She explained that she felt every one of them had a responsibility before God to take whatever steps they could in the midst of their household duties to make others aware of the importance of voting. She said that it was necessary to convey to each one that it was a matter of conscience and could even be a sin of omission to neglect to go to the polls.

In a very practical way she proposed an approach that many have found successful. She suggested that each one of the dozen housewives take it upon herself to telephone fifteen or twenty friends, neighbors, or acquaintances—especially those who ordinarily didn't vote—and impress upon them the importance of their ballet. This telephone campaign met with immediate success. It was used not only in preparation for a presidential election but also in getting people out to register for primaries, school district, and other local elections.

To do all of this required only a few hours' work over the telephone on the part of each of the dozen women. There is no way of ascertaining how many others who were thus contacted carried on the campaign to their own circle of friends. If a million housewives in America also spent a few hours before registration and election time encouraging, persuading, or prodding those who ordinarily would say "My vote doesn't count," it needs no stretch of the imagination to visualize what far-reaching effects for good might be achieved.

You can do it. If you are conscientious about your country, you will do it.

More Is Needed

Interest of this kind on the part of the citizenry is indispensable. Yet something more is needed. More workers must be found to participate in the political campaigns that *precede* most elections. Much depends on the type of worker in this field. The more interested he is in serving the best interests of the public, the more efficiently and honestly he will campaign. On the other hand, if his only interest is his own per-

sonal advantage or that of a political machine, he may inflict
no small harm on the public.

While only a comparative few will become workers in
political organizations, everybody can become acquainted with
the general setup so as to be better fitted to play a role in
keeping politics clean. Unfortunately, for the vast majority
of the public the words "politics" and "politician" often con-
note something questionable or even sinister. Yet the definition
of politics, as we have learned, is the art and science of civil
government. If politics is to benefit the people at large, it
must have the same integrity and prestige as the legal, medical,
or any other profession.

People Make Politics

Politics will never be any better than the people in it. The
only way to improve its quality is to encourage more persons
with high ideals to take an active part in everything that
comes under the heading of legitimate politics.

One practical way to get into the realm of politics is to
start at the bottom and become a worker in the precinct.
There are 131,693 precincts or election districts in the United
States. *One of them is yours!* Each one of these is the basic
political unit and usually contains from three hundred to six
hundred voters. The total number of party workers on the
precinct level is about eight hundred thousand persons. Their
business is to ring doorbells, be good listeners to voters' problems, be familiar with the issues and candidates, and remind
prospective voters how and where to register prior to casting
their votes. Occasionally they will see service on a speaker's
bureau, as organizers or solicitors of funds.

The more willing they are to start at the bottom, to serve
in the ranks and generally play an insignificant role, the more
valuable they will be in the long run because of their experience and hard knocks. By fulfilling an earnest desire to serve
the public in getting the best type of voters to the polls, they
may well prepare the way for a political career for themselves
in which they can render even greater service to the public.

Those who are willing to go into politics even on a small scale would do well to make a study of all the possibilities. Once started, you'll find plenty of ways and means. Your library, your newspaper can help you in this matter.

Merely complaining about "dirty politics" accomplishes little, if anything, except perhaps to allow it to become more "dirty." Those who could make it better are discouraged from having any part in it. If the average good citizen refuses or otherwise fails to take an interest in politics, then there are no two ways about it—things are bound to go from bad to worse. Those who criticize and do nothing are probably more responsible for any resultant disaster than those who actually promote it.

The only strength of the enemies of democracy is the weakness of those who should support it but fail to do so. . . . You can certainly do something about that!

3   GOVERNMENT NEEDS THE BEST WORKERS

One day a teacher in a junior college asked the young men in his class how many of them would consider taking up a career in government. To his surprise, 95 per cent replied, frankly and emphatically, that they weren't interested in such work.

Less than six months later, however, more than 50 per cent of the students questioned were in government service . . . they were in various branches of our armed forces, and many had already seen action in Korea!

Probably the least to blame in this attitude were the young men themselves. Maybe nobody meant any harm, but they could not have been given any particular feeling of responsibility toward their government in their childhood. In nearly every survey made it is revealed that the average young American frequently acquires within the confines of his own home a lack of interest in and respect for government service. During the impressionable years from twelve to eighteen he hears little that is favorable or constructive about government. On the contrary, he is frequently exposed to remarks that do anything but heighten regard for his own government. He can easily build up antipathy toward rendering a personal service in such a vital sphere of influence.

A Significant Trend

One encouraging side to the picture is that while the majority of the parents interviewed in the various surveys did not want their children to go into politics, at least 20 per cent of them did take the very sensible view that "unless good people get into government and run it for the benefit of all, democracy will die."

It couldn't be put any plainer than that. About the only way to raise the level of government service is to increase this proportion of 20 per cent of the parents who think so sensibly and so affirmatively until they number at least 65 per cent.

Moreover, despite their present attitude, most American parents are blessed with a great deal of common sense. They will see that they have the power within their own home circle to make an important contribution to save our nation.

A Dallas Father

There are many heartening examples that come to Christopher headquarters as proof of this. One instance in particular came to our attention after a talk some months ago in Dallas, Texas.

In the course of my remarks I attempted to point out that much of Europe's tragedy today is traceable to the fact that the average good parent became more and more discouraged with the performance of government and tried to keep everyone they could from having anything to do with the running of their various countries. The net result was that conditions became much worse. Eventually the way was left open for these same countries to be "sold out" to those whose one objective is the enslavement of all mankind.

In concluding the Dallas talk I tried to draw attention to

the fact that American parents, without realizing it, are following the same dangerous pattern.

The next day one man who had been in the audience sent a telegram to his son in New York urging him to accept an opening in government that had been offered him. The father admitted to friends that he had been adamant in refusing even to discuss the desire of his son to embark on such a career. Then he suddenly realized that opposition on his part could have fatal results if duplicated by enough other parents. The Communists could wish for nothing better than to have such effective co-operation in keeping new blood out of the main arteries of government life.

In Hollywood Too

Several years ago, when the Christopher movement was just getting under way, I spoke to a group of motion-picture writers, directors, and producers in Hollywood. I laid special emphasis on the immense service they could render by picturing those in government jobs as people of trust and responsibility and deserving of every encouragement in the fulfillment of their duties.

Without the slightest hesitation, one of the writers stood up and said to his confreres in the film industry: "Nothing could be more simple. I've been here in Hollywood for twenty years and this is the first time anything so elementary and so constructive ever occurred to me. I can't remember more than one or two pictures in all that time in which we have done anything but make light of people in government and even belittle men. We didn't mean any harm, I suppose, but I'm afraid we've been responsible for shunting off many a fine prospect and stopping him from getting into government. Why shouldn't we take a different slant? We could easily play up the guy in government who is in there pitching for all of us instead of playing him down. After all, his job is hard enough."

The more each of us becomes interested in seeing to it that all phases of government are staffed by the best type of citizen, the better off we will be in the long run. Everyone

can play a vital part in this important project. While only a
few can make the football squad in college, yet the more interested the entire student body is in getting the best possible
team, the better chance there is for winning the game. As the
players make up the team, so the workers make up the government.

We make heroes out of good football players and a big
fuss over a good coach. Why not do the same for good public
servants? They could do with a little of that rooting.

If occasional investigations into corruption and crime in
government do no more than arouse the anger of the citizen,
little will ever be accomplished. Until each person realizes
that he himself is responsible for conditions and takes a more
active interest, not much progress will be made. But once he
is fully aware of the seriousness of the situation, rolls up his
sleeves and works to get the best possible administrators of
government, then he will be making headway. If he himself
is not in a position to render such a service, he can find and
encourage others to do so.

Depend upon Men

When the Constitution of the Commonwealth of Pennsylvania
was being framed William Penn made this wise remark:
*"Governments rather depend upon men than men upon gov-
ernments. Let men be good, and the government cannot be
bad. . . . Though good laws do well, good men do better; for
good laws may want [i.e., lack] good men and be abolished
or evaded by ill men. But good men will never lack good laws
nor suffer ill ones."*

Here are a few pointers that may be helpful to those interested in providing better workers for better government:

1. Try to think of yourself as a "committee of one" in encouraging more high-quality persons to take up purposeful
   careers in government. You can do it any place—in the
   home, in a letter, in a conversation, in a business conference, in a classroom, in a garage, or on a street corner.

2. Stimulate others to be one-man recruiters. You will find most people disposed toward such a positive approach. The man in the street, the woman in her home, the student looking forward to the future, are for the most part sincere and of good will. Whatever their lack of technical or political knowledge, they can usually improve themselves by study and training. As someone put it, "If the majority of men were not upright seekers after the common good, no government, regardless of how powerful, could even exist. The police force would have to outnumber the citizenry."

3. Stress the necessity of getting as many young people as possible to take up government work as a lifetime career with the sole objective of providing efficient, honest, and economical government for the benefit of all. In times of emergency it is necessary to supplement a regular staff with specialists who can serve only on a short-time basis. But even special assistance like this depends on those who are dedicated to government on a continuing basis. A supply of new blood is constantly needed.

4. Encourage little government workers—messengers, typists, file clerks, guards, and similar public servants—to work for the best interests of everybody. Every one of them counts. In their hearts they want to do the right thing. Most of them now think that nobody cares. Yet each one doing one good stroke, speaking one good word, can start a trend that may have mighty effects.

The more interest the majority of the citizens take in seeing to it that every branch of their government, from top to bottom, is staffed by the best available career workers, the better government is bound to be. The home, the church, and the school are in a unique position of advantage to foster such a trend.

There will always be a tendency on the part of most of us to limit our interests to getting rid of inefficient or corrupt people in government. Important as that is, it is far from enough. To win a game of any kind, much more has to be done than "throw out" the poor players. It is of far more consequence to keep adding more good players to the team and putting heart into those who are already there.

In considering the ever-present need for additional workers of ability and high purpose, it is most important not to overlook the fact that there are large numbers now in government who are fulfilling their responsibility to the American public in an honest, efficient manner. If it were not for them, the situation would be well-nigh hopeless. They rate your gratitude and your constant help.

4   THIS IS YOUR BUSINESS TOO

In Trenton, New Jersey, some months ago there was considerable difficulty in finding a jury to sit at a murder trial. One person after another gave some reason why he felt he should be disqualified. After the questioning of thirty-eight prospective jurors had resulted in the seating of only one, Superior Court Judge Ralph J. Smalley could control his skepticism no longer. As each gave his reason for dodging jury duty, the judge couldn't refrain from saying: *"Is that your real opinion or are you saying that just to be excused?"*

The business of evading responsibility is becoming so widespread that it constitutes an open invitation to those bent on the worst types of abuse. There are certain duties that must be fulfilled by good citizens if democratic processes are to be preserved. Everytime a good citizen succeeds in dodging jury duty or some other obligation, he is unfair in expecting someone else to bear the burden that he should carry. Furthermore, he exposes the welfare of all to the troublemakers who never fail to take advantage of each and every opportunity.

Jury duty involves the exercise of one of our fundamental God-given rights which government insures and, as such, should be the responsibility of every citizen. Federal Judge Harold R. Medina, who rendered such a service to his country in the trial of the eleven Communist leaders, recently called upon the average citizen to take an active part in the administration of justice, particularly with reference to jury duty. "Every single member of the community," he said, "must shoulder his or her own individual responsibilities if we are to have 100 per cent justice—the only kind of justice worth having."

The downfall of a country is usually attributed to circumstances that are well known to all. More often than not, however, the root of the trouble is to be found in countless little instances of negligence, carelessness, or oversight on the part of the average citizen in the performance of his duties.

One of the best indications that the ordinary citizen is doing very little in an effective way to save his country is evident in his oft-repeated phrase: "What can I do?" First of all, it is an open confession that, while sharing in the fruits of democracy, he is failing to contribute to the preservation of the roots that make the fruit possible. "What can I do?" clearly reveals that one is doing very little. Those who are dedicated to a cause, whether good or bad, are fired with ideas that they individually can put into effect. One never hears a man devoted to destruction say, "What can *I* do?" He is already doing it!

They Are After the World

Why is it that those who are missioners of evil display such unusual initiative and resourcefulness? Many reasons might be given, but chief among them is the fact that they are out to take the whole world while most of us think and act in terms of a small locality. They have big vision, while our outlook is often small and narrow. Consequently they are ever on the alert. They see in every facet of government a steppingstone to their ultimate objectives. No effort is too insignificant. It may be only a remark to a fellow worker belittling our form of government, or a letter to a congressman opposing a measure that he, better than most others, sees would bolster good government and hinder the inroads of those who would undermine it.

The missioner of evil realizes that he as an individual is important and that while he will have guidance and direction from time to time in the furtherance of his unholy cause, it will be up to him most of the time to make the best of every situation. This very feeling of individual responsibility to the bigger cause carries him through many obstacles and difficulties that almost paralyze with fright and discouragement those who have no cause outside themselves.

The very first requisite for anyone who would be a vital force, however small, in seeing to it that we get the best government possible is a love of all—for the love of God. Fear alone is not sufficient. Fear is usually concerned only with self, whereas love—true love—is by its very nature concerned with the well-being of all. Love is thoughtful and all-embracing. It is constantly looking for new means of extending itself and more often than not discovers them. Love is persevering and never gives up. Love is daring and is ready to take all sorts of risks if it can serve the best interests of one and all. "Greater love than this no man hath, that a man lay down his life for his friends" (John 15:13).

With the driving force of such high purpose, those who are fired with love of God and country should be more eager and alert than those bent on evil. They, more than any others, should be on the lookout for every opportunity to do what they can for the benefit of others.

Americans should never be discouraged. The valiant souls who gave this country its start never flinched. They did not run away from countless troubles and evils. They pitched in and set things right. It's time to do a bit of that again.

Read a little history and take note of the impossible situations that were cleaned up by the early Americans. Too many think they had an easy time of it. Our problem today, serious as it is, is small compared to theirs.

The Part You Can Play

We should not wait for an angel to tell us what to do. God expects each of us to use our imagination. There are many ways in which almost anybody can participate in promoting better government. We do little more than mention them here because we feel that, so far as possible, each person should discover for himself what best can be done in his particular circumstances.

(a) *Encourage a more respectful attitude* As we repeat over and over again, the tendency to criticize government is growing even among those who are ordinarily very loyal. Consequently there has developed among many a lack of sympathy —an aversion toward public service and anybody connected with it. A bad situation, therefore, has become steadily worse.

A man with a weak heart is only hurting himself if he does no more than make fun of his heart and neglects to protect it. If his heart stops, everything stops.

(b) *Loyalty to government begins in the home* Children pick up most of their prejudices in the home. If an ever-increasing number of young people show a reluctance to undertake a career in government, it may be due to the fact that they frequently hear derogatory remarks about all phases of government from the lips of their father or mother. If ever they should express a desire to devote themselvs to a life of public service, their parents' reaction is frequently a chilly one. "Don't be foolish. Don't stick your neck out," is what they're told. "You'll never get anywhere in politics. You'll only get hurt." Thus children are conditioned over a period of years to do nothing but take care of themselves.

Again extensive harm is done to young people by discouraging them from taking any part in government because "there's not enough money in it." Emphasis in this direction gradually stifles the generosity and loyalty that are so essential in anyone who is worthy of the name of citizen.

Parents have the destiny of their children almost entirely in their hands for practically one third of their lives. Since this is the formative and therefore the most important period, they have countless opportunities to foster in them a firm sense of loyalty and patriotism that will make them a contributing force of good in the lives of all.

(c) *Pray for someone in government* Pray that more persons of character and competence take up careers in government. The possibilities for good are enormous in this sphere. In one sense it can be a real apostolate. "The harvest indeed is great, but the labourers are few. Pray ye therefore the Lord of the harvest, that he send labourers into his harvest" (Luke 10:2).

You can also accomplish much by praying for someone already in government service, praying that he will live up to the high responsibility of his office. This type of assistance is appreciated more than you realize. Anyone in a position of authority, as well-intentioned and as well-equipped as he may be, feels his inadequacy at times and looks for more than human guidance and support. This was brought out in a forceful way in a letter sent by a young marine officer from the Korean battle front. "As a machine-gun platoon leader, I have nearly fifty people, fifty lives, under my command," he wrote. "In your prayers ask that I'll have the intelligence and the courage to carry those men through battle safely. You know, in the Marine Corps discipline is so strong that no matter what I order my men to do, they'll do it without question. So you can see the importance of my having the courage to lead them and the intelligence to keep them from an impossible situation. Of course I'll always be able to get advice from my other officers, but there will be many little things that will definitely be up to me. I'm confident that I can do it, but your prayers, everyone's prayers, will help me more than anything else. Perhaps this sounds a little dramatic, but I know you'll realize its importance."

(d) *Make your voice heard through letters* A means at the disposal of all, and one overlooked by most, is the influence for good that can be achieved at the cost of a little time and a three-cent stamp. A simple, spontaneous, constructive letter, whether it is sent to the local councilman or to your representative in Congress, makes much more of an impression than you think.

One member of the Senate has said that "all senators read their mail. They are quick to spot and give special weight to unprompted, openhearted letters, whether they are scratched on rough paper or written on embossed stationery. They all make tabulations on how the spontaneous mail runs when a controversial issue is approaching a vote."

Once when some members of Congress were taking a very noncommittal attitude toward a recent investigation, they started to get letters from the people back home urging them to take a firmer stand and warning them that otherwise they would find substitutes for them at the next election. This forceful reminder from the grass roots was just enough to make them shift their position to a more definite and constructive one.

(e) *Organize a study group*   It is startling to find how little Americans know about their own government. Most of them, fortunately, are very well disposed. But they are somewhat like the man who said he would die for the Bill of Rights. When someone asked him what these rights were, he quickly replied: "I don't know, but I'd die for them just the same."

You could do something to dispel this ignorance. You could get a group together that would meet regularly as a career-guidance school or study club and look into the meaning and functions of the democracy that makes your liberty possible.

Many Americans are only vaguely aware that their priceless heritage was won in hard struggle and that it took much thought, wisdom, and considerable courage to establish on this continent the extraordinary form of government with which God has blessed us. But there is danger ahead if those who share its benefits have little idea of its origin, the source of its strength, the detail of its structure, the weaknesses it must guard against, and the never-ending duties that must be performed by all its citizens.

Thomas Jefferson spoke well when he said: "If a nation expects to be ignorant and free, it expects what never was and never will be."

(f) *Encourage the schools to do their part* Repeated warnings are made in the public press that the foundation of American strength gets too little attention in the curricula of most educational institutions over the country. Little or nothing is taught about the spiritual heritage that is ours. The inspiration of the Founding Fathers and of our early documents is ignored. There is probably no malice in this. It simply reflects the "take it for granted" attitude that has become the custom in so many walks of American life.

A little effort by you and others like you may accomplish much in correcting this defect. One lady, Mrs. Elizabeth E. Malament, made her voice heard not long ago with a healthy effect. The newspapers picked up her contention that the New York State Regents examination in American History failed to contain any questions on the improvement of democracy, that basic fundamentals were left out, and that because of these omissions the emphasis in classrooms might be dangerously wrong. Mrs. Malament pointed out: *"There was no question on the Declaration of Independence, no question on the Bill of Rights, no question to test pupil understanding of the meaning of democracy, the struggle to achieve it, the vigilance required to keep it."*

Some time ago we made an inquiry from Christopher headquarters to find out to what extent the Declaration of Independence was required teaching in the schools of America. It had been our impression that the Declaration of Independence, the Constitution, and the Bill of Rights were required teaching in practically all schools in every state of the Union. When someone questioned this, however, we decided to look into the matter.

We started telephoning the Board of Education in a large city. We were referred to three different departments. Nobody knew. Next we tried a leading university. Here again we were passed on to three different people without any success. On our third try we contacted a teachers' college. No success there, either!

A very pleasant gentleman at still another teachers' college frankly told us that he didn't know but suggested someone who might. That person didn't know, either! We tried information bureau of a metropolitan newspaper. They admitted they didn't know and recommended that we try the Board of Education. . . . This "run-around," far from discouraging us, made us more determined than ever to find out the answer.

Finally we wrote to Washington—to the United States Office of Education. The reply we received shocked us. An official wrote that while the Declaration of Independence may be given incidental attention in various courses, yet instruction concerning it is specifically required by law in only nine out of the forty-eight states. Startling, isn't it?

Recognizing a deficiency or complaining about it is not enough, however. Everyone should set before himself a positive program of action. The following recommendations will suggest still more to the alert citizen.

1. Check to see if the Declaration of Independence, the Constitution, and the Bill of Rights are integral parts of the policy and teaching of every school, from kindergarten to university, to which you as a citizen pay taxes or make gifts.

2. Where the letter and spirit of these American fundamentals are not faithfully taught, you as an individual, as an American citizen, can exert effective influence, no matter how small. You can help save our country by insisting that these fundamentals be not ignored, belittled, or denied in any way.

3. Persuade every organization to which you belong or with which you may be acquainted (veterans' groups, labor unions, fraternal organizations, women's clubs, parent-teacher associations, youth movements, et cetera) to concentrate on the one objective of having these basic Ameri-

can fundamentals taught and respected in all phases of
local, state, and national activity.

The part that education can play in strengthening government was underlined by Dr. T. R. McConnell in his inaugural
address as Chancellor of the University of Buffalo, when he
said: *"The momentous issues that divide the democratic and
totalitarian systems are profoundly moral and spiritual. And
it is these intellectual, moral, and spiritual issues that the universities, devoted so largely to professional studies; the faculties, so fully absorbed in their specializations; and the students,
so intent on their particular interests and careers, frequently
ignore."* Dr. McConnell went on to say that higher education
should emphasize these values not merely in a special course
but throughout all its courses, if it would make an important
contribution to American life. He said: *"The university has an
obligation to engender in all of its students . . . an understanding and appreciation of the ideas, the institutions, and the
values which are the background and substance of a free society."*

(g) *Use the public forum.* There are many ways to use
the lecture platform in order to keep people conscious that
continuing good government can be had only if it gets the
necessary attention. It is a never-ending challenge that is not
met in a day or a month but must be carried on day after
day, year in and year out.

In regard to the lecture platform, if you yourself are not
qualified to give talks, you may be able to learn with very
little coaching. In any event, you may be able to encourage
those with speaking ability to address groups on the important
features of government that are referred to here. Those who
are intent on disrupting our democratic processes make frequent use of the lecture platform. From long experience they
have learned that the spoken word imparts a special conviction that can be conveyed in no other way.

(h) *Interest your newspapers* Messages to the letter col-
umn in newspapers should not be overlooked. They are an-

other means of stirring up interest in good government. If your local newspapers do not already include it, you may see fit to request that they adopt the custom of carrying a daily box or section showing how legislators, in both state and federal government, voted.

At election time encourage the newspapers to present information that will familiarize voters with the background and principles of those who are running for office.

Every means, private and public, used to develop intelligent public opinion gives much-needed support in securing the type of government that the great majority of our people desire. You, whoever you may be, can render some service in this way. Yes, everybody can do something.

III. POLITICS AFFECTS YOU WHETHER
YOU REALIZE IT OR NOT

III.   POLITICS AFFECTS YOU WHETHER YOU REALIZE IT OR NOT

1 WHAT YOU THINK ABOUT POLITICS MAKES A BIG DIFFERENCE

Some time ago I gave a talk in New Rochelle, New York, on various means which the average citizen might employ in order to have good government. In the course of these remarks I attempted to point out that government on any level is usually good or bad in about the same proportion to the number and quality of the people who take an interest in it; that failure on the part of good people to interest themselves in what concerns the common good of all can be a serious sin of omission.

After the talk, a businessman came up and, in a friendly way, reprimanded me for having overlooked mentioning what he regarded as the greatest obstacle to good government: namely, a correct understanding of and an intelligent interest in politics by most wives and mothers.

"Without ever intending it," he said, "they are doing more harm to the country than a carload of Communists. They do everything in their power to keep their husbands, sons, and daughters away from anything and everything connected with politics. To them there is no such thing as good politics—and I can vouch for this firsthand. My wife's a fine, sensible woman, but she certainly has a blind spot on the subject. Why, there's been many a time that I wanted to do my bit to clean up a bad political situation, but each time she would raise such a fuss I just gave up. I know I should have stood my ground, but—well, I was guilty of the same old appeasement that's going on everywhere.

"Back of it all," he continued, "is the mortal dread on the part of a wife or mother that anybody connected with her may be ridiculed or kicked around and lose a little prestige in the community. They hardly give a moment's thought to the fact that by keeping the good people out they are helping the corrupt politicians make a bad situation worse.

"Furthermore, they complain about our sons going off to war every few years, many of them to die. But for some strange reason they don't see that if only a few of them had taken a bit of rough treatment in politics, they might have prevented countless others from losing their very lives."

The more I reflected on the earnest plea of this businessman, the more obligated I felt to do something about it. It was a project, I soon realized, that held out considerable promise and hope. Those concerned were essentially good people. The basic problem was primarily one of misunderstanding. Conveying the truth to them might go far toward removing that major impediment.

As Things Stand Now

First of all, it seems wise to recognize what the present attitude toward politics is on the part of most wives and mothers. Here are a few observations that give some idea of how things stand:

1. One survey showed that 82 per cent of American parents who were asked if they would approve of their children taking a part in politics stated emphatically that they would "disapprove."
2. A recent poll revealed that five out of seven people interviewed believe that all politicians are dishonest.
3. It is bad enough that the majority of people have become accustomed to thinking that "politics is dirty." But it is

even worse to spread this impression and further distort the public mind toward politics by using words and expressions that serve no purpose beyond promoting greater disrespect on the part of everybody. The very people who could and should be doing everything in their power to improve conditions in politics unfortunately stigmatize even a good political leader as a "boss." To them a political party is never anything but a "machine"; a volunteer in political work is a "ward heeler"; all political income is "graft"; all election promises are "political propaganda."

4. In his book *The Legislative Way of Life*, Mr. T. V. Smith says that according to the present public attitude, "Democracy is government by politicians for citizens who too often reward them with disdain. This disdain of politicians is a dangerous disease. It is peculiarly dangerous for a democracy."

A great many people are of the opinion that political parties are an unnecessary evil. This unrealistic attitude could prove very dangerous to our system of government if carried to its logical conclusion.

If everyone was non-partisan, who would do all the spadework, make the necessary preliminary investigations and recommendations that the average busy citizen has neither the time nor the adequate experience to do for himself? Who would go through the long process of finding out what candidates were both competent and available and would best serve the public interests? Who would provide information on important issues to be voted on? Who would see that the natural apathy of the voter is overcome and that he takes time out to register and cast his ballot?

The fact that there is, and probably always will be, abuse in our present system of political parties is a poor reason to advocate getting rid of them. The system is not evil in itself. The only need is to increase the number of good workers already in politics. In any event, in our present system the political worker is essential. As Malcolm C. Moos of Johns Hopkins University said: "No one has ever discovered how democratic government can function without him."

5. The disregard and even scorn for participation in political life shown by the home is reflected more and more in the school. A study of the careers of 218 graduates of a Washington, D.C., high school, ten years after they had left school, showed that of the 97 who went through college not a single one had gone into or shown any interest in the political life of his country. Another survey of 1,800 college students forty-five years after graduation disclosed that only one had become a leader in political life. And it so happened that he was the student who had the lowest grades in his class.

6. In the 2nd Assembly District of Brooklyn the eligible voters totaled 154,628 for both parties. In 1950 only 9,183 persons voted at the primary, which involved the election of the leader of the district, who is a member of the executive committee of his party for the county and state. As leader he, in turn, helps select the candidates for the Assembly and, with one or two other district leaders, also helps select the candidate for the New York Senate, the candidate for the City Council, and the candidate for the Municipal Court. This little handful of 9,183 was affecting, for better or for worse, the destiny of the other 145,445 voters because they were the only ones to express their opinion with regard to who should be their political leaders.

7. In the average precinct 65 out of every 100 are registered voters. Of this 65, only 40 vote on election day. Of the 40, only 16 vote in the primaries, which is an average of 8 in each party. Of these 8, a candidate needs only 5 to win a primary. Thus 5 per cent of the voters really decide who shall govern the other 95 per cent. In the light of these facts, the remarkable thing is not that our country has corrupt and incompetent public officials, but that there are so many honest and effective ones.

It Can Be Changed

Can this harmful and dangerous attitude be changed? We believe that in a comparatively short time it can—if enough people make it their business to "build up" rather than "tear down." A first step in finding a cure for cynicism and indifference toward politics is to bring about a proper understanding of its place in a democracy like ours. Government "by the people and for the people" is possible only with an alert and intelligent electorate. People who are politically indifferent unconsciously lay themselves open to dictatorship.

It has always been the Christopher thesis that positive, constructive action offers the only lasting solution to any problem. By bringing in light, darkness is automatically removed. *The more the love, truth, and justice of Christ is brought into government, the less chance there is of the opposite holding sway.* Our Christopher thesis, therefore, is that the big job to be done with regard to all phases of activity connected with government is "to get good workers in" rather than to become too preoccupied with chasing out evil or questionable workers, important as that task undoubtedly is.

This point of view was verified in a curious sort of way about two years ago by Artie Samish, who has been referred to in an article in *Collier's* magazine as "the secret boss of California." When Samish was asked what could be done to get rid of the unusual influence that he exercised over the legislator through lobbying, he answered very frankly: *"There is one way. The people must take more interests in the men they elect."*

Before the average person takes such an interest, however, he must get a correct view of the important and necessary role that politics plays in providing good government for him and for everybody else. Once he gets that, he is automatically disabused of many false and injurious notions. He would do well to get clear in his mind what politics is.

Keeping First Things First

But even before considering the proper role and function of politics and the attention that should be given it by anyone who claims to be a good citizen, it seems well for all to refresh themselves from time to time on the broad perspective on which a sense of personal responsibility depends: namely, one's relationship to God and to his fellow men.

It helps us to regard man as God's handiwork, as created in God's image and likeness. The Creator has implanted in every individual His basic law. This fundamental principle is the foundation of the *natural* law. *All* law must be based directly or indirectly upon this truth.

Any government, political movement, or piece of legislation that violates this primary law of the divine worth of the individual violates the natural law. The natural law is the law of God written in the heart of man.

The more one bears in mind the eternal destiny of each and every human being and that his stay here on earth is only the beginning of a life after death that will never end, the more interested he will be in trying to bring as much peace and order as possible into the lives of everybody. He will feel that he is an instrument, however small, in seeing to it that God's "will be done on earth as it is in heaven."

Personal Accountability

Because in his heart and soul he feels an accountability to God and man, he will make it his business to enter every possible facet of life and make his personal contribution of time and effort toward the well-being of all. With such a high motivation, he will think not only in terms of the present and what affects him directly, but also he will show a genuine and continuing concern in protecting and preserving for countless millions of Americans yet to be born the blessings of government that others have passed on to him. The extension and intensification of this sense of personal responsibility to all, regardless of the cost, is a basic requisite both for a proper understanding of political life and a loyal participation in it.

In a speech in Indianapolis on February 11, 1861, while en route to Washington to take office as President of the United States, Abraham Lincoln delivered a message that seems to be even more significant today than it was then. Here is a portion of it: *"I wish you to remember, now and forever, that it is your business, and not mine; that if the union of these States and the liberties of these people shall be lost, it is but little to any one man of fifty-two years of age, but a great deal to the thirty millions of people who inhabit these United States, and to their posterity in all coming time. It is your business to rise up and preserve the Union and liberty for yourselves, and not for me. I appeal to you again to constantly bear in mind that not with politicians, not with Presidents, not with office-seekers, but with you, is the question: Shall the Union and shall the liberties of this country be preserved to the latest generations?"*

Points to Remember

With these considerations in mind, one is likely to be better disposed toward a few elementary ideas about politics, such as the following:

A. For the administration of government within the framework of democracy, various persons with similar ideas gather together in groups to decide on a common policy and to find those among them best fitted to apply these policies to the running of government. These groups are called political parties.

B. Political parties are the chief instrument of democratic government. Whatever defects they may have, no better formula has yet been found. Should our present political system collapse, our form of government might be seriously crippled, even disappear.

C. Regardless of the many disparaging remarks that people make about political parties, they are the most practical means yet found to discover, nominate, and elect individuals who will serve in their stead in the administration of public affairs. Political parties, if conducted properly, can serve also by holding public officials responsible for the manner in which they perform their duties.

D. The conduct of politics will never be much better than the integrity and devotion of the men in it. There is probably no more corruption in politics than there is in business, labor, the professions, and most other walks of life. The truth is that with Adam's fall, all mankind fell. Corruption is a definite part of life.

E. Much corruption in political parties originates from the outside as well as from within. One of the best ways to keep politics clean is to not seek privileges or favors from politicians. Those who are often loudest in condemning "dirty politics" are more to blame than all others because they seek special privileges. More often than not it has been found that a corrupt worker in politics "got that way" because someone not in politics corrupted him.

F. To exert any force, political parties must have workers who will become politically active and strive in various legitimate ways for what they consider the best interests of all concerned. Voting is not enough. Party workers, while conforming as far as possible to the worthy objectives of the organization, must be ever alert not to put party advantage above the best interests of the country or the locality. Moreover, for every person who takes up a career in politics there are five hundred who could assist on a part-time basis. How about you?

G. One who engages in politics must be prepared to follow a positive approach and not be content to play a negative role on the side lines. Theodore Roosevelt gave a strong recommendation on this when he said: "The prime thing every man who takes an active interest in politics must remember is that he must act, and not merely criticize the actions of others. It is not the man who sits by his fireside reading his evening papers and saying how bad our politics and politicians are who will ever do anything to save us; it is the man who goes out into the rough hurly-burly of the caucus, the primary, the political meeting, and there faces his fellows on equal terms. The real service is rendered not by the critic who stands aloof from the contest but by the man who enters it and bears his part as a man should."

What One Woman Did

One of the many hopeful features of our Christopher work is to find countless persons who, with just a little encouragement, suddenly become imbued with a high sense of purpose and do a more thorough and constructive job in political circles than those who have engaged in this work over a long period of time. An instance of this was seen recently when a lady in the Midwest reviewed the Christopher book *You Can Change the World* for a woman's organization of the Presbyterian church to which she belonged. She laid special stress on the part that Christian women should play in bettering politics.

Next she brought the Christopher idea to a study club of which she happened to be a member. She pointed out the great need for individuals and groups to be vigilant and alert in everything that concerned our country's welfare. "She ended the program," one lady wrote, "with an earnest appeal to the club, which is seventy years old and which has always adhered to intellectual pursuits for their own sake, to come out of its ivory tower and be a real force for good."

A political committee subsequently was formed among the women of the church. Its purpose was to inject Christian principles into government life. One of the group's first projects was a "get out the vote" program before a recent election. Complete details were given to each member, showing what a prospective voter should know—how, when, where to register; who is eligible to vote; what are national, state, and county offices being filled; how to work the voting machine; the boundaries of the five voting precincts of the suburb in which the church is located, and the location of the polling booths. This newly awakened political worker visited the

county clerk's office and received correct detailed information
on all the voting procedure as well as some forms and bulletins
to help her in her talk.

Biographies of all candidates running for office, printed in
the city's leading newspaper, were pasted on large posters
for the information of anyone who desired it. No specific
candidates were indorsed.

Another member spoke briefly on "What Just One Vote
Can Do." Announcement was made that baby sitters and
transportation would be provided for all who could not go to
the polls otherwise. This made it possible, on election day, for
a man just out of the hospital and an almost blind woman to
call the chairman for transportation and cast votes that would
not have been cast without this arrangement.

A telephone squad undertook to phone the entire church
membership either the evening before or the morning of election day. This effort was well received and praised by the
members. And if there was a member of the church who didn't
vote, the committee doesn't know who it was!

At the next meeting of the committee a woman who had
recently moved into the community told the chairman: "After
your talk, I went right to the village hall and registered. I
never would have bothered if it hadn't been for what you
said." Another said: "Entirely because of what you told us that
day, I accepted a job on a campaign committee I didn't feel
like taking and have been just slaving, getting out literature
and helping in every way possible."

Be for What They Are Against

One of the objects of those bent on undermining our country
is to banish and expel from all public and private life the sub-
lime truth upon which our nation is founded and upon which
all Christian civilization depends for its survival. The truth
that they wish to eliminate above all others is one that we
draw attention to over and over again in this book: that God
is the source of all our rights and that one of the chief functions of government is to protect us in the exercise of these

God-given rights. The divine concept of man which is the basis of our form of government has been the bond and rallying point for the followers of Christ down through nineteen hundred years and the one that held the Jews together for centuries before that. Our enemies recognize this and are therefore determined to eliminate this truth at all costs.

If men will devote themselves to a lifetime career in politics in order to exterminate this noble concept, certainly the least that those who believe in it can do is to bring back into the realm of politics a love of God together with justice and charity for all.

This was the kind of politics referred to by Pope Pius XII when, on September 11, 1949, he said to a group of Belgian pilgrims: "Let the laity turn its attention to the family, social, and scholastic questions; let it become active in science or art, literature or radio and the cinema; let it engage in political campaigns for the election of legislative bodies."

Only a short time before that the Holy Father reminded the women of Italy, as well as the world, of their duties in social and political life when he said: "The fate of the family, the fate of human relations are at stake. They are in your hands. Every woman has then, mark it well, the obligation, the strict obligation in conscience, not to absent herself, but to go into action, in a manner and way suitable to the condition of each, so as to hold back those currents which threaten the home, so as to oppose those doctrines which undermine its foundation, so as to prepare, organize, and achieve its restoration.

The more you delve into and discover the true meaning, the true significance of politics, the better citizen you are likely to be. And, by the same token, the better politics will be.

While you will not be blind to the influences that are ever at work trying to corrupt the political system, yet you will not exaggerate them either.

You will not shun politics and overemphasize the failures of those who participate in it. You will regard this as a sickness to be cured rather than avoided.

The very detecting of any illness in the body politic will spur you to look for a remedy rather than to take a futile attitude and abandon all hope.

The price of playing a part in politics, if it is done well, will not be a small one.

There are bound to be heartaches and heartbreaks.

But in the midst of it all there will be that deep sense of satisfaction in knowing that you have served the high cause of God and country and that your reward will last for eternity.

2 THE MORE YOU KNOW ABOUT POLITICS, THE BETTER FOR EVERYBODY

"A man has to play a more active role. It isn't enough to talk ethics and clean government in the classroom and then go home and forget about it. You have to do something about it yourself." So spoke a professor of political science in one of our prominent colleges.

Recently this educator put his convictions to the test in his own district, where there are almost a quarter of a million people. He decided to run for district leader despite the fact that he had no organization, no backing of any kind. His objective was to improve the political "tone" of the whole area.

He wasn't completely without assistance, however. While it was true that he had no political party to support him, he did have what he later described as "the darndest hard-working group of backers a man ever had in a political scrap." He was referring to his former students, who, while they might have been a little "green" about clubhouse politics, were still schooled enough in the various phases of political science, thanks to him. So he got them together and determined on a course of action. They enthusiastically agreed to hustle around the district from early morning till late at night, telling the people about the professor who wanted to be district leader and improve conditions for them. The professor himself spoke on street corners, over the radio, in school auditoriums—anywhere people would listen to him.

The result? The educator won a tremendous victory over the machine candidate. Today he runs his district very much like he did his political-science classes. He tries to get everyone interested in what is going on. He holds meetings, forums, debates—anything and everything to get the people thinking about problems of government—and he works constantly at selling them on the idea that all decent citizens ought to get into politics. He tells them: "I want as enlightened a group of voters as I can get."

Red Hands in Mississippi

Another interesting example of what people have done to make their influence felt in politics concerns the city of Madison, Mississippi.

The women there had been afflicted for some time with a chemical substance in the city's water supply which reddened their hands, face, and clothes. They complained and complained, but the city did nothing. A group got together and entered a full slate of candidates for city office at the next election. If the city officials wouldn't help them to get something done, they'd do it themselves! And what's more, they succeeded. They won the nomination for every city office but that of city marshal. There is every reason to believe that they will get the kind of government they want and deserve.

This incident may not be of world-shaking proportions. It may not even be a sufficient reason for changing a city administration. Yet the important thing to remember is that once enough people become interested in public affairs, they usually have it within their power to effect the changes they desire.

The Party System

Our present system of government depends on political parties. Throughout most of our history, parties of any great consequence have been two in number.

Splinter parties, however, are free to bid for popular support. But Americans have shied away from them because of the weakness and instability that results from too much division of strength. When there are too many parties, experts point out, it is extremely difficult to fix responsibility in the event of mismanagement of public affairs.

The backbone of political parties consists of the *committees*. At each successive level the committees formulate policy and nominate party candidates. In order, these committees are:

1. Precinct committees
2. Ward, city, town or township committees
3. County committees
4. Congressional district committees
5. State committees
6. National committees
7. National convention committees

The personnel who make up these committees are elected at the various primaries and are responsible for the selection of candidates—from the President on down to the local alderman. Despite this important role which committees play in the life of our nation, it is a fact that far too few committee members know what their jobs are and what they contribute to the general picture. They belong and serve, but often are at a loss to explain how and why.

There is a very real danger in this lack of understanding. As Woodrow Wilson once pointed out: *"No more vital truth was ever uttered than that freedom and free institutions cannot long be maintained by any people who do not understand the nature of their own government."*

The Precinct Leader

Basic to any understanding of the mechanics of government is the undeniable fact that elections are won and lost at the "grass roots" level—and this is where the first level of committees, namely the precinct committees, comes in. The entire pyramid of party organization rests, as mentioned in the preceding chapter, on the 131,693 precincts which cover this nation and upon which all the other committees are "built." The man who is the head of the precinct is the "captain" or "committeeman." The exact title varies from one community to another, but whatever he is called, the fact remains that he is the connecting link, the first contact between the voter and the party organization.

Do you know who your precinct leader or committeeman is? Or are you one of those people who just doesn't bother?

Precinct leaders are chosen by the voters in the primary elections. They get their names on the ballot in the usual way —that is, by petitions. These petitions are circulated by the precinct leaders themselves, together with petitions for all the other candidates put forward by the party machine.

It follows, therefore, that one good way for the average citizen to get into the arena of politics is to run for the job of precinct captain on his party's ticket. The precinct captain's principal job is to get out the vote on election day. It is also up to him to select poll watchers and workers for several paid jobs at the local level connected with the holding of an election.

On the City Level

The next level above the precinct is the "ward" in the urban areas and the "county" or "assembly" district in other sections. Precinct committeemen are usually under the ward leader.

In a city these ward leaders, in turn, combine to form a city committee. Again, in pyramid fashion, this latter committee selects a central executive committee which is really responsible for party policies and slates. In any typical large American city this executive committee wields enough power and controls enough votes to be most influential in state and national politics. But remember that this pyramid so far has had its foundation on those at the lowest level—namely, the precinct captain and his assistants. One could not exist without the other.

The County Committee

With the exception of the New England states, where the

town overshadows the county, one of the most important units of government is the county committee. It conducts campaigns, takes care of nominations, and controls all the machinery of the local party.

The county committees are composed of a committeeman and committeewoman from each election district in the county. In large cities, however, it may be the ward leaders rather than the district leaders who are chosen to serve on the county committee. In those areas where women are given recognition within the party organization, the size of the county committee may be doubled, a woman serving with a man leader from each election district. A woman may be vice-chairman of the county committee whose job it is to direct the activities of the women in the party.

The members of the county committee are usually chosen at the primaries, but in a few states they are selected by local party conventions rather than by the voters themselves.

There are over three thousand counties in the United States, and some forty-five thousand officials serve in various county capacities, almost all of them on a party basis. Their duties, on an increasing scale of importance in regard to the national scene, parallel the activities of party workers and officials at the lower levels.

The Congressional Committee

Every two years congressional elections are held throughout the country. Because of this, the parties in many states have separate congressional district committees. These committees have their personnel drawn from county committees and, with the latter, co-ordinate their activities with those of the state and national organization. How important a contribution a sound-thinking, patriotic man or woman can make to the general welfare at this level is graphically illustrated in the following account which came to our attention not very long ago.

Out in one of our Midwestern states a Christopher-minded man on a local congressional committee was assigned the job of drawing up a preliminary sketch of the various party candidates for public office. This worker proceeded to draw up the list with, however, one exception. He deliberately left off the name of a candidate who had made a habit of associating with any number of leftist organizations and fronts. The candidate himself was strongly suspected of being a secret member of the Communist party.

When the party bosses demanded that he include the leftist's name, this district worker refused and gave his reasons why. Moreover, he stuck to his guns at the time of the regular party meeting when the matter again came up for discussion. And it was no easy decision. The leftist commanded such a following among a certain class of voters that the party organization was willing to sacrifice principle for expediency. The party had to be maintained in power at all costs.

Eventually the leftist's name went on the list of eligible candidates. And no sooner had it been done than the worker who had opposed his nomination threw himself into the task of defeating him for public office. He gathered all the material he could about the leftist's affiliations from the secretary of his state. Then he had a notice inserted in the local paper on the Thursday before the election, which announced that he would speak on the radio at a certain time the following Saturday night.

When Saturday arrived this courageous man went on the air for twenty-five minutes—at his own expense—and informed the public of the leftist candidate's record. He pointed out that he took this unusual step fully conscious of the fact that for thirty-five years he had loyally supported his party. Now, he emphasized, it was a matter of loyalty to party or loyalty to country. He was choosing his country and, to further show his determination, he was urging every voter in the district to forget party lines and repudiate the leftist office seeker.

Thanks to his plea, the leftist was soundly beaten by almost forty thousand votes. The district worker lost something too. He sacrificed not only money but the friendship of those in his party whose patriotism and adherence to democratic principles left something to be desired. But this worker didn't care, because his conscience was clear. He had done his duty as God gave him the light to see it.

State and National Committees

The next important rung on the ladder of operations in both major political parties is the *state committee*. This committee is composed of representatives of the county committees, sometimes one or two from each committee or sometimes in ratio to population or party power within the various counties.

This committee heads the party organization within the state, conducts the campaigns, and, as part of its campaign work, raises money, arranges meetings, publishes and distributes pamphlets, leaflets, and so on. The state committee is constantly in contact with the various county committees and tries to keep them working together harmoniously. This power to keep the state political machinery working smoothly varies from state to state.

The state committee is, of course, most active in those years when a governor or a senator is elected. In presidential election years it is more or less overshadowed by the national committee.

Each of the two major political parties has a *national committee* composed of one man and one woman from each state. Each committee serves as the spokesman for the party. Whichever party happens to be in power at a given time, the national committee of the party is the official mouthpiece for the President and makes recommendations in regard to appointments, ranging from cabinet posts and ambassadorships down to the federal jobs at the local level.

In any presidential year the national committee maintains an extensive headquarters, with hundreds, perhaps thousands, of workers, and special divisions such as a speakers' bureau, publicity department, radio and television bureau, women's section, and so on. In non-presidential years the national committee still maintains a headquarters, but obviousⁿly on a much smaller scale.

In a presidential year the national committee and the national convention committee work in close co-operation, since the convention committee is charged with the responsibility of issuing the call for the national convention, selecting the convention city, and picking the date of the convention. In addition, this convention committee is concerned with the multiplicity of details connected with the actual holding of the convention itself.

The Voters Decide

The jobs on all the committees, from the precinct on up to the national level, are held by men and women from all walks of life. They have made politics their avocation—yet their selection still rests in the hands of the average citizen who votes for them at the various primaries. It is essential, of course, that every person in politics have the proper training, ability, honesty, and balanced judgment in order to serve the people he or she represents.

To run for public office does not necessarily entail the backing of a political party. But such backing, when possible, does smooth the "bumps" in one's political roadway.

State election laws specify how many signatures are necessary for a person to run for the various offices and when such signatures must be obtained. Anyone who secures the required number of signatures in the prescribed time can have his name put on the ballot. And from then on the success or failure of a candidate will depend on his ability and perseverance in rounding up people to vote for him.

Theodore Roosevelt once said: *"When a band of 150 or 200 honest, intelligent men, who mean business and know their business, is found in any district, whether in one of the local organizations or outside, you can guarantee that the local politicians of that district will begin to treat it with a combination of fear, hatred, and respect, and that its influence will be felt."*

A Word about Primaries

Many political writers have emphasized the importance of the direct primary in the mechanics of government. Anyone who undertakes a career in politics, either on a part-time or full-time basis, should be aware of this, just as they should be aware of all the details connected with election regulations. Those who abuse politics are well versed in this procedure. The sound-thinking man and woman who is out to change the world for the better can be no less.

One political observer, Frank R. Kent, set forth the importance of the direct primary in these forceful words:

"To think that the general election is more important than the primary election, as most voters do, is to magnify the wrong side of the political picture. It ought to be reversed, and instead of, as now, many more voters voting in the general election than in the primaries, the public interest should be concentrated on the primaries first, and the general election second . . . Primaries are really the key to election. There is no way for party candidates to get on the general election ballot except through the primaries."

This is your field. Here is where *you* count.

Election Regulations

It is difficult of course, for one person to be fully acquainted with all the details concerning election regulations. But each and every citizen has the obligation to know at least the basic facts—facts such as what qualifications the voter must possess, what regulations the state has provided for registration, when elections are held and for what offices, and so on. These points may seem academic at first glance, but it is surprising how few people are really and fully aware of them. And yet if a person is interested, all facts pertaining to elections and candidates may be secured at the office of the town or county clerk.

From the Bottom Up

A more comprehensive knowledge of the whole field of politics is needed, of course, to work effectively for better government at every level. Yet even a fundamental knowledge, combined with a general knowledge of the structure of political parties and the various committees, which has been given here, should provide the basis for sound, constructive action. One of the ablest congresswomen in the 81st Congress has acknowledged that she got her start in politics as a result of her detailed knowledge of the election laws.

Her home was in New England, where the caucuses which convened to select candidates for public office had much the same complexion as that of the old town meeting, with citizens from all walks of life participating. At one caucus which she attended an opportunity arose to challenge the accuracy of the party leader's interpretation of the election regulations. Although this was one of her very first meetings, it turned out that she knew the law better than did the party leader, for the simple reason that she had made it her business to "bone up" on the election regulations at home.

As time went on she became more prominent in the party's affairs. She became party chairman, and from that point on her progress from post to post within the party was practically assured. She became a leader of the women in the state, and at the state convention a few years later the delegates demanded that she be nominated for the elective post of Secretary of State. After serving in that capacity with considerable distinction, she ran for a seat in Congress, where she is today.

The way wasn't always easy in her political career. Those who know her acknowledge that there can be no question about that. But her determination to make felt her influence for good brought worth-while results. In fact, her whole life has been a shining example of the power of one individual. And her life likewise calls to mind the words which someone once wrote on this very same topic:

"It's true that you are just one person. But multiply one by a million and you have a million. Multiply a million by zero —and you have zero."

3   EVERYONE CAN DO SOMETHING IN POLITICS

The best way to show what can be done in politics is to point out what has been done by individuals who already have accomplished more than a little in helping to change the world for the better. Here is one example:

For several years now Al Hess, a restauranteur in Harrisburg, Pennsylvania, has been talking up a new law to his patrons, most of whom are politicians, legislators, and various minor government officials. He is pushing this new law because he feels that people in general know too little about their government, particularly about the Constitutions upon which their government is based. He has been urging all who would listen to him that a bill be passed to require the teaching of both the Federal and State Constitutions in the public schools. He is convinced that if youngsters are given a good education in regard to these documents—how they came into being, what they mean, and how they affect the lives of every man, woman, and child—the result would be sounder government.

Al Hess has impressed everyone who has heard him with both his sincerity and his logic, and just recently his suggestion spurred someone to action. That someone was a member of the State Legislature. The day after leaving Al's restaurant he introduced a bill at the Capitol to require the public schools to teach the Federal and State Constitutions to Pennsylvania children.

This was certainly a step in the right direction, but Al Hess didn't stop there. He keeps urging all the members of the General Assembly who stop by to "get that bill out of committee and vote on it. We've got to get it passed. Then . . . when these kids begin to grow up, we're going to have a better state!"

Everyone Counts

The party system of government, while it is the agency of our political life, still does not cover the entire area of political activity. Some of the strongest political forces in the United

States today have little or nothing to do with parties. They are groups of average people, citizens in all walks of life from truck drivers to teachers, from mechanics to manufacturers. The one thing most of them claim in common is that they are working for the public welfare. Regardless of their affiliations or geographical locations, they can accomplish much for the general good if they are not selfish groups. They can sponsor candidates who will put the people's interests first and their own welfare second. They can get laws passed, bills initiated, projects of various kinds inaugurated.

The task, as we see it, is to make democracy live in America once more as it did when our country first was founded. This entails active participation in the political life of the nation—running for public office, working in political organizations, voting, and so on. But it entails something more. If one sentence could describe it, it would be: become government-conscious.

Most people, fortunately, are becoming more aware of the role that government plays in their lives. And most of them are well disposed toward doing something about it. A survey made a few years ago showed that two out of every three citizens said that they would be willing to serve without pay on civic committees dealing with housing, education, labor-management problems, public welfare, and other vital subjects.

Yes, they were willing to offer their services—but the fact remains that only a small percentage actually ever did anything. They apparently were always waiting for the other fellow to start things moving.

A Kentucky Teacher

One person, however—a schoolteacher in Kentucky—is an exception to the rule. Within the four walls of her classroom she is doing her bit in the field of politics. As she related in a letter to us:

"Since being caught up with the Christopher idea, I've been hammering away here at the boys to take up careers in the vital fields, especially in government. It's hard getting a new idea into people's heads. Most of them are interested in getting just a "job," and politics seems off somewhere on Mars to most of them—indeed, sometimes it seems as if I could say that about all of them. But I'll keep at it until they graduate. I feel confident that some of these boys will go into careers where they can influence others for the better."

A Doctor's Advice

A few years ago some of the people in Richmond, Virginia, became concerned about certain conditions in their local government. In a gathering one night a man stated that he didn't think businessmen had a right to complain about the subject that was on everyone's lips and yet not do anything about it. The very next day a delegation of some of his associates called to inform him that they had chosen him the chairman of their committee "to do something about it."

At first this man refused on the grounds that he was too busy, only to be told that he was being guilty of the same fault he ascribed to everyone else. So he had no choice but to accept, which he did somewhat reluctantly. And he did make one condition: he couldn't do the job alone—he would have to have someone to help him.

The man selected to be his assistant had just returned from Washington, where he had been working for the government. He immediately informed the committee that he would have to refuse the assignment. "I couldn't possibly do it," he said. "I've already neglected my own business too long as it is. Besides, my health won't permit it. I really need a good long rest."

At this point the man who had agreed to do the job provided he got help invited the second man out for a ride. His destination, though he didn't announce it at once, was his doctor's office, where he surprised his friend by insisting that he have a physical checkup. When it was over he asked the doctor: "Is there anything wrong with my friend here that would prevent him from working on a local committee to get better government in the city?" "Absolutely not," came back the prompt reply. "As a matter of fact, it would undoubtedly do him a world of good. It would get his mind off himself and his own worries, which, I gather, are considerable."

To date the two men have done a wonderful job in arousing the local citizenry to the need for better government in their city.

The Power of One Woman

On April 28, 1949, Representative Clifford Davis of Tennessee, speaking on the floor of Congress, paid public tribute to a woman whose devotion to her country should be an inspiration to young and old alike. Referring to an article which had appeared in the *Saturday Evening Post*, Representative Davis told his colleagues that he had known the author of the piece, Mrs. Josephine Crisler, for many years and added: "Would that we had more Josephine Crislers in the world."

Mrs. Crisler's article, which was autobiographical, was entitled: "I Saved the Panama Canal." It wasn't as boastful as it sounded, as Mrs. Crisler was quick to point out. It was a simple statement of a fact. "I know it sounds fantastic," she wrote, "but before you wire me the name of your favorite psychiatrist, hang on until I get that documentary proof out of the desk drawer and I'll tell you what happened."

Mrs. Crisler went on to explain that she was a Washington, D.C., housewife whose husband—a former insurance executive —had been in the government for more than a dozen years prior to his death. Her story began in 1938 at the time of year when her three children, all boys, were cramming for their exams. Apparently they hadn't noticed how preoccupied their father had become. But she had, and finally she learned the reason why. Her husband then had been in government service a little over two years and had held a most responsible position. Conscientious by nature, he spent every waking minute trying to devise ways and means to enable his department to operate more economically and efficiently.

One night he and his assistant discovered that millions of

dollars could be saved on one operation alone. Naturally they were elated—until the next day when his secretary, who was a long-time government employee, laughed and said that it would be difficult under the management of that particular department.

Mrs. Crisler's husband refused to accept such an opinion. He persisted in his efforts. Among his other duties he was chairman of the personnel-selection committee charged with filling approximately thirty-five thousand jobs, and he became increasingly worried about a situation that arose when there was a change at the top of his agency. It was not a change for the better. His new boss apparently had many friends who had to be put on the pay roll, although they soon demonstrated that they had no intention of working for their money. Most of them began to use their time and the services of a stenographer or two to help them write books and do work on their doctorates. Moreover, most of the new employees were noncitizens and often could hardly speak a word of English. Despite the fact that civil-service regulations specifically prohibited the employment of such persons, and that Mr. Crisler went to great lengths to quote the regulations to his superiors, the applications were approved—and this at a time when there were many better-qualified Americans seeking government employment.

The result of Mr. Crisler's persistence in trying to live up to the letter and spirit of civil-service requirements brought about reprisals. Duties and assignments were taken from him, he was studiously ingored, given the "silent treatment." Finally, when he still stuck to his guns, the inevitable happened. His whole job was abolished.

As their savings dwindled and their situation became exceedingly grave, Mrs. Crisler decided to do something about it. She went to the only place she felt she could get action—the office of a senator from her home state. The senator wasn't in at the time of her call, but she told her problem to his secretary. She explained about the type of people who had cluttered her husband's old agency, and she added some other information she had obtained which cast serious doubts as to the loyalty of many of these so-called employees.

The senator, when he heard of it, was as outraged as Mrs. Crisler. His own investigation showed that there were well over ten thousand aliens on the federal pay roll! And many of them were poor security risks. Therefore he caused to be added to an independent offices deficiency bill then pending in Congress the following rider, which said, in part: *"No part of any appropriation contained in this act or authorized hereby to be expended shall be used to pay the conpensation of an officer or employee of the United States . . . unless such a person is a citizen of the United States . . . or being eligible for citizenship has filed a declaration of intention to become a citizen or who owes allegiance to the United States."*

The bill went through. And just as quickly there began an exodus from arsenals, war plants, navy yards, airfields, laboratories, experimental research and social agencies from New York to California and from Canada to the Canal Zone.

Some feel that this sweeping legislation went too far in excluding all non-citizens, many of whom were diligently working for the best interests of America. However, it did serve a purpose. Less than four years later the United States was at war. At a staff conference in the Pentagon a group of officers who had met to discuss the threat to our national security from subversive forces within our borders and territories recalled the law which a certain senator from Tennessee had caused to be enacted on the floor of Congress. And one senior officer gravely remarked: *"Gentlemen, you can say whatever you please but, in my opinion, we have that senator to thank for the fact that we have the Panama Canal today."*

In truth, Mrs. Crisler did a great service also. "As long as that law remains a law," she said, "I've still got my finger in the dike. Maybe women ought to get mad more often."

These examples are just instances of what good can be effected once people make up their minds to pitch in and do the job. Despite certain imperfections of our democratic system of government, the fact remains that we still have one of the best types of government in the world. If government is defective in any way, the fault lies chiefly with us, the people. As J. Edgar Hoover recently pointed out. "The American people, if they desire competent, efficient, and effective administration of justice, must be willing to provide financial means, moral support, and a practical realization of the responsibilities of citizenship."

Four Basic Rules

To make one's influence felt in the field of politics, whether it means running for public office, working in a political organization, serving on a civic committee, or encouraging pupils in a classroom to think of making politics their career, there are four basic rules that may be helpful.

1. Acquire a working knowledge of the political setup in your locality, city, and state.
2. Get facts—about candidates, issues, et cetera.
3. Offer your services for the essential chores and "leg work."
4. Maintain the basic principles of morality and fundamental Americanism.

While it is true that one must be well disposed toward taking up a career in politics, the fact still remains that the best of good efforts will fail to achieve maximum success unless the problem is approached properly. Adherence to the four basic rules listed above should prove a guide to effective action.

You can join your district club or a political group of your own choosing. Attend meetings, however dull, until it all seeps through and makes sense to you. Your very presence helps. Even if you can't make government service a career, you can still make your voice heard. Your individual influence for good will be felt by those who are in the service.

From the Home

In the past there has been much propaganda to the effect that politics is no place for a woman. Actually the reverse is largely true. The average woman, in her daily contact with grocers, shopkeepers, teachers, as well as with her next-door neighbors, acquires a unique insight into community problems from individual "case histories." And that experience can be translated into political action for the common good.

Even the busiest woman can do something in this way if she uses the head and the heart that God gave her.

Politically tough precinct captains have admitted that women, by and large, tend not to seek political privilege. One logical explanation may be that women are more intimately concerned with the welfare of the home—which, after all, is the backbone of our society. Consequently they are more keenly aware of the advantages of good government since government touches the lives of all, young and old alike.

There is virtually no segment of life that is not in some way affected by politics. And politics can be good or bad, depending on the caliber of the men and women who make politics their individual, personal responsibility.

4 A CAREER IN POLITICS CAN CHANGE THE WORLD

Up to November 7, 1950, John W. Costello of Jamaica Plain, Boston, was just another student in the senior class at Holy Cross College in Worcester, Massachusetts. A twenty-three-year-old war veteran, majoring in political science, he seemed known more for his athletic ability than for anything else. A standout swimmer and a second-string end on the football team, he had earned much praise from his gridiron coach, Dr. Eddie Anderson, for his "scrappy and aggressive play."

On November 7, 1950, however, John Costello's aggressiveness and capacity for hard work paid off in something else besides sports. That day saw him elected to office as the youngest representative in the Massachusetts State Legislature, capping a campaign almost without parallel in the Bay State's political history. Running in the primary against fourteen other candidates in the 19th Suffolk District, he succeeded in capturing the Democratic nomination, which, in that section, was tantamount to certain election.

According to Costello, his election was not just "one of those things" that sometimes happens. It was the result of a campaign born of a long desire "to do something constructive." He had always been keenly interested in politics. As he said, "From the time I was fourteen I used to follow elections through the newspapers and through comments by my father." He enlisted the aid of some sixty young men, his school and neighborhood friends, for a door-to-door campaign. More than one person scoffed at the idea and said it was a waste of time and couldn't be done. He was told he was too young, but his answer was always the same. He pointed out that many men in public life had sought office in their twenties. He cited the governor of the state and a few others to prove his point.

As it turned out, his youth was an asset rather than a liability. Only a person with his fire and energy could have maintained the rigorous schedule he laid out for himself. From early in the morning until late at night he kept at it. Often he was mentally and physically at the point of exhaustion, yet never once did he become discouraged. From his bank account, accumulated from his pay and terminal leave allowance while in the Navy, he paid out some four hundred dollars for campaign literature, leaflets, and other routine expenses connected with his candidacy.

His family, too, caught the spark of his purpose. His mother and two sisters addressed campaign literature and made telephone calls to friends. And his father, an attorney who had managed campaigns for a number of state officials, gave him invaluable advice on the practical aspects of electioneering.

Student and Legislator

All these efforts finally spelled victory. He won in the primary over the other fourteen candidates and went on to be elected the following November. When he was sworn into office in January 1951, there arose the problem of how he would continue with his classes at Holy Cross and also attend the sessions of the State Legislature in Boston, an hour's ride away. But he solved this problem, as he had all the others, by hard work and sacrifice. Fortunately he had only morning classes during his final semester. On the days that the Legislature convened at 11:30 A.M., he dashed from school the instant the bell rang and skipped lunch entirely. When the Legislature convened at 2 P.M. he had a little more "leisure" time—long enough, at least, to get a bite to eat.

Today, at his own request, he is serving on the Legislative Committee on Education. His aim is to help coordinate the American Government and American History courses in the public schools throughout the state. "People aren't interested in government," he said, "because they aren't educated in it." He feels that if people are instructed in government while they are young, more good men and women will be drawn to that profession.

Representative John W. Costello is living proof of the truth of his words.

For those who would make a specific area of politics their objective, there are innumerable opportunities for effective action. It has been estimated that nearly a half million people are needed to man the essential party jobs all over the country. And *this is considered to be the minimum figure*. Around election time the total rises to *two or three million*, returning to the lower figure only when the elections are over.

It may be true that not all of the half million "year-round employees" work at their jobs constantly, day in and day out. The political needs of the community determine their attendance. Without these loyal workers, no party could hope to continue as an effective political force.

Two Roads to Take

For those who intend eventually to run for public office, the schooling they will get in politics at the lower party organization level will prove invaluable. This, of course, is not the only way to plan a career in the political life of our nation. Actually there are two roads to political office.

One is the "low" road which has just been described—starting at the bottom of the political ladder and working up to more responsible posts until the time is opportune to actively seek public office.

James A. Farley, the former National Democratic Committee chairman, who knew from long experience the joys and advantages of pioneering in politics, made this recommendation recently: "In the vital realm of politics . . . it is essential that the torch of leadership be passed on to others, preferably to younger men.

"If younger men are not trained step by step to take over leadership there is danger that the race may be set back or lost," he added.

"Leaders do not spring full-grown into public office . . . but must patiently climb to eminences of trust through accomplished performance in positions of trust whether private or public."

The "high" road is considerably more direct but more hazardous. It should be followed only by those who have attained some measure of leadership or prominence in civic organizations, welfare councils, and the like, and have been identified in the public mind with public issues. In a state which has open or non-partisan primaries there undoubtedly are good opportunities for this direct method of running for office for those who have managed to develop an enthusiastic popular following.

Politics, like any other career, whether it be medicine, law, business, or science, should be planned if it is to be a success. Whoever plans to take this "high road" should not at the start expect to make a living from politics alone. Some job or profession will give him the income and independence he will need until he arrives at his goal of a full-time political career.

Meanwhile, in his spare time, he should try to gain a sound knowledge of political science, parliamentary law, the fundamentals of public speaking, and a working acquaintance with the rules which govern good public relations. This will prove a valuable aid, although it is not absolutely necessary.

Where to Start

The precinct—or election district, as it is sometimes called—is the basic political unit of the state. It might be a block long or it might be several blocks. There is no doubt that many elections are won or lost in the precinct. The role of the precinct captain is generally underestimated by the average voter. To become a precinct captain and do the job honestly and well is to assure eventual success in other areas of political life.

The precinct or district captain who makes the voters in his area his personal concern—not just in matters of voting but in everything that affects their general welfare—will do much to restore a firm moral tone to this vital field.

In politics, it should be emphasized, it is not flash or brilliance that counts the most, but loyalty, integrity, and steadiness of purpose.

If the post of precinct captain is one's immediate objective, it might be wise to arrange a meeting with the district leader and discuss the matter with him. More often than not he will help, especially if the seeker is a good party worker. When the opportunity arises to present the applicant's name to the party's nominating committee, he will do so.

The important thing to remember is not to be impatient when results are not immediately forthcoming. If a person stays on friendly terms with his leader and continues to be a good party worker, his chances are much better than if he broke away and tried to accomplish his objective on his own.

Part-Time Politics

For those who find it impossible to take up politics as a full-time career, there are many other important ways to work effectively to insure good government for all.

Three months or so before the elections, certain committees are activated and workers are asked to lend their assistance. Those who are interested should speak to the precinct captain or district leader and express to him their willingness to serve.

Some of the more important committees to which they might be appointed are as follows:

1. *The Speakers Committee* This committee prepares its members to discuss the issues of the campaign at public meetings and forums. It is not necessary to be an accomplished orator to serve on this committee. Clear, simple, sincere speaking is sufficient. He has to believe in what he says, and he has to have something of interest to say to his listeners.

2. *The Publicity Committee* This committee writes the news releases, leaflets, radio scripts, and letters to the editors. Press conferences are also arranged by this committee.

3. *The Finance Committee* This committee handles the general fund raising for the campaign, which is accomplished mainly by solicitations, holding dances, picnics, selling buttons, et cetera. If the party's program is sound and its candidates have popular appeal, fund raising is less difficult.

4. *The Businessmen's Committee* This committee usually raises funds for the campaign from fellow members of the business community. Money is raised by trades—grocers from grocers, furniture dealers from furniture dealers, et cetera.

5. *The Labor Committee* This committee is composed generally of leaders of the various labor unions in the community. Its job is to persuade members to vote for their candidates. It will invite candidates to union meetings to speak and meet union members, and will arrange mass meetings for its candidates. Pro-labor candidates will often receive contributions of men and money from labor groups.

6. *The Law Committee* This committee is the lawyers' committee of the party. It briefs district captains and poll watchers on the regulations affecting rights of voters, residence requirements for voting, et cetera. This committee

advises the party with respect to the law governing the holding of outdoor meetings, filing of nominating petitions, financial reports of candidates, et cetera.

7. *Veterans' Committee* This committee is composed of leaders and members of veterans' organizations and un-affiliated veterans. Its job is to secure the vote of veterans for its candidates. It usually appeals to the veterans by pointing out the pro-veteran stand of its candidates on housing, veterans' benefits, et cetera.

8. *Nationalities Committee* This committee operates wher-ever there are foreign-lauguage groups in the community. It supplies speakers and news releases for these groups and their own publications.

9. *Women's Committee* This committee appeals to the women's vote. It holds luncheons, teas, and other affairs. Its special task is to bring to the attention of the voters the party's stand on nurseries, schools, libraries, health and welfare legislation.

10. *Committee of Young People* Young men and women ranging from twenty-one to thirty-five years of age are in-vited to join and work through this committee. Here they are offered a variety of jobs—public speaking, ringing doorbells, distributing literature, et cetera. In regard to this latter committee, it might be well to add here the very point young Representative Costello brought out earlier—namely, schooling of young people for govern-ment.

Through the Schools

Some colleges already have courses which are geared (1) to prepare their graduates for government; (2) to accommodate college graduates now in civil service who wish a broader training as a base for further advancement; (3) to train college graduates in private business whose work deals intimately with governmental agencies; (4) to prepare students in grad-uate divisions of their universities to enter the technical or scientific services of the government on a full-time basis.

At a Conference on Practical Politics conducted not long ago in New York under the joint sponsorship of the Democratic and Republication parties, Paul E. Fitzpatrick, Democratic State Chairman, had this to say: *"The public servant and the political leader are just as important members of our society as the doctor, the scientist, the business executive. And, like any professional person, a good public servant should be trained for his career of service to his people."*

Of course merely being trained for government service will not of itself guarantee good government. It is far more necessary to be spurred on by a sense of purpose which aims at leaving the world a bit better for being in it.

It Really Works

One man who confessed that he had at first been somewhat skeptical "about the practicality of the Christopher approach" found that when he put that approach to the test "it really worked." In his letter he wrote:

"Last December, when I decided to give it a trial, I was surprised. With no political background or influence, I wrote to the newly formed ESA and offered my services as an attorney. I had served as an enforcement attorney with the old OPA for about two years and while there had become disillusioned about the viewpoint of those who were formulating the policy of that organization. I left it to return to private practice.

"When I made my decision to go back into government, however, I was astonished that my offer was accepted. Within the last two weeks I have been appointed Chief Enforcement Attorney for the ESA in——. Although the salary I will receive in government service will nowhere approach my earnings in private practice, I feel that I have a real opportunity to carry into effect the Christopher ideal."

The more men and women of high purpose who make government their individual, personal concern, the brighter the hope for a nation and a world at peace. In addition to competence and efficiency, they will give to the government at every level a firm sense of loyalty, which in these critical times is of paramount importance in our struggle for survival.

Aim High

Those who make politics their career, either on a full-time or part-time basis, should ever keep in mind that what they do can have a world-wide effect. Therefore they should think beyond their own small circle. Their vision should be global, with the welfare of *all* mankind their concern.

The value of such a concept was beautifully expressed by Daniel H. Burnham when he wrote:

"Make no little plans: they have no magic to stir men's blood, and probably themselves will not be realized. Make big plans, air high in hope and work, remembering that a noble, logical diagram once recorded will never die, but long after we are gone will be a living thing, asserting itself with ever-growing insistency."

Bold, constructive action in the area of politics is needed now as never before in our history. To echo the words of Emerson: *"This country was founded by the bold and cannot be maintained by the timid."*

IV. THE BEGINNINGS OF GOVERNMENT

IV. THE BEGINNINGS OF GOVERNMENT

1 WHY HAVE ANY GOVERNMENT AT ALL?

There is a legend that one day Frederick the Great of Prussia was walking along a road on the outskirts of Berlin when accidentally he brushed against a very old man. "Who are you?" asked Frederick out of idle curiosity as the two came to a halt.

"I am a king," the old man answered.

"A king?" echoed Frederick. "Over what principality do you reign?"

"Over myself," was the proud reply. "I rule myself because I control myself. I am my own subject to command."

The beginning of all free government, for which men over the earth have always yearned, is within each individual. The more he sees the necessity of governing himself, the more likely he is to see the need for direction and guidance through government in his relations with others.

In the paganism in which nearly three quarters of humanity still remains, man has little or no voice in how he is ruled. Because he is unaware of his own worth as an individual, he is easily dominated. He takes a passive, an almost hopeless attitude toward everything. He feels that a fate rules his life and that it is impossible for him to better his condition. He feels he has no freedom of will and in many respects is reduced to a life not much higher than that of the animal.

More than three thousand years ago one man who possessed such a deep reverence for a Higher Power devoted his life to bringing peace to his people. He realized that in order

139

to have law and order among them they would need some plan
or code as a basis for self-government. He was well aware
that he did not have within himself the wisdom or the ability
to formulate that plan.

The Mosaic Law

In his humility this man, a young Hebrew called Moses, appealed to God for assistance. God rewarded his trust and gave
him on two tablets of stone a basis of government that was to
serve down through the ages as a guiding star to keep each
and every one reminded of his minimum obligations to his fellow man and his Creator. By sacrificing himself for the common good of all, Moses showed how through one individual
the destiny of a whole people might be changed for the better.
Not only did he bring his brethren out of their enslavement in
Egypt, but he made them a free and independent nation, the
first to honor and worship a single God.

But having a code of laws, even from God Himself, doesn't
automatically solve the problem of providing society with that
order on which harmony and peace depend. More than knowledge is necessary. The will to do must follow. In performance
comes the test.

However, there is always hope when men know and respect
a code like the Ten Commandments, even though their observance of it may be imperfect. All the people who play golf
know at least some of the rules of the game. The vast majority
who play golf are mediocre golfers, try as they may to improve.
But they still keep playing, always hoping to do better. The
point to be remembered is that they wouldn't try, wouldn't
even play, if they didn't know the fundamental rules.

Rebellious by Nature

Man, weak and rebellious as he is because of the weakness of
his nature, knows deep down in his heart that he and everybody else ought to follow the moral law. But that doesn't make
him like it any better. As a matter of fact, more often than not
he has a keen aversion for any kind of control at all.

This was graphically illustrated not long ago when a newspaper editor, finding himself with space to fill in his evening edition, ran the following without editorial comment:

1. I am the Lord thy God . . . thou shalt not have strange gods before me.
2. Thou shalt not take the name of the Lord thy God in vain.
3. Remember that thou keep holy the Lord's day.
4. Honour thy father and thy mother.
5. Thou shalt not kill.
6. Thou shalt not commit adultery.
7. Thou shalt not steal.
8. Thou shalt not bear false witness against thy neighbour.
9. Thou shalt not covet thy neighbour's wife.
10. Thou shalt not covet thy neighbour's goods.

A couple of days later this editor received a letter from a subscriber who obviously didn't recognize the Ten Commandments when he saw them in the newspaper. "Cancel my subscription," the letter read. "You are getting too personal."

Tendency to Resist

When considering government, therefore, it is well to bear in mind that the ordinary human being usually doesn't want to be bothered with any control, any restraint. All through history he has shown a tendency to resist it, and even revolt against it when it runs counter to his own inclinations. He tends to be apathetic or indifferent when it concerns merely the welfare of others and implies no gain to himself. Most Americans have probably never once read the Ten Commandments. Were they to do so, they might come to feel inwardly disquieted—a feeling, incidentally, that may often be the first step toward self-improvement.

Difficult as it may be for man to put up with government of any kind, history shows he can't get along without some form of it, even in the most primitive society. Whether he realizes it or not, man is a political and social animal. He is a product of group living under all its legitimate restraints which are invoked to preserve the common good.

Factors That Help

Man is born of a group—the family—and gets his entire training and means of livelihood in a group—the home, the farm, the school, the community. Without group living his survival would be difficult indeed, with few if any opportunities to develop his talents and strive for the pursuit of happiness.

Government comes easier to those with a spiritual background because, realizing that they are children of God and heirs of Heaven, they have learned the necessity for self-respect, self-improvement, self-reliance, and discipline. Not only that, as children of God they are constantly reminded by Christ Himself that "Thou shalt love thy neighbor as thyself." And although this runs counter to their own selfish interests, they have learned by many a sad lesson that men enjoy the measure of peace allotted to them here on earth only when they show the same interest in the well-being of others as they show in their own.

The very laws of nature remind man that the order essential for the survival of the family was even more necessary when a number of families, early in history, gathered together in a clan, a tribe, or a colony. At the very outset such a merging of interests took place as a matter of course, since it immediately became apparent that certain measures would have to be taken for the health, safety, and general well-being of everyone concerned.

Since most of the people had to be busy running their homes, doing the farming, building, carrying on trade or engaging in other occupations necessary for their livelihood, they chose others to act for them in the performance of the elementary duties vital for the preservation and continuance of the community. Yet even then it was recognized that if this arrangement was to work out satisfactorily, everyone involved would have to keep ever conscious of the role of those individuals set aside to represent the community. It had to be borne in mind at all times that in whatever capacity they acted, they were employed by the majority to serve their best interests. In the full sense of the term, they were public servants, charged with the responsibility of serving the public. They were made to understand that whatever authority they possessed was delegated to them by the people themselves.

Still Your Business

In modern society most people are too preoccupied with their own affairs to arrest lawbreakers, use weapons to preserve law and order, or regulate the movement of traffic. The community therefore appoints policemen, and delegates to them the power to carry out these functions.

In the same manner we, as members of the public, delegate the power to make laws to our elected representatives, assign the tax-collecting function to the collectors, and turn over the administration of justice to our elected or appointed judges.

The delegation of authorities like these is a matter of convenience for each of us. It is important to remember, however, that the original powers still reside in us as political rights. By that fact alone we can see that turning over authority to someone else and then forgetting all about it will not discharge the functions of citizenship. We must remember always that the fact that we have the rights imposes an obligation on each of us to see that those rights are properly exercised.

Naturally, because those delegated to serve the public good would have no time to earn a reasonable living for themselves, the community relieves them of that responsibility by providing compensation. Originally this compensation was based on the average earnings of individuals in the community. So long as the community kept the relationship on this basis—i.e., that those engaged clearly understood that their primary function was to serve the best interests of all as a public trust—it was felt that there would be a fair assurance of good government for all.

If the people of the community failed to take sufficient interest in the activities of their public servants, they might neglect their duties or seek personal advancement by enlarging their sphere of jurisdiction. Then the compensation and acquisition of power over their neighbors would become their primary interest and their job as protectors of the interests of the community secondary. Thus they would become the masters instead of the servants.

Our Debt to the Greeks

Anyone interested in the origins of government would do well to look back into early Greek history. All of us are indebted to the Greeks for working out the first formula of self-government.

In the beginning they lived in tiny settlements as a free people. To discuss matters of public importance they gathered together in the market place, where each one had an opportunity to express his views. An elder of the village was chosen to conduct the hearing. In case of war, one man among them was picked to lead them until the emergency was over. Eventually these villages grew into cities, with a subsequent development of a governmental system.

With this expansion into a more complex society, certain abuses crept in. There arose a small class of rich people and a large class of poor, and the head man disappeared from the scene entirely. His place was taken by the class of rich folk, who were called nobles, who were usually a warlike group given to bickering among themselves and producing temporary kings. These kings, with but a few exceptions, soon earned the reputation of tyrants in their rule of the Greek cities. Finally the system became unbearable.

The people of Athens decided that a good house cleaning was needed to recover their once-held voice in the government. They chose Solon to write a code of laws to improve the condition of the peasant without destroying the prosperity of the nobles. His code not only protected the "demos"—the people—but forced the average citizen to take an individual interest in his government, to attend council meetings, and to recognize fully his responsibility in achieving the safety and prosperity of the state.

No longer could he remain away. and say, "Oh, I have too much to do today," or, "I'm tired and need a rest." Each man had his part to play and was expected to do his share. This government taught the Greek people independence and the necessity for relying on the individual for the preservation of their state. Thus were sown the first seeds of democratic government.

Strength and Weakness of Roman Empire

The next great civilization to develop was the Roman Empire, some five hundred years later. Also founded on a code of laws, it was to rule most of the then-known world. Order was established, roads were built, trading and commerce prospered, the arts were cultivated. To be a Roman citizen was deemed a prize treasured above all else.

Paul the apostle stood on his rights as a Roman citizen when he appeared before Portius Festus, the Roman governor: "I appeal to Caesar," insisted Paul (Acts 25:11). Festus had no choice but to reply: "To Caesar shalt thou go."

The Roman Empire suffered from human defects which eventually brought about its destruction. It became a dictatorship, its morals vanished, its culture disappeared.

A New Concept

At this critical hour in history, when civilization itself seemed to totter, when men began to question the very reason for their existence, an event took place which was to change the whole course of history from then until the end of time. Into the world was born a tiny Babe. At His birth in Bethlehem the angels sang: *"Glory to God in the highest; and on earth peace to men of good will"* (Luke 2:14). Thirty-three years later Jesus Christ stood before a Roman governor, Pontius Pilate, on trial for His life. And yet, in standing trial, he brought a new concept of government to the world. *"Thou shouldst not have any power against me,"* He said, *"unless it were given thee from above"* (John 19:11).

The advent of Christ gave suffering mankind a goal in life, and an eternal purpose. It provided the answer to why God put man on earth: to know, love, and serve Him in this life so as to be happy with Him forever in the next.

And so Rome, whose empire was built on the sands of dictatorship, where the authority to govern was not recognized as coming from the Author of all Creation, went down to destruction. And across the world went the divine message which Christ came on earth to bring. Men were made to realize that they were stewards of a common God-given heritage. Their power to govern, they realized, came from God, and from Him alone.

Recognizing the Need

Today, when the whole Christian concept of government is being challenged by those who would wreck our society, Americans are becoming increasingly aware that the more they know about the true origins of authority and the more interest they take in government, from top to bottom, the better it will be for everybody. They are becoming conscious that, in order to live harmoniously, they have to conform to an organized structure of government in a free society. Failure to recognize the need for this pattern, they realize, produces social chaos. Without an organized political society based on sound principles, no normal social intercourse can exist.

2   EVERYTHING STARTS AT THE GRASS ROOTS

A young Manhattan lawyer, Oren Root, began to read a few speeches of the late Wendell Willkie in the spring of 1940. Mr. Root liked what he read about the prominent business executive. His admiration went deeper a few weeks later when he saw one or two magazine articles about the same man. Gradually in Root's mind grew the conviction that Willkie was an individual of presidential caliber. Once he had reached this conclusion, the young attorney decided to do something about it.

At best he had but a very vague idea of how one went about the job of launching a candidate in the race for public office, especially when that office was President of the United States. Moreover, he realized that another factor made his task more difficult: Mr. Willkie did not have the slightest idea of what he, Root, planned to do.

The young lawyer started by discussing the matter with some of his friends and acquaintances. Most of them favored his idea, but they tempered their approval by stating that they didn't think Willkie had a ghost of a chance of being nominated, for the simple reason that he was not and never had been in politics.

Other difficulties and obstacles subsequently presented themselves. Yet Root refused to be deterred. He felt there was much to gain and little to lose. He quickly set to work to see if opinion in favor of Willkie could be organized. He prepared a short statement giving his reasons why he thought Willkie would make a good President and had it printed. Twenty blanks appeared underneath the statement in which could be inserted the names and addresses of anyone in favor of the idea. He mailed them to some eight hundred people whose names he had selected at random from college directories, fraternity catalogues, and alumni lists. Root, of course, had no money of his own to spare. Realizing that the project might run into considerable expense if the idea caught fire, he put the name of the printer and the price of additional copies on the statement so that anyone could order more.

The response was immediate and encouraging. People began calling and writing for more information. Newspapers picked up the story. This thoroughly unprofessional attempt to reach the grass roots met with such quick and widespread success that it astonished everybody.

The only one who wasn't too pleased about it was Wendell Willkie, who read about it in the newspapers. He was very

upset and promptly sent for Root. It was the first time the
two had ever met. He asked Root to put a stop to further
activity, explaining that it was making him look silly. He was
interested, to be sure, in the great privilege of being President of the United States, but he felt he didn't have a chance
of being nominated.

He Had the Right

Root respectfully stood his ground and argued that as an
American citizen, he, Root, had the right to select anyone
whom he felt was qualified for the office and to do whatever
was within his power to promote his candidacy.

Meanwhile the campaign that had been started by a one-
man committee began to snowball. The switchboard of the
law firm with which Root was connected was so flooded with
enthusiastic telephone calls about the Willkie project that
regular business came almost to a standstill.

For Root the only alternative was to leave the firm and
open a small office of his own on Madison Avenue, where he
continued working on the Willkie nomination. Volunteers
came in off the street. Soon there were a dozen people working
on the staff. An advertisement a friend inserted in a newspaper, inviting financial aid from anyone interested in the
project, brought in ten thousand dollars in small contributions.
Two million persons ultimately signed statements similar to
the eight hundred originally mailed out.

Within a short time people in every section of the country
were organizing Willkie clubs. And out of these clubs came
a spirit and enthusiasm that swept across the country right
into the Republican convention and resulted in Willkie's nomination for President of the United States.

It was a clear demonstration of the power of the grass roots
which is the basic strength of our country. The entire project
was started and completed within three months. Oren Root
prepared and mailed out his simple statements to eight hundred people in April. Willkie was nominated in June.

Voice of the People

It is usually around election time that the term "grass roots" comes into prominence on the pages of American newspapers. Candidates for political office suddenly remember that the grass roots can make or break their careers, and so they give the matter their earnest attention.

To give a hard and fast definition of what is meant by the term isn't easy. Generally speaking, however, the grass roots are associated in the average person's mind with rural America, with the ordinary, down-to-earth citizen who is close to the soil and to his neighbors. The grass roots is believed—and with considerable truth—to represent the heart of America, the voice of a people still holding fast to the early concept of democratic government. Since the grass roots expresses the power of the individual for good, it can have a significant impact on our society.

There is a tremendous reservoir of power for good resting in the hands of the man in the street, the woman in the home, the pastor in the church, the teacher in the classroom, the farmer in the field, the doctor, the lawyer, the truck driver, the businessman, the artist. It is seldom brought into play because more frequently than not the individual underestimates the influence that he personally can exert for the benefit of all.

It was to arouse this sense of personal responsibility and individual initiative that the Christopher movement was founded. We say over and over again that *you can change the world*—that whoever you are, in whatever circumstances you may be, you can, by the grace of God, render a service to the well-being of your country and your world that no one else can make.

Our Limitations

However, while we recommend that each one make his voice heard and do whatever he can to bring about better government, we repeat frequently that it is our strict policy to refrain from recommending what party one should join, how he should vote, what position with regard to politics he should take, or what issues he should support.

We limit ourselves to the urging of each to base his judgments upon the spiritual and natural truths upon which our nation is established. We therefore encourage each person to stand on his own two feet, make his own decisions, and have the courage of his own convictions. We feel that the more deeply he personally and individually is convinced of his own accountability, to God and his fellow man, the better his judgments will be. The more he realizes that it is his job to safeguard and strengthen his country, the more imagination and resourcefulness he will display in initiating or co-operating with measures that are for the common good.

It is fascinating to see the steps that individuals will take when they get the slightest bit of assurance that they really count, that they can do something to better a situation. Each one seems to go about it in a slightly different manner—which in itself reflects the imagination and enterprise of an interested person. Their desire to reach beyond themselves and share with others expresses the purpose that makes the difference.

The Power Is There

Imagine if you will a great outdoor arena where perhaps thirty thousand people have gathered on a summer night to hear a famous opera star sing. The audience lights are darkened, the singer steps on-stage and a single spotlight picks him up. Then the tones begin to flow, golden and appealing, over every corner of the vast arena. And the audience falls silent as the music comes welling forth.

What is this single thing which can hold an audience of thirty thousand enthralled, Nothing more than the human voice. Every individual in that audience has a voice: some good, some bad, some mediocre. Fundamentally all of the voices had the same beginning. The opera singer dominates a huge audience because he has developed his voice, his stage presence, and his memory. It is, then, not the fact that he has a voice and we have none, but rather the fact that his degree of vocal development exceeds ours.

Possibly only a few of the audience could hope to match the singer's proficiency. But in that audience are voice students who are trying to match it. They know the old saying: "Every professional was once an amateur."

They also know that diligence, hard work, and a burning desire to attain the heights may someday make them the opera star's equal. If they had no voices to begin with, their quest would be hopeless. But all of us have the basic ingredient, the voice itself. It is how we develop it, how we share it with others, and how we hold steadfastly to our purpose that makes the difference.

From a High-School Teacher

Here is an example of how one person motivated by a love of country can see a danger that many might overlook. A high-school teacher in Springfield, Massachusetts, took the time and trouble to write the following letter. We feel we can help make her voice heard over the country by presenting it here.

"As a teacher of history in a large high school I am becoming increasingly aware of a great need for us to do something quickly about this national situation. I mean the growing disrespect toward our leaders in city, state, and federal government.

"If it becomes much worse, it can well be an opening wedge for the Communists to use in their favorite method of "divide and conquer."

"This unhealthy attitude toward all people in positions of authority will stop many a man of high motives from running for public office.

"As I talk with many young people, I am shocked at this growing disrespect which I know is only a reflection of what they hear from their elders.

"Although we know there are individuals who abuse

the power of their office, nevertheless we must not overlook the great service being rendered by the large number of good, honest people in public office who are doing their best in these troubled times.

The People Speak

Another example of the power of the grass roots to initiate a change for the better was put in plain evidence when the Senate Crime Investigating Committee indicated that it was bringing its work to a close a few months ago. The flood of mail from people all over the United States, demanding that the investigation continue, literally engulfed the members of Congress, with the result that official Washington began making plans to see that the committee's work continued in some form or other.

Still another manifestation of the power of the grass roots can be found every day in the week in the actions of *grand juries* from one end of this county to the other. Grand juries are one of the safeguards of our liberties. Chosen from representative and intelligent members of the community, they are a vital factor in seeing that the scales of justice operate fairly and well. They have the power to subpoena witnesses and possess the mighty weapon of punishment for those who defy their authority.

And speaking about the measures taken to stop the increase of crime in America, grand juries are the means whereby the ordinary citizen can do much to wipe out corruption in his community. In Cleveland about eighteen years ago a grand jury was called to sit on a case involving a taxi driver who had been beaten up by four underworld hoodlums. This particular grand jury did not confine itself to the case at hand, however. It endeavored to trace the hoodlums' connections, and in doing so threw the spotlight on the whole structure of organized crime in the city. More than that, it brought about a general house cleaning which went so far as to affect even some of the local officials, who were thrown out of office for protecting known criminals.

In Brooklyn some years ago the infamous Drukman case so shocked the grand jury that when it disbanded it brought formal charges against the district attorney. When the state later exonerated him, these same jurors paid their own expenses to the state capital to protest. The visit made such a stir and received so much comment in the press that the district attorney's office was changed from top to bottom.

Service on a grand jury demands the best that our citizens can offer. It is the answer to those who may be shocked at crime and corruption but who also ask, "What can I do about it?" Grand juries are one weapon which our citizens have to insure better government and a better, safer life for all. All they have to do is use it.

The Beginning of Responsibility

Basically, it all comes down to the matter of developing or awakening in the American people a sense of their responsibility to the community. And this sense of responsibility to the community cannot be strengthened unless there is first a responsibility to one's God.

About the only big obstacle in stirring the grass roots to action is the tendency on the part of the vast majority to feel that "I don't count," "I'm only one little person and nobody will pay any attention to me," "What I do or don't do won't make any difference anyhow."

This underestimating of the power of even one individual probably accounts more than anything else for the plight that most of Europe is in today. The average person failed to make his voice heard. The grass roots never brought into play its inherent strength. It inclined to follow rather than to lead. Because it neglected to assert itself, it was easily dominated.

In China some years ago this same attitude—that what one person does or fails to do is relatively unimportant—brought starvation into many a home. And while primarily it concerned an agricultural problem there, its lesson can just as easily be applied to the field of political activity in America today.

A Million Times One

It so happened that the average Chinese farmer raised just enough rice for his own needs and that of one other family. Half of his crop he kept for himself, since it sufficed for him and his family both in good times and bad. The other half he sold to merchants, who transported it to a distant province which could do no farming of its own and which had to depend on others to raise most of the food that it consumed.

When a famine threatened, the rice farmer decided to keep his entire crop for himself. Though he meant no harm, withholding that portion probably meant starvation for another family. If it had been restricted to only one family, it would have been bad enough. But approximately a million other little farmers likewise decided that nobody "will miss the rice that I would sell, so I will keep it for myself." Because a million farmers thought this way, it was estimated that approximately a million other families suffered. Many were wiped out, because each of them in turn had been deprived of the little food that meant the difference between life and death for them.

In order to arouse the grass roots, it is necessary to stress over and over again the truth that even the least person can exert far-reaching effects for good. He should never forget even for one moment the old saying that "While I am only one, yet I am one. I cannot do everything, but I can do something. What I can do, I ought to do. And what I ought to do, by God's grace, I will do."

Every effort should be encouraged that will remind the average citizen that he counts, that he is important, that he has a particular mission to perform, that "freedom is everybody's business," that government will never be any better than he makes it.

The total population of the village, the city, the state, the country is nothing more than the average citizen multiplied over and over again. Make him conscious of his responsibility to fulfill his obligations as well as exercise his rights, encourage him to take a stand in matters that vitally affect all—getting out to vote, urging others to participate, fighting for business-like methods in government, and cutting down on every unnecessary expense—and the big job of getting better government is well in hand. Neglect the average citizen and there is littl hope of ever improving the situation.

The Highest Hurdle

Probably the greatest obstacle of all to an alert and active citizenry is a certain defeatist attitude that the average man entertains toward his own capabilities. In a way, the main difference between the great man and the ordinary man, the successful one and the failure, lies in just this.

The biographies of most of our great men and women who stand out in public service could be told in terms of their defeats as well as of their triumphs.

The Classic Example

Many cases in the annals of those who have dedicated themselves to government could be given. But the one that can serve as a model for all of how a man in public service actually built his life and accomplishments upon defeats is that of Abraham Lincoln.

The following litany of failures that punctuated his life throughout thirty years is a living and eloquent example of the successful use of defeat in achieving victory.

ABRAHAM LINCOLN

1. Failed in business 1831
2. Defeated for legislature 1832
3. Again failed in business 1833
4. Elected to legislature 1834
5. Sweetheart died 1835
6. Had nervous breakdown 1836
7. Defeated for Speaker 1838
8. Defeated for Elector 1840
9. Defeated for Land Officer 1843

10. Defeated for Congress 1843

11. Elected to Congress 1846

12. Defeated for Congress 1848

13. Defeated for Senate 1855

14. Defeated for Vice-President 1856

15. Defeated for Senate 1858

16. Elected President 1860

Lincoln had great native talents and gifts. Not the least of them was his courage in not letting defeats get him down. Likewise, a measure of greatness is awaiting every man who will rise above his failures.

You too, in God's Providence, can, despite all obstacles, do great things for your country—for your world!

3 THE ROLE OF THE VILLAGE AND TOWN

Picture yourself someplace in New England, in a small colonial town, two hundred years ago, the year being 1751 instead of 1951. The roads are muddy, the sidewalks nonexistent. Over there is the blacksmith's, there a confectioner's or sweetshop, there a bakery, there an inn. And there, in the very center of everything, is the town meetinghouse with its wooden-pillared front and crudely carved bulletin board.

This meeting hall typifies the nearest approach to pure democracy that America has yet seen. Within its walls the people of colonial and post-colonial times gathered to debate public issues, to vote on laws for their welfare, and to nominate candidates for local government office. It expresses in specific form the words which Abraham Lincoln was to utter a century later when he pledged that "government of the people, by the people, and for the people" would not perish from the earth.

Meeting of the People

Tonight in this New England town the people have gathered for their annual meeting. Notices announcing the event have been posted well in advance, so that no one may plead ignorance of what is to take place. A new slate of town officers is to be elected, the amount of money to be spent in the coming year is to be determined, the tax rate is to be established.

One of the men prominently mentioned as a likely candidate for public office is smiling and waving to his neighbors inside the hall, showing his pleasure at the confidence they have placed in him. And he is conscious too, perhaps, that if, without good reason, he were to refuse to serve if elected, there would be imposed on him a fine of five dollars—a considerable sum of money in those days. He and all the other menfolk in the town, you see, are obliged to take turns serving the public welfare. That obligation was deemed the best guarantee of individual participation in government.

The meeting itself conforms to a fairly recognizable pattern. Proceedings are opened with a prayer offered by the meeting chairman. Then the items on the agenda are announced, beginning with the candidates to be considered for office. What remuneration, if any, goes with each office is also established. Some posts draw pay, most do not, and this is a boon to the townspeople who pay the taxes. The town clerk, who is ex-officio registrar, is seated at the end of the platform, where he keeps the statistics and informs the chairman of what money is available for public use. The clerk, it should be added, is also the town treasurer.

Nominations are then accepted from the floor, seconded, and the names are duly recorded. Then comes the vote, on the result of which is determined what men shall act in an official capacity on their neighbors' behalf. The winning candidates are then sworn in.

The rest of the meeting runs long or short, depending on the issues to be discussed. Occasionally tempers flare high and sharp words are spoken. But the people do have a chance to be heard. Tax proposals are voted upon and other business settled to the satisfaction of the majority concerned. And then the meeting is closed, as it began, by a prayer for divine guidance with thanks for favors received.

From Those Beginnings

This, in brief, is what a typical New England town meeting might look like to a visitor from the present-day world. And while our society has grown more and more complex with each passing year, the spirit, if not the procedure, of the town meeting is recommended as the best insurance of good government. In the town meeting everyone participated in one way or another.

You may ask, how did they find the time? What happened to the fields, their livestock, the sick ones at home, their "pressing business" while attending the meeting? Often as not meetings were held at night or on week ends, but also men and women considered that *nothing* was more important than how their town was to be run, by whom, at what cost, and with what rules and laws.

Today, only by making government our individual, personal concern can we insure sound administration for ourselves and for our children.

Most of the features of small local government can be traced back to the colonial period. Some were, of course, designed to meet the rugged pioneer conditions which the early settlers encountered. Others were copies or adaptations of earlier English models. All, however, were geared to supply the immediate needs of the local citizens. The colonists chose selectmen, assessors, constables, fence viewers, and other town officers, adopted the few ordinances necessary for security, and voted the necessary taxes.

Basic Services

Contrast the simplicity of these services with the complex needs of even the smallest town or village in these United

States. Government services today affect most of the daily activities of every individual—man, woman, and child. These services include:

Safeguarding personal right and liberties	Education
	Safety laws
Protection of property	Local improvements—side-
Public health	walks, roads, et cetera
Water supply	Recreation
Apprehending criminals	Libraries
Traffic controls	

When the cost of these services is examined, the role of local government assumes its proper significance. In 1940, the last year of normal prewar expenditures, the total spent by federal, state, and local governments in the United States was seventeen and one half billions of dollars. And of this sum, 40 per cent was spent by local governments. Until the second World War, as a matter of fact, and except for two extraordinary periods—the first World War and the depression of the 1930s—local government expenditures constituted a larger sum than the amounts spent by state or federal government!

The amount of money spent, of course, does not fully gauge the town's or village's importance in the national scene. In addition to local, tangible services, small communities perform other equally significant functions in a free society. They provide stages for civic action, a school of citizenship. It is an undeniable fact that more people have an opportunity to participate in civic affairs here than anywhere else. They have more opportunity to realize in practice that government is what we individually do, not what we let others do for us.

Divisions of Local Government

It is not easy to define accurately what constitutes a village or town. Not only do the words themselves take on different meanings in different areas of the country, but the classification also often varies with each state.

In some states this classification is decided directly by population. It varies from forty-two to ten thousand. New York State, for instance, might have a town of ten thousand, while in Nevada or Utah such a unit would be classified as a city.

Other states classify communities according to the responsibility they are willing to assume. If they undertake their own police protection, water supply, and other public services, they are sometimes regarded as a village or town.

There are nearly nineteen thousand towns and townships in the United States. In addition, there are 16,220 cities, 109,-000 school districts, and about 8,300 other special-function districts, for a total of 155,000 units of local government at the grass-roots level.

In the South and South Central region of the United States the area structure of local government is the county; in the North Central, the combined county and township; in New England, the town. In addition there are school districts, municipalities or cities, and other special-function districts. But the village and town remain the smallest and most cohesive units of local self-administration and, as such, constitute the basic community groups in the whole national structure.

Recently there has been a large drifting to big cities in search of employment as our economy has become more centralized and industrialized. Yet for millions throughout the country who have clung to their own small communal life, the town and the village represent their only contact with government. Since the communities are comparatively small, there is both the opportunity and inclination for each individual citizen to take the matter of government personally and make it his own concern. This personalized attitude should be extended to *every* phase of government life.

Not Wholly Independent

Towns and villages, while small and more or less self-govern-ing, are not, however, independent of any outside authority. Do you realize that towns and villages can incorporate and exist only by permission of the state legislature? This is a point which any aspirant to local public office should bear in mind. In poorer communities, especially, the state often has to step in and assist in matters which the towns and villages are unable to handle themselves.

Furthermore, towns and villages frequently pool their re-sources to maintain hospitals and poorhouses. Good public relations beyond one's own small circle is therefore of first importance.

Geographical Differences

Just as towns and villages are not wholly independent units, so in various parts of the country their functions differ to a fairly wide degree. Not only that, even their name designations are different.

In Mississippi, for example, the primary districts of gov-ernment are not known as townships but as "beats." Tennessee calls them "civil districts." The term "election precincts" is used in Alabama, Colorado, Florida, Idaho, Maryland, New Mexico, Oregon, Utah, Washington, and Wyoming. Texas calls them "Justice's precincts" and "Commissioners' precincts." Delaware uses the designation "representative districts," while Georgia calls them "militia districts," and Louisiana, "police jury wards."

Diversity of Functions

Some townships have been incorporated merely for school pur-poses. Some have no political organizations as we understand them generally. Some serve simply as judicial districts. Still others are used solely for purposes of assessment. There are thousands of towns and villages, however, which have a full administrative organization and stand in relation to the local citizenry on a basis as complete, governmentally speaking, as is possible under modern conditions.

In regard to this last group, especially, it would be well for the man or woman contemplating a career at the local level not only to become better acquainted with the functions which local government generally performs but to become an active participant in public affairs. In other words, strive to *do* as well as to *know*, keeping ever in mind that experience at the lower levels of government is an excellent apprenticeship for effective action in more responsible governmental positions.

Incidentally, your close interest in those who run local government can do much to guarantee the best type of officeholder. At the same time, by this positive method you will help to eliminate questionable characters and prevent them from reaching higher branches of government. All big crooks start as little crooks.

Protection of Life and Property

Throughout our history, maintenance of law and order has been regarded as the chief function of local government. One proof of this is that the colonial governments never maintained a police force nor has the federal government maintained one. As a matter of fact, it wasn't until recently that a limited number of states arranged for a state police organization. Since crime and criminal tendencies start with the individual, the closer law-enforcement agencies are to the people the better the chance of protecting society. Organized crime which cuts across local boundaries requires the attention of state and federal authorities. But, so far as possible, maintaining law and order should rest with the local sheriff or constabulary.

Judicial Functions

The administration of justice has always been and still is a primary function of local government. The whole theory of common law, with its minor courts and jury system, is based on the belief that the citizen can and should have his disputes settled in a fair and equitable manner—settled, that is, with the aid of his neighbors. And by settling such disputes locally, not only is higher authority relieved of the responsibility but the whole procedure is in line with the idea that communities, insofar as possible, should take care of their own problems and not allow outside agencies to take care of them. Likewise, the private citizen should care for his own problems whenever he can and not let others do the job for him. It all comes down, basically, to a matter of self-reliance. And that's where *you* come in.

Agricultural Extension

Originally, the promotion of agriculture in areas favorable to it was a state and federal function. Now, however, it is carried on locally by the township or county agricultural agent, who is employed jointly by the state college of agriculture, the U. S. Department of Agriculture, and the several county boards of commissioners or supervisors. He is in charge of all extension activities carried on within the county. He works under the direction of state leaders of major phases of the program, such as home economics, extension of 4-H club activities, and is administratively responsible to the extension division of the state college of agriculture. These programs carry considerable weight in the community since, being educational in character, they cover a wide variety of activities.

The Christopher-minded man or woman who aspires to such a post as county agricultural agent will see countless opportunities for guiding youthful minds and imparting a sense of direction and purpose to work for the common good and not for one's self alone.

Public Welfare

In the early days of our country, public welfare had none of the aspects of social-service care as we understand it today. Those in distress were assigned to almhouses, poorhouses or poor farms. In fact, most New England towns had a poor farm as part of its community life. In modern times, however, the spirit of charity has dictated that people in distress be helped to become self-supporting and self-respecting members of the community. This task has often brought the state and federal government into the picture to take over local relief. Sometimes, of course, these agencies are necessary. But too many people have let the solution of their own problems go by default because they were unwilling to assume their individual responsibility.

This point is stressed here because the person with a Christopher purpose making public welfare his career should have a clear-cut idea of his role and the role of his profession in the community. It all comes down to a matter of doing the right thing for the right reason.

Maintenance of Schools

A few years ago the U. S. Commissioner of Education stated that there were some 143,445 separate one-room schoolhouses scattered across the country. He made the additional point that there were almost as many separate school districts, the largest grouping being in Illinois, which had some 12,138 in all.

Despite the fact that of late the extension of state subsidies to local education has cut into local control over such matters, for the most part the citizens of towns and villages have insisted upon choosing by popular vote the members of the local school board or board of school directors; they have joined parent-teacher associations and, in other ways, have demonstrated a deep concern over the problems of the local schools. This field, in particular, offers countless opportunities for those with a Christlike purpose.

Recreation Programs

Increased leisure among workers means that local units have the duty to develop recreational facilities and programs for their use, in order to assist those so inclined to make pleasant and profitable use of their spare time. Such programs are expensive, naturally, but not so expensive as to warrant failure to inaugurate or continue them. Much of the incidence of crime among adults—not to speak of those of teen age—would be sharply reduced by providing the opportunities for pleasant, wholesome recreation at little or no cost to the individual concerned.

Other Functions

Under the heading of strictly administrative work come such functions as election staffing and clerical and recording duties.

On election staffing, local authorities are responsible for the printing and distribution of the ballots, the determination of the number and the size of voting districts, and the reporting of the returns after the polls have closed. In this same classification can be included election judges and officials as well as poll watchers and other functionaries.

Finally, in the matter of clerical and recording functions, these have always been part and parcel of local responsibility and are performed either by the town or county clerk. Where a township comprises the whole county area, additional clerks, of course, are required—clerks to staff the various courts, the various administrative boards, and so on.

From the Bottom Up

The importance of a clerical post in a town or village cannot be overestimated. One young man we know, who had caught the Christopher idea, made it his business to concern himself directly with the government of the village in which he lived.

He knew so little when he started that he had to ask one of the local policemen where a certain political organization had its headquarters. Since the political organization ran the town, it might be thought that such information would be general knowledge. But to this young man it wasn't. Once he knew, however, he took it upon himself to attend the next organization meeting, and there he discovered how apathetic in general were others of the community to matters which should have concerned them.

Using his initiative, he bought a mimeograph machine and, with a friend of his, printed handbills calling on the hundreds of members to bring about a change in the organization. He aroused so much interest in the village generally that party officials began a house cleaning all on their own.

Later one top official asked the young man if he would like to be village clerk—a post which in any small community is the most influential one obtainable. The official explained that he realized the village had need for men like him, and hence the offer. The young man accepted. But he did more than that. He started going to school at night at one of our leading universities to train himself in public administration. He intends, he told us, to make government service a lifetime career.

As more men and women with this young man's sense of purpose and dedication make government their individual, personal concern, this nation—and the world—will be safely on the highroad to lasting peace.

4 COUNTY GOVERNMENT PLAYS A NECESSARY PART

"We in local government are right close to the people here," a pleasant middle-aged county clerk in one of our eastern states told me not long ago. "But I don't rightly know if we have any tie-in with the national government."

When I respectfully pointed out that the county, as a unit of the state, was an integral part of the government of our country, he drawled: "Well, I guess we're supposed to be, though we're really more hitched to the state than anything else. And I reckon, according to law, I'm actually a state officer, but I've never thought much about it that way."

Then he added: "Like I said before, we're close to the people here. The governing body in this county is a board of supervisors. Each town is allowed to elect one supervisor, and each ward in a city is allowed one. In this county we only have two cities but we've got an awful lot of supervisors—forty-nine to be exact—more than any other county I know of. Why, one of our little cities has twelve supervisors while right in the neighboring county a city twice its size has only six. It doesn't make sense to me."

The clerk then added, "Y'know, besides the two cities I was telling you about, we've got thirteen villages and thirty-three towns in this county—and there are a lot of little hamlets too—and they all organize for special benefits. When they want electric power they incorporate under an electric district. The same way with water, sewer, fire, and school districts. When they want to have sidewalks, roads, and even policemen, they can petition the state for a franchise to set up a township. The way I see it, the more people take an interest in their community, the better sort of government they're gonna get."

What this county clerk said was only too true. And what he might have added, perhaps, had he realized it sufficiently, is that just as the citizens at the local level get better government in proportion to their participation in county affairs, so the entire state reflects their interest or disinterest. The county, it should be emphasized, is vital to the smooth functioning of state administration.

Of English Origin

The idea of county government was inherited from England, where it was originally a convenient geographical area for administering royal business—such as the collection of taxes and the administration of justice. Today the county, in theory, serves much the same purpose. It is (1) a unit for the administration of state laws and the maintenance of law and order; (2) a convenient district for judicial administration; (3) a district for the administration of charitable relief; (4) a convenient geograpical unit for the recording of deeds, surveys, mortgages, and so on.

The county, strangely enough, does not have the independence of a town or village. It is like the town or village, however, in that it exists solely by authority of the state. It is unlike the town or village in that it has no true chief executive. The one person who comes closest to being such is the county sheriff.

This position, above all others in the county, requires an honest, efficient man, since the sheriff's jurisdiction usually covers such a wide territory with innumerable opportunities to exert influence. The fact that he makes a number of contacts in the course of his duties is given as one reason for this power. But it was also pointed out that the state, wittingly or not, has often helped the situation along by allowing sheriffs to succeed themselves in office.

No Standard Pattern

Generally speaking, there is no standard pattern of county government in the United States. The top governing body in two thirds of our counties—which, incidentally, number some 3,050—is a board of commissioners or supervisors. In one tenth of the counties there is a board of town supervisors, and in another one tenth there is a judge and commissioners. In the rest, authority is held by judges, courts, or non-judicial officers chosen in various ways.

Room for Improvement

These officers are almost always chosen by election. These same jobs—which include such posts as judge, attorney, court clerk, superintendent, assessor, treasurer, sheriff, weigher, and surveyor—do require men with special knowledge and administrative skill. Sometimes political candidates possess the necessary qualifications. Sometimes they do not. Therefore their selection should be a matter of most careful consideration for the voter when he prepares to cast his ballot.

The solution lies in observing one fundamental rule of good government; elect policy makers and appoint skilled administrators and technicians to carry out those policies.

This fundamental rule is one which the man or woman

who has a high purpose should always bear in mind in taking up a government career.

By following such a course, or working toward it, the average citizens will always retain control of the reins of government *since they can always change officials at the next election if enough of them decide to do so*. They will also establish a pattern of uniformity which cannot help but result in more efficient county government.

It should be mentioned here, however, that while an aroused citizenry can do much to restore matters of government to the hands of the people—where such matters rightfully belong—consciousness of the obligation to participate in government affairs should not be acted upon on an "emergency" or "crisis" basis alone. Citizen participation should also be on a "continuing" level each and every day of the year, in good times and bad. This approach in periods of calm will help to avoid confused or misdirected government in times of national emergency.

A Significant Point

One interesting feature is that four fifths of all the counties in the United States—or roughly twenty-four hundred of them —contain no municipality with as many as ten thousand inhabitants. These twenty-four hundred are rural in character. The majority of our counties have to do with the government of farmers, and the rural county is the typical county.

In regard to geographical limitations, figures vary as widely as do the characters of the different county administrations. The largest county in the United States is San Bernardino, California, with an area of more than twenty thousand square miles. This county alone is larger than the states of Vermont, Massachusetts, Connecticut, New Hampshire, and Rhode Island put together. The smallest county is Arlington, Virginia, with an area of twenty-five square miles. The average area of all the county units is approximately one thousand square miles. In the western region of the United States these counties are large in land size but small in population, while in the eastern section of the country the opposite is usually true.

These statistics are given simply to furnish a clear mental picture of the area, administratively speaking, of government at the county level. The more a person knows of the general layout, the better he will be able to understand local situations. Every time a tax is considered, an important factor is the sparsity or density of the population. The same goes for the geographical location and the nature of the various industries and their financial status.

Important to Remember

As was pointed out earlier, the county is invariably formed for the convenience of the state to facilitate the administration. As such, counties may be said to be agents of the state with sharp limits put on their powers of operation. However, while legally in this position, counties have experienced some modification within the last few years.

In a number of states, laws have been passed to increase the optional powers of counties, so that in a number of cases a county, by adopting such statutes, might almost reach the stature of a true municipal corporation. This is especially true since many of the laws concern local conditions which are best handled at the local level.

The fact that few rural communities seem to have availed themselves of these new-found powers offers a tremendous opportunity for people of sound ideas to take the initiative in seeing that the many opportunities for local self-government are realized.

Spheres of Influence

At the top of the county governmental structure is found the county board. This board is designated officially as the board of county commissioners or as the board of county supervisors. The membership of these boards varies from three or four people to upward of a hundred or a hundred and fifty, depending on the size of the county in question.

In the larger counties board officials are full-time, salaried personnel. In the smaller counties the members frequently are part-time officers, paid on a fee basis. Needless to say, membership on any board—which is secured by popular election—is most to be desired by anyone of high purpose seeking to put his ability to the widest possible use.

Next in line of importance in the average county governmental structure are what are called "row offices." These include the posts of county clerk, treasurer, auditor, receiver of taxes, board of assessors, legal officers, district attorney or state's attorney, and the public defender, where such exists. Then there are the offices of sheriff, coroner, clerks of court, recorder of deeds, superintendent of schools, health officer, and the enginer or surveyor.

Again It's Your Decision

In most states all these officers are chosen by direct vote of the people. That means that people like you have the reassuring opportunity to get the type of administration that you demar.d. Since all these jobs require special skills and training, the sound, God-fearing individual can do much to insure good, clean, honest government by aiming at them.

When such posts are filled by dishonest, incompetent men whose only qualification has a distinctly self-seeking flavor, the duty to see that they are replaced with honest, efficient officials becomes a matter of paramount importance.

A man who now holds one of the most important jobs in a certain New England county told us that the people who originally elected him had done so without his consent. He was the local postmaster at the time and had absolutely no desire to be anything else. But since the people put so much confidence in him; he admitted he felt obligated to accept the post and do the job as best he could.

As county supervisor he was, of course, a member of the county board, and it didn't take him long to become aware of an unhealthy state of affairs among the members. The majority party had formed a coalition with the minority party members and controlled every phase of county administration. Favors were exchanged in return for political support, and the people never had a say in how things were run.

"I was an insurgent right from the start," this supervisor told us. "I refused to go along with the rest of the board. In fact, I caused them so much trouble that they supported me for another county post—a higher one—just to be rid of me. I found out that it was their intention to dump me into the ash can at the end of my first term. But by then I was fighting mad.

"When they withdrew their support, I ran independently— and won. And ever since I've followed the same procedure and have yet to be defeated. But more important than that, two other men on the board joined up with me and the three of us fought the opposition. They tried everything in the book to ride herd on us, but it didn't take. Eventually we got control of the board back in the hands of the people."

A Young Attorney on the Job

In another county, this one out in the Midwest, the board there had for years been in the control of a small group of politicians who had power not only to make all political appointments in the area but also were able to dictate the nominations of candidates for public office. On the surface this was all done legally. The delegates who were sent by the various political committees (this county was in effect under one-party control) all were supposed to have a say in who was nominated and who was not. Actually, however, the executive committee, controlled by the group of politicians mentioned above, selected their own hand-picked candidates, from among whom the delegates could make a choice. Consequently, no matter how the vote went, the committee's candidates always won.

This condition went on for years—until a short time ago, when a certain young attorney was sent as a delegate to the primaries. He had a firm sense of purpose, together with the courage to back it up, and he made it his business to learn what had been going on. When the list of candidates was called off, he got to his feet and told the gathering that he represented a community which expected him to vote for the best possible men. He explained that he knew nothing about the candidates whose names had been submitted and would the executive committee therefore furnish him with a résumé of their qualifications.

Encouraged by his stand, other delegates began to voice similar demands. As a result, the super-smooth operations of the executive committee were completely upset. So much so, in fact, that all the nominations finally came from the assembled delegates. The executive committee—and those behind it —lost control of the county, which went on to have the best slate of officials it had had in years. And the young attorney himself later became district attorney. Today he is an outstanding district judge.

Powers and Functions

Since the county board, then, is the very center of county administrative life, there is every valid reason for knowing just what it can do and cannot do—in short, assessing its powers and functions.

The laws establishing the machinery of county government usually vest the county board with the "management of county affairs" or charge it with the "supervision of county affairs." However, while such wording on the surface is most specific, putting the implied powers into practice is something else again.

At the present time—and the practice has become more and more widespread—the tendency is to commit the running of county affairs to numerous officials who are elected by popular ballot.

This does not mean, however, that the county board is useless or without power, for it still remains the core of government structure at the local level and it does have many duties to perform. Some of these include:

1. GENERAL SUPERVISION. The board does not have, as was mentioned above, power over elected officials. Nevertheless it does have power over the officials it appoints to various posts. Moreover, in recent years new functions have been added to the list of county employees, and the law usually provides for their appointment and control by the board.

2. POLICY MAKING. Though subservient to state authority, the board retains many matters of policy making in its own hands, matters such as building projects, county legislation, purchasing of equipment and determining its use.

3. AWARDING CONTRACTS. This function involves the expenditure of considerable money over the course of a year's time. An honest, competent board can insure that graft and corruption will have no part in their contract decisions. By the same token, when the board fails to measure up to the high standards expected of it, the results can be disastrous for the average taxpayer as well as for the entire community.

4. GRANTING POOR RELIEF AND ADMINISTERING WELFARE. The supervision of poor relief, the management of orphanages the care of special dependent classes, such as widows, veterans, crippled children, and the blind, comes under county board jurisdiction. And it is almost understood that the board's control of finances in such matters determines the county's entire welfare policy.

5. PURCHASE OF SUPPLIES. The duties here, while not of a spectacular nature, are important in that the honest, efficient county board can fulfill its obligations to the taxpayers in seeing that their money is spent wisely and well. The post of most importance in this area is that of purchasing agent.

6. CLAIM ADJUSTMENT. In few counties are the means to handle the claims of the citizens geared to satisfactory performance. In some counties the whole matter has been reduced to a system under which one person—usually the county clerk—receives and files all claims, investigates

them, and recommends payment or rejection. This is a function that stands in need of prompt, soundly conceived solution.

The County Clerk

The post of county clerk, secured by popular election, is one of the most influential in the entire county area. It is true that it does not involve the exercise of independent action, nevertheless it carries considerable influence in county administration.

For one thing, the clerk is the secretary to the county board. He prepares the business for their meetings, gets all the papers and records which they will require, sees to it that the meetings are properly announced and the meeting place itself is in readiness. The minutes of these meetings, incidentally, are permanent records in the county clerk's office and are open to public inspection.

Even though the county clerk does not have independent action, since he is not a member of the county board, he can exert great influence. Moreover, precisely because he is in closer touch with county affairs than any other officer and is apt to have more knowledge of county business than even the board members themselves, his suggestions and comments carry considerable weight in the actual board meetings.

Other Duties

In addition to the duties listed above, the county clerk has the task of carrying out the board's decisions, originating the desired correspondence and following it through. In the larger counties the clerk has a staff of stenographers, assistants, and bookkeepers under him to facilitate his work.

Another duty involves that of being superintendent of the courthouse. His offices are in that building at the county seat, and he is responsible for the courthouse's maintenance—heating, decorating, and cleaning.

Then, too, the clerk must keep all the records of county administration, issue warrants, receive claims, assist in the operations of the tax machinery, participate in the conduct of elections. In this latter task he must make up the official ballot, receive the names of the various candidates for filing, distribute the ballots, and tabulate the final returns.

Finally, the county clerk, prepares reports of the county's transactions, issues licenses, takes care of the paper work in general.

Obviously, then, the county clerk occupies a most important part in the machinery of local government. His is not the only important post, of course. All county jobs are important.

V. CITY GOVERNMENT DEPENDS ON YOU

V. CITY GOVERNMENT DEPENDS ON YOU

1 A JOB OF "GOOD HOUSEKEEPING"

Running a city government seems, to the outsider, a complex and mystifying business. The purpose of this chapter is to show the average citizen that it is essentially simple, with no mystery about it at all.

Any American housewife should have the fundamentals of city administration at her fingertips. If she sweeps her sidewalk, disposes of her garbage, checks her water supply, makes sure of proper schooling for her children, and protects the life and property of her family, she is doing what every city government does. The only difference is that she performs her daily tasks as an individual.

The city does the same things on a much larger scale. City administration is essentially a housekeeping job. And there are many skilled housewives who feel justified in believing that they could do a better job of running their cities than the city administration does.

If you are to play an active, intelligent part in local government, whether you live in a small town or in a large city, it is important that you first become acquainted with its assets and its liabilities.

On Your Own

A few years ago a friend met the mayor of New York one Friday night in Madison Square Garden. Then, as now, Friday night was was "fight" night at the Garden.

"What kind of a job is it to be mayor of New York?" he asked him.

"Well, it's something like the championship bout we're going to see," was the mayor's reply. "A boxer steps into the ring at the Garden trained as finely as experienced hands can make him. All through his training he has had the good counsel and wise advice of old-timers in the ring who know every angle of the game.

"If he gets into trouble during the bout, he has skilled seconds who know how to get him out. Their keen eyes are alert for any sign of weakness in his opponent. Through long experience they know how to take advantage of an apponent's weakness.

"Now—with all this sound preparation—he comes in here to fight a main bout at ten o'clock on a Friday night. The referee calls both boxers to the center of the ring and makes sure that they understand the rules. Then both boxers go back to their own corners. Then they ring a little bell for the start of the first round. And—when that little bell rings—you're on your own! That's the kind of a job it is to be mayor of New York."

The comparison was apt. A boxer's seconds and handlers could be compared to the political advisers around a candidate. The public—personified by the referee—is there to see that any man gets a square deal if he abides by the rules.

The Individual Can Do Much

But in the final analysis it is the individual in each case who has to make the decisions and suffer for them if they are wrong, benefit by them if they are right. The individual can do much to control the ultimate decisions of his city's administration.

The average American is likely to think that public administration is a field separate and distinct from everyday life. This tendency is sometimes encouraged by the professional politicians. If they are not men of principle, they are likely to rejoice inwardly each time they hear a businessman say:

"I could never go in for politics, all that backslapping and glad-handing. Besides, look how public officials are smeared."

As a result, the impression has become general that politics and public administration will always be dominated by those who are interested in little except feathering their own nests.

Political machines are often administered with a degree of incompetence that would be fatal to any ordinary business. What saves the dishonest politician is that his revenues keep on coming in no matter how inefficient and bumbling he may be.

Another thing that saves him is his organization and what the organization chooses to call "party loyalty."

Twenty years ago young men and women entering politics were taught this lesson in the form of a story.

The Lesson of the Beehive

As the tale went, a district leader journeyed from New York to the country to visit a friend. When he got off the train he found that he still had to drive about twelve miles along country roads to reach his friend's home. The only conveyance at the station was a buckboard drawn by two horses, with an elderly countryman as driver. The two made a deal, and the leader sat up alongside the driver as they started off.

A little way out of town, a large horsefly lit upon the left ear of the off-horse. Without a word the driver flicked out a long whip, cracked it once, and removed the fly so deftly that the horse's ear did not even twitch.

"You're pretty accurate with that whip," the city man observed admiringly.

"Oh, it's mostly practice," the driver replied. "Don't have much else to do, driving along these country roads."

A little farther on they saw a bullfrog at the right-hand side of the road, jaws wide open and ready to swallow a passing butterfly. Once again the driver drew his whip, cracked the bullfrog on the lower jaw, and drove the jaw down far enough to let the butterfly escape.

"Well, I'll be blamed," marveled the New Yorker. "Never

in my life have I seen such uncanny accuracy with a whip."

Presently, at the left of the road, they came upon a long row of beehives. On top of the first hive perched a single, solitary bee.

"Go on," the politician urged. "Let me see you take out the whip and knock that bee off the hive."

"Bees?" said the driver. "No sirree—no bees. They've got an organization!"

How It Works

What is the place of the city political organization in the whole scheme of government? Understanding its capabilities and its limitations provides a clearer grasp of the whole subject.

When a city organization in a big municipality is really clicking, its powers are almost without limit. However, it is only in the largest cities that we see this. For most of America's 106 cities with populations of 100,000 or above, the city organization's power does not extend beyond its own borders.

The city organization draws its primary strength from control of the city administration. On winning an election, the leader names the city commissioners. Almost without exception they are district leaders of the party in power. They hold down the top departmental spots, with some hard-working subordinates really running the individual departments.

Through the election of its members in city government to the State Legislature, the city political group can acquire a powerful voice in state government. By electing city members to both houses of Congress, it gains a voice in national affairs.

Basic to All Public Service

The city organization, therefore, is the basic unit in all public administration. Power on the national and state levels is based upon the primary political strength of the city.

We must look first to the city, then, if we want any improvement in the general caliber of public administration. It is most important, as already pointed out, to remember that there is a sharp distinction between "politics" in the bad sense and "public administration," which can be achieved through good politics.

The businessman who shies away from politics might easily be attracted by public administration. The reason for this is that public administration, properly conducted, would use the efficient techniques that the businessman knows by heart.

"Well," the businessman may ask, "why shouldn't I leave politics to the politicians? I need all my time to conduct my own business."

Everybody Is Involved

The answer to that is that all of us are in partnership with the government, whether we like it or not. Actually we have no choice on whether we will turn our backs on politics and public affairs. Why? Because government, first of all, affects the destinies of all of us. In addition, it operates on our money, each day and every day. It has no other source of income.

The farmer, the cattle raiser, the country housewife, and the city businessman all pay part of their incomes for government. In recent years the government's share has leaped so high that it takes one dollar in every five for federal income taxes alone. Is it reasonable, then, for any of us to say:

"I have a partner in my business who receives 20 per cent of all my income, but I do not intend to bother about what he does."

It would be far more logical for us to say: "Let's get down to brass tacks. The expense of government takes one fifth of my earnings in income tax alone. Maybe it is all needed. Maybe it's not. I don't know. But just the same, I guess I ought to examine this cost closely and to apply to it the same standards of economy and efficiency that I practice in my own business. After all, whether I am dealing with the one fifth that is paid out or the four fifths that I retain, it is still all my money."

Learn from Taxes

And this is merely the beginning of the tax story. Federal taxes aside, every wage earner is affected by state and city taxes that concern and sometimes control his daily life.

You may ask: "What can I, as a single, small individual, do about it?"

First of all, you should avoid extremes. A certain increase in taxation has been necessitated by the growth of government, by the debts and inflation caused by two World Wars and the present national emergency, and, last but by no means insignificant, by the ever-increasing demands for services and benefits from government on the part of the payer himself.

Next, you should acquire a clear picture of what happens to your money under varied and often duplicating tax schemes. It is up to you to find out what taxes are essential. While recognizing the need for legitimate expenditures, never forget that the abuse of taxation has wrecked many a country. As the late Senator William E. Borah said: "The marvel of history is the patience with which men and women submit to the burdens unnecessarily laid upon them by their governments."

This observation was made years before the tax burden on individuals was as heavy as it now is. Another legislator, Senator Walter F. George, said: "You can confiscate only once, but you can tax perpetually."

Taxes Give an Insight

Taxation on the city level is the key to understanding any city administration. Once we understand how these taxes are levied and collected and how they are used, we will be able to give intelligent scrutiny to how "our town" operates. Since the city must tax to live, taxes always tell a story. If you know the tax structure of your city, you will get a very practical insight into municipal government and you will see very clearly that "government is your business."

2   A CASE HISTORY OF TAXATION

There is hardly a better way toward a fuller knowledge of city government than to look into its tax structure. This has always been an evaluable index of the condition of a city's health, and it still is today.

Benjamin Franklin said, "In this world nothing is certain but death and taxes." If Dr. Franklin were alive today, he might cast about for an even stronger way of putting it.

The information on this subject, as well as on various phases of government and civil service presented in this book, has been secured from those who are experts in these matters. I have had to do a lot of digging to get this material, but in doing so I have learned and relearned many of the ABCs of government. You can do the same. But you, too, must dig. Skip these pages—unless you wish to familiarize yourself with the strengths and weaknesses of your government.

These chapters will at least give you the ball. It is up to you to take it from there and run. You can get all sorts of advanced books on civics. You can send for any number of pamphlets from Washington, D.C. You can acquaint yourself with the history of your town, state, and country, and of the men who have played a part in the making of its history and its laws. It can be a fascinating second calling in your life. You will be the better for it—and so will *your* country.

An Upward Trend

All over the country the trend is toward an increase in the cost of government. Some regard this as reasonable. Others claim it is excessive. This is one more instance in which you must decide for yourself. But before jumping to any final conclusions, you should find out what the facts are.

For instance, it is important to know that since World War I the value of the American dollar has dropped to a current purchasing power of fifty-five cents. In considering city finances it is well to remember this fact, because it takes almost twice as many dollars to run a city administration as it did in 1939.

As a case history, you may care to look at the New York City sales tax and run back through its brief history. It illustrates how a tax, for better or for worse, comes into being and grows.

Whether you live in the smallest village or in the largest city, this example may give you an added insight as to how you are involved in government through taxation.

The New York City sales tax at 2 per cent made its bow in 1934 when the effects of the nation-wide depression were still strong. As proposed, it was for a one-year limit only. Its proceeds were to be devoted exclusively to relief of the poor and homeless—and to no other purpose. That provision was written into the law which imposed the tax itself.

People said: "Ah well, it's for a good cause, and after all, it's only two pennies on the dollar."

In the first year of operation of the sales tax those pennies added up to $44,000,000. As general conditions improved, the need for emergency relief funds diminished. People thought the tax would be going out of existence one of these days. The city administration, however, found that those pennies were vitally necessary to its continued existence. Once, just before a city election, the rate was dropped from 2 per cent to 1 per cent. Within five years it went back to 2 per cent.

Up They Go

For several years the State Legislature renewed the tax on a strict year-to-year basis. As before, the proceeds were marked for emergency relief only. Then, under the late Mayor Fiorello H. La Guardia, New York City persuaded the Legislature to remove the "relief only" restriction. From that time on the tax proceeds were used for general city purposes. At the same time, real-estate taxes were increased. Other city charges followed the same pattern.

In the 1949-50 fiscal year the sales tax at 2 per cent had raised $132,206,843 "in pennies." On May 1, 1951, the city raised the rate to 3 per cent on almost all purchases over eighteen cents.

The additional 1 per cent is calculated to add $60,000,000 to the tax for the remaining eight months of this year. On those figures it appears that the sales tax is running up pretty close to $200,000,000 a year.

What can one person do about government? That $200,-000,000 is what a penny can do. Even the lowliest among us has more importance than a penny. With proper application, people can do what pennies can do. People should be able to do far more than pennies.

More on the Tax Story

In Washington there is talk of a proposed federal sales tax of 5 per cent, and the sponsors say it would raise $5,000,000,000 each year. The 5 per cent rate is not impossible—Canada has had a 5 per cent sales tax for years. In Britain, highest-taxed country in the world, the "purchase tax" is 100 per cent of the sales price on all luxury goods.

In the District of Columbia there is a sales tax on a twenty-five-cent magazine. Georgia has a new 3 per cent sales tax to raise $170,000,000 a year for schools. Ohio residents know the sales tax well. People in St. Louis have been paying ½ of 1 per cent on their annual gross earnings as a city "earning tax."

The history of the city tax proves several points. First, when a "temporary emergency tax" goes on the books, it is likely to become permanent. Secondly, while the rate may be moderate at the start, if it goes anywhere, it will tend to go up.

Is all this justified? Yes or no, it is your business as a citizen and taxpayer to find out.

If You Won't, Who Will?

What can we learn from this experience? First, when a new tax is proposed, it is up to you to find out what it is for and how it will work. You can do this as members of taxpayers' groups, as members of civic and trade organizations, as individuals in a parent-teachers group. You can tell the city's governing body that you wish to be heard; file formal notice in writing if necessary. You can go to the public hearing and speak your mind.

If you consider the new tax unnecessary, you can make your voice heard. If the tax is justified for a limited time, you can insist that the enacting law carry its own expiration date. If

the purpose is to be limited, you can help to make sure that
the tax bill specifies one purpose and one only. These are some
of the things that you as an individual can do. "Let George do
it" just doesn't work.

Another View

It must be remembered, however, that there are two sides to
every tax story. Recently a letter to a Providence, Rhode Island, newspaper complained about the shortage of policemen.
It was signed "Disgusted Taxpayer." It drew a prompt reply
from another citizen who signed himself "Disgusted Policeman." He wrote: "The public is disgusted by the shortage of
policemen and all they can say is, 'We are paying taxes.' Well,
I am paying taxes too!

"Our present pay is $57.50 a week. I clear $46 and I just
can't make ends meet. I'm single, too. Imagine a family man
trying to live on that wage."

The "Disgusted Policeman" went into details:

"Here's a list of what I have to buy to do my job: Overcoat
—$75. Shirts—$5 each. Trousers—$28.50. Ties—$1.50. Shoes—
$14. Tunic—$49.50. Hats—$5."

For this, the policeman said, the city granted a clothing
allowance of $30 a year. Whatever the tax, in this policeman's
opinion, it wasn't enough to pay policemen a living wage.

So the debate will always rage on. But it is each citizen's
responsibility to see that all the facts are learned and recognized if the best interests of all the people are to be served.

What One Person Can Do

One city resident, concerned about his city's growing indebtedness consulted an expert and learned how to analyze the
figures in his city's budget. At that time his city was being run
by one of the nation's most notorious politicians. Within a few
days the well-prepared citizen went to a budget hearing to ask
some pointed questions. When he asked them, the police threw
him out.

Not easily discouraged, the same civic worker turned up for

the budget hearing the following year. Once more he was evicted, but this time more gently. In the end his efforts succeeded. He was elected to a city post where his persistent pursuit of good government made substantial and beneficial changes in his city.

"Taxation for revenue only" is still a sound principle. Some economists have enumerated the rule that two extremes should be avoided: first, for a city to carry a surplus of income over expenditures which would serve as a soft cushion, or, second, to borrow on future generations by floating bonds for present indebtedness. They say every city should operate on a "pay-as-you-go" basis.

Cities should not have surpluses of income over expenditures. Still they manage to wind up the year with a surplus. How do they do it? Chiefly by underestimating tax receipts. Budget makers almost never shave down to the last penny. As an individual, you can check last year's tax estimate against the amount actually collected. If you find the "cushion," that will tell you what to do about this year's estimate.

Look into This

Items of "miscellaneous expenses" in a city budget always warrant careful scrutiny. If the expenses are legitimate, there is no reason why they should not be itemized. Another point worth investigating is "transfers from accrued funds." A salary account, for example, may not be fully used in a year because of deaths, retirements, or transfers of employees. Many cities take these "accruals" out of the account they were voted for and use them to pay for new jobs or new services not included in the original budget. On a day's calendar of city business the "transfer of accruals" item may look harmless. But sometimes it isn't.

Again you may wonder: "Isn't the individual pretty helpless against all this? After all, the politicians know the inside story of city administration, and I don't. They seem to have all the advantages."

True enough, they do have some advantages. But there's

another way of looking at it. We all know the function of the "cat's whiskers." The cat will not stick his head into a space that his whiskers will not clear. Now, it doesn't require all his whiskers to tell him where the danger spot is. Just one whisker is enough for that. And if just one person discovers a danger to his city, others will follow his lead.

Still Paying

You should also know something about the use of city bonds for major improvements, as against the use of cash on a pay-as-you-go basis. On some New York City bonds issued for a fifty-year term, for instance, each bond dollar has cost the taxpayers $2.53, more than two and a half times as much. Still, when your city wants to build a school, the chorus always goes up: "Let's finance it with a bond issue and reduce the taxes."

To the voters the bond issue sounds attractive. They figure they won't be around when the due date arrives, so perhaps their grandchildren will pay it.

New York is still paying on bonds originally issued to build a bridge in Brooklyn. The bridge has long since been demolished and replaced, but the bond payments go on still.

After World War I, New York State issued state bonds to pay a bonus to the veterans of that war. The last of these bonds was retired in 1949, four years after World War II ended. This makes little or no sense. Let the words "bond issue" be equivalent in your mind to "red light." Don't be deceived by the temporary attractiveness of the bond issue. You and your children will pay for it with your money.

In 1951 the city of New York is spending $252,000,000, or 18.7 per cent of its total city budget, on one item—debt service. Debt service means the money the city has to pay each year on its outstanding bonds and corporate stock issued by the municipal corporation.

Helpful Hints

As a taxpayer your primary interest should be to scrutinize all taxes carefully and see that your community gets a fair return in services for the money expended. Your best insurance for honest city administration may be summed up in the following suggestions:

1. Keep a sense of proportion. Avoid being too critical about taxes. Bear in mind that costs of city, state, and federal government are increasing just as is the cost of living.
2. Watch your city budget carefully, however, and compare it item by item with previous budgets. Where an amount increases, get an explanation. Scrutinize all proposed bond issues with care. Find out how much the bond dollars will cost you. Don't approve a bond term longer than the life of the project it finances.
3. Keep a close eyes on city real-estate purchases and check the amounts paid against a fair going value.
4. Watch the financial relationships between your city, your state, and the federal government.
5. Guard against overtaxation by resisting the building up of any surplus, unless the money is actually used for capital improvements on a pay-as-you-go basis.
6. Make sure all bonds are fully justified.

These are the key points in a most important phase of any city administration. Devoting some of your time and attention to them not only may save you money but will also provide a better community for you and your family to live in.

3 WHAT YOU CAN DO

The cost of government should not, of course, distract us from a full view of government iself. Make sure that you don't take a disinterested attitude toward the proper functioning of the public affairs of your city as a whole.

Do whatever is in your power to come to grips with each problem as it turns up. There are countless ways in which you, personally and individually, can do something for the benefit of all. More often than not, you will underestimate your own capacity in this respect.

Every Cupful Counted

Two years ago New York was gripped by the greatest water shortage in its history. The drought in that city focused national attention upon water as the nation's No. 1 national resource. Until water ran short, everyone had taken a plentiful supply for granted. But when the city's giant reservoirs dropped to 33.4 per cent of capacity the shortage became alarming.

The city administration asked New Yorkers to save water, by the cupful if need be. Housewives were asked to do their dishes in a pan instead of letting the taps run. Water for swimming pools was barred, street flushing was abandoned, and the householder was forbidden to use his hose on lawn or garden.

The city asked the co-operation of its residents on a voluntary basis. It requested each individual to save as much water as he could. The city had no idea of putting a man in jail because he watered his lawn; it just asked him not to while water was so short. Normal consumption ran close to 985,000,000 gallons daily.

Then what happened? "Dry Thursdays" became the vogue. The newspapers published daily front-page boxes telling the people exactly what their water situation was. Residents in one section vied with those of another to see who could save more water.

Every Little Bit Helped

Through the combined efforts of some 7,500,000 individuals, New Yorkers saved 55,000,000,000 gallons of water. That quantity was enough to put all of Manhattan's twenty-two square miles under a solid blanket of water twelve feet deep. On the average the saving amounted to 300,000,000 gallons daily. This saving was not accomplished by any race of supermen. It was accomplished by the housewife who made one pan of water do for her dishes, by the individual who decided he didn't really need that last drink of water before going to sleep, by the gardener who figured that his lawn could get through one more day without a sprinkling.

The city officials decided that this was a very fine example of individuals collaborating for the common good. That is, until they measured the results of the conservation campaign in money. Then they found that New Yorkers had also saved themselves $2,500,000 in hard cash on their individual water charges.

Whose money was this? Before, it had always been collected each year as part of the city's revenue of $46,000,000 from the sale of water. As a result of the "save water" campaign, the city's people had not only saved the precious fluid but a goodly amount of cash as well.

It is pointless, therefore, for the individual to say he is helpless. This accomplishment was performed by individuals, because only individuals could have done it.

Four Men in a Restaurant

In a different field, the story of another instance of individual accomplishment came to Christopher headquarters. One night in April 1947 a small group sat around a table in a well-known restaurant just off Times Square. In the group were Andy Burke, publicity director for the New York County Democratic Committee; "Chick" Bowan, a young lawyer; Joe Gilhuly of the restaurant firm, and Bill Conklin, a political reporter on the New York *Times*. Burke had been reading of the granting of a police permit for the "May Day Parade" held by the city's Communists annually on May 1.

"It burns me up every time I think of these Communists parading through the streets of New York and showing their contempt for the rest of us," Burke said to his friends.

As they agreed, Conklin said half jokingly: "Why don't you do something about it, Andy? You're connected with a big political organization. Maybe you could organize a counter-demonstration. Let's see—you could get the veterans; the anti-

Communist unions would support it; the churches would help out; and maybe you could even borrow a couple of elephants from the circus, since it's in town."

"Maybe you've got something there," Burke replied. "Anyhow, it's worth a try and I think I'll go to work on it."

From Small Beginnings

Burke did. He formed a committee, set up headquarters, and got a prominent man to serve as committee chairman. He canvassed the unions, the veterans' organizations, and the nationality groups in which New York abounds. From the churches he got school bands and marchers. In a few weeks he had the parade lined up. On May Day the Communists straggled down Eighth Avenue. The first Loyalty Day Parade—complete with two large circus elephants—moved on Fifth Avenue with the solid backing of the citizenry. That was the origin of the parade which last May Day celebrated its fourth anniversary with General of the Army Douglas MacArthur among the dignitaries in the reviewing stand.

The original idea emerged from a group of four friends in a friendly chat over a restaurant table. One of them had the idea; another picked it up; the remaining two helped out, and in a matter of weeks the idea became an actuality.

Up to the time it did, the Communists had May Day all their own way because the great body of loyal Americans had no way of expressing their patriotic feelings in a counter-demonstration. But once given the opportunity, they leaped at it.

From this small beginning four years ago, the 1951 Loyalty Day Parade drew a crowd of marchers estimated by police at 150,000 and a gathering of spectators numbering more than 1,000,000.

Everyone Counts

Every city administration has within its ranks thousands of hard-working, good-living employees who do their honest best for the city that employs them. These are the "career employees," the wheel horses who perform the actual work of running the city and perform it well. By and large, they are motivated by a love of God and country.

The positions they hold have been gained usually after a lifetime of plugging through one competitive civil-service examination after another. As a group they exercise the responsibility for good city administration regardless of the party in political power at the moment.

Many of these individuals have literally devoted a lifetime to the study of city administration. It is not uncommon to find an unsung accountant who can rattle off budget figures for a series of years without hesitation.

A fire captain may invent a new type of hose nozzle useful in fighting stubborn fires underneath wooden piers. A police officer may develop a new timesaving technique in police administration. Even a street sweeper may figure out a better type of broom than the one that has been used for years.

Something You Can Do

With these considerations in mind, let us review our own attitudes toward the honest, efficient, and intelligent city employee. How seldom do we take the trouble to write a note to a department head commending the actions of one of his employees. How little do we realize that our note might be the basis of an official commendation that would help this good employee up the ladder.

If we believe that graft and corruption in public administration should be discouraged, do we not also owe an affirmative duty to those whose daily work is characterized by honesty and intelligence?

In practice, certain small groups of city employees can be compared to money, on the basis of the old adage that "bad money drives out good." A dishonest policeman can take his graft from day to day without censure from his honest co-workers. In most cases they will merely shun the grafter.

But when a dishonest policeman is operating, the reputation of honest men suffers. Why? Because the public lets it suffer.

The honest policeman gets little or no encouragement from the public, which employs him, to go on being honest.

As a result police morale goes down; some honest men quit their jobs, and the grafters become more solidly entrenched. This does not apply to the police alone. It applies equally well to any city department, whether it be a tax department, building department, welfare department, or any other.

Encourage the Good

If we want good city government, we must encourage the employees who have the power to make it good. We should express our appreciation and recognition of their good work whenever we have the opportunity. Far too many of the honest employees believe they are laboring alone in the wilderness with no public appreciation of the work they are doing. It is up to us, the public, to correct that impression by giving recognition where it is due.

Some years ago in New York City a small group formed the Citizens Budget Commission to exercise a public check on the city's budget spending. Among other things it pioneered cash prizes for individual city employees who developed money-saving techniques in their own departments.

A Big Saving

Every year each department head submitted a list of economy suggestions made by his employees to the Commission. The Commission sorted the entries and gave cash prizes as well as public recognition to those who deserved it.

In 1948 the Commission recommended city economies from its own studies which saved the city an estimated $1,160,000. Another survey showed that five of the largest city departments could save $30,000,000 a year by improving their methods.

In another field, the Commission recommended a new plan for the systematic disposal of tons of old and useless city documents. Instead of burning the old paper, it was sold for pulp to the paper industry and realized $127,000 in six years.

At the same time, the way was cleared for the city to save large amounts in the rents it formerly paid on warehouse space for the old records. The old paper was found to occupy 20 per cent of the working space in fifteen city buildings, in addition to the vast amounts stored in outside warehouses. The dead working space had a rental value of $200,000 a year.

Many Benefits

This type of civic activity confers a positive and tangible benefit on any city. Equally or perhaps more important is the intangible effect it has on the morale of the city employee who finally sees public recognition of his efforts.

Any worker, no matter how minor, is in a position to make his own job a better job, especially if he has a Christ-like purpose. All it requires is that he think about it a little and try to devise better and quicker methods of accomplishing it. This type of effort, taken in the aggregate, mounts up to staggering sums of money saved.

A Few Rules of Thumb

It has been aptly said that a democracy in which the citizens do not participate can become a "rule of the indifferent by the unscrupulous." To prevent this on the city level the individual citizen must bestir himself and acquire the virtue of *civic courage.* Toward this end we list a few prescriptions that may prove helpful:

1. Arouse popular interest in municipal affairs, first in yourself, then in your community.
2. Watch for undemocratic and dishonest election methods.
3. Object to unnecessary centralization of power in any part of the government.
4. Keep an eagle eye for all forms of graft and corruption.
5. Point out the need for new methods in government and wastefulness of antiquated systems.
6. Study the records of all candidates.

7. Keep honesty and public service uppermost in your own mind and in those of all city officials.

8. Pray for the courage to always stand for what is right in civic affairs and to condemn what is wrong.

4 INSIST ON THE BEST

About half of all Americans live in or around 140 cities of more than 50,000 population. If you had the time and interest to look into it, you would find that there are 4,000 separate governments and nearly 12,000 school districts in these 140 metropolitan areas. This means that there is an average of 114 different government units for each of the 140 districts, and each of them with separate taxing powers.

A volume could be written on this phase of government alone. You should familiarize yourself with at least some of the more important patterns followed in governmental units.

Take, for instance, the three principal forms of city government; (1) Mayor and council; (2) Commission; and (3) City manager.

Mayor-and-Council Pattern

The elected mayor-and-council form is the pattern most generally followed. This is headed by a mayor with wide powers which tend to become wider. Normally the mayor has an extensive power of appointment over heads of city departments and agencies. He may also exercise a veto.

Usually the head of the council and the city's chief financial officer are elected with the mayor by popular vote. Each councilman is elected from a segment of the city and devotes his primary attention to the residents of that segment. In addition, some members of the local governing body may be elected from the city at large.

Commission Form

Secondly, the "commission" form of government centers on the election of a commission, usually of three to five members.

The city commissioners exercise wide municipal powers in both the legislative and executive fields. Each commissioner heads a department.

City functions are grouped into as many main city departments as there are commissioners. Ordinarily this system is accompanied by the initiative and referendum on municipal ordinances, plus the power of the people to dislodge any commissioner through petition and popular vote.

On September 8, 1900, a hurricane and tidal wave inundated the island city of Galveston, Texas, with a loss of six thousand lives. Five prominent business leaders were named to take over the administration of the city. This governing body remained and became the first example of the commission type of government.

In the next twenty years about one hundred additional communities adopted the commission form.

City Manager Formula

In order to overcome many disadvantages, a third plan called the "city manager" plan was put forward. Under it, a small council of perhaps five policy-forming individuals were elected by popular vote. From among their number, or from outside, they chose the city manager.

The city manager usually would be a trained expert who had devoted years to the scientific study of municipal administration. When Sumter, South Carolina, adopted it in 1912, it became known as the "Sumter Plan." Dayton, Ohio, adopted the city manager plan about 1915 to cope with the aftermath of a serious flood. The community has operated under this plan ever since. Dayton was first among cities to put its laborers on an annual pay roll. Before then standard practice was to hire vast numbers of "laborers" before election and lay most of them off right after election. Dayton was the first city to give its employees vacations with pay and first to furnish a Legal Aid Bureau for poor litigants.

The city manager must stay on his toes. Unlike the elected official, he cannot "coast" once he is in office. He can be fired summarily without cause, and he is completely subject to the policy-forming council of elected representatives.

In Six Hundred Cities

Many smaller communities use the services of the Municipal League, established in 1894 as a clearinghouse to serve all local civic organizations. The League keeps abreast of the most modern techniques in municipal administration and is ever ready to proffer advice and help to communities that ask for it. In an average year the League receives more than fifteen thousand inquiries dealing with complicated municipal problems.

More than six hundred American cities now function under the city manager plan. Since 1912 the city manager plan has made local government responsive to the wishes of city residents. It is operating in townships as well as in cities. In the East we also see the institution of the county executive in New York counties like Nassau and Westchester. These officials function like city managers, but their field is the county rather than the city. Both city managers and county executives occupy the same position in government that the manager of a private corporation holds in relation to his board of directors.

The earliest American cities followed the English pattern of organization and government. In the first half of the nineteenth century American city governments were largely remodeled on the state government idea, with local governing bodies of two chambers elected by popular vote. More recent developments in the forms of local governments are tailored to the needs of individual communities.

New Methods Step Up Efficiency

Cities are the same as any large enterprise. Methods of governing tend to become static as the old-timer teaches the newcomer the same methods that were used in the distant past. It is to your interest, as a citizen and taxpayer, to insist on the most efficient methods possible and to see that the cost of government is cut without cutting the essential services it provides.

This can be done by discarding old techniques in favor of newer methods. If your city keeps its tax records and sends out its tax bills by hand, perhaps it could benefit by installing business machines. Take a good look also at the methods your town uses to buy materials. Most purchasing systems are so cumbersome that it costs more to make out purchasing forms and certifications than the purchased article is worth.

Another angle to watch is city specifications so drawn as to exclude all but one favored product. The specifications should read so that a number of products may fit them, and not merely one that has a political connection. Many cities have found it economical to centralize all their purchasing activities in one purchasing agency which buys for all departments and offices. Dishonest politicians don't like that idea.

A Few Can Start a Change

City administration can be improved if only a small number of individuals work at improving it. A city employee can, with a little imagination and diligence, improve it from the inside.

The ordinary city resident, by studying his city government and exercising a voice in it, can improve it from the outside.

The greatest lesson to be drawn is that it does take only a few to accomplish much. An actual minority of New York's registered voters elected an independent candidate. It took only four men to launch the Loyalty Day Parade which now draws more than one million people. It took only small minorities to overthrow the country's major political machines in the last twenty years. It took individual initiative to pull New York out of its serious water shortage. It takes only a few civic-minded people to check graft, to develop new methods, and to effect economies in city administration. In close national elections 2 or 3 per cent of the registered voters can make the difference.

It's for You

All these personal relationships come together to give us our relationship to the city government. Protection of life and property is a primary duty of the city government. Here we find the courts, fire and police protection, and, more recently, the civilian defense agencies concerned with the same function.

This protection may include a welfare department to care for orphans and aged people unable to care for themselves. The city's public-health and hospitalization functions center on the same point: protection of life. Street cleaning, garbage disposal, and sewage disposal also fall into this field.

In connection with the protection of property, the city has its building code, which provides primarily for the safe construction of your home or the office building where you work.

Zoning ordinances guarantee that if you buy residential property, its value will not be impaired by the construction of an industrial establishment next door.

If you alter your home or office, a building inspector from the city stands by to make sure that the changes meet minimum safety requirements. Public education is primarily a city function, aided by state and federal grants.

"The poor man's court" is usually found in cities, with some courts considering only cases involving twenty-five dollars or less. Here the unpaid workman can collect his pay, the landlord-tenant dispute is ironed out, the unlicensed street peddler is brought to book.

You Decide

There are endless possibilities to serve the common good in the field of city government. There is little glamour in most of the jobs, and often little thanks or appreciation is shown for the devotion and energy that have been expended over a long period of years in this area of public service. But that is the test of real loyalty to God and country—to carry on despite lack of recognition.

One important consideration that should be the concern of all citizens in these times is to see that those in city government, in low ranks as well as in high, are provided with the same monetary compensation that they would receive for similar service in civilian life.

As was said at the outset, the final decisions are made by the individual. An individual equipped with a purpose in life will find that ideas for improving his own little sphere begin to flow through his mind.

If his ideas are reasonable and represent an improvement over the past, others will follow his lead almost automatically. Apathy and indifference are the chief enemies of progress.

If you find a bad situation in your city administration, do something about it. Do not dismiss it by saying you can do nothing. Others like you are making their individual influence for good felt every day.

VI. STATE GOVERNMENT VITALLY AFFECTS YOU

VI. STATE GOVERNMENT VITALLY AFFECTS YOU

I WHAT IT DOES FOR YOU

In dealing with government, the average American feels a personal relationship toward his mayor or city manager. If the citizen has a complaint, his instinct is to run right down to city hall and tell the mayor all about it. By contrast, the President seems far beyond the reach of a personal approach by the taxpayer. Few would dream of going to Washington to tell the President their troubles, and many would think twice before writing the President a letter.

To the average man state government falls between the complete accessibility of the mayor and the almost complete inaccessibility of the President.

Still, state government exercises more control and direction over our lives than any other level of government from local to national. Each American state is a sovereign power in itself. Each possesses all the authority that any temporal government may invoke. For national unity, the states have delegated some of their original sovereign powers to the federal government. They have delegated other powers through constitutional compacts with their own citizens. These aside, the state governments have sovereign power within their own confines.

In a book of this size it is impossible to do more than draw attention to the various branches and functions of government. However, since state government is so basic to our American system and yet so little understood, we felt it advisable to treat it more thoroughly.

If the reading of this chapter requires more than ordinary attention, we trust you will be amply compensated by the practical knowledge gained. Fundamentally, all our forms of American government—town, city, country, and federal—are built along the lines of state government described in this chapter.

The State and the Nation

First, let us consider the sovereign powers delegated by states to the national government when the latter was first established. Among these we find:

1. The right to declare war and make peace.
2. The right to deal directly with foreign nations.
3. The right to regulate commerce within the states.
4. The right to raise and maintain armies, except state militia.
5. The right to coin money and to tax imports and exports.
6. The right to make laws on naturalization of citizens, bankruptcy, and patents and copyrights.

Some of these original grants of power have become amplified through the years by custom, usage, and judicial decisions. Some are in the process of being amplified or curtailed today through court decisions. However, the great bulk of original sovereign power remains with the states themselves. Each state exercises a wide jurisdiction over its own inhabitants.

Virtually all states are barred by their own Constitutions from invoking some sovereign powers whose exercise might conflict with the Constitution of the United States. Among these are:

1. The right to deprive any person of liberty, or condemn him to penal servitude except upon conviction of a crime following a fair trial.
2. The right to discriminate between citizens on the ground of color, religion, or economic condition.
3. The right to seize private property for public use without payment of fair compensation.

4. The right to compel any person against his will to contribute to the support of any religion or to observe its tenets.
5. The right to bar citizens from peaceful assembly for the redress of their grievances.
6. The right to deny any person accused of crime his right to be represented by counsel; his right to confront his accusers; and his right to have witnesses called in his behalf.
7. The right to limit freedom to speech, of religion, or of the press, except such exercise as might invade the freedom of others.

The states have forsworn exercise of these "rights" which are implicit in the definition of sovereignty. By so doing, they have established the essential difference between free government and authoritarian government. The authoritarian government not only has these rights but also exercises them in behalf of a strong state. By contrast, we place the individual above the state and put the whole power of government behind the principle of upholding his individual rights.

The State and the Individual

Your state government is concerned primarily with the individual. Many do not understand how the state functions in relation to the individual. We know in a general way that the state stands between the local and national governments, but how does it affect the life of the individual resident of a state?

If you drive a car, it is registered by the state, your driving license is issued by the state, and the major highway you drive over has been built by the state. As a parent, the state prescribes your duties to your children. Your children may go to schools constructed partly by state aid and study under teachers whose qualifications are set by the state. To advance and graduate, your children must meet certain minimum educational qualifications established by the state.

Through its wage-and-hour law, your state fixes the conditions under which you earn your daily break. The state will not permit you to work in an unhealthful or poorly constructed building, because it sets standards for factory- and office-building construction. Through its penal code the state decides what is law-abiding conduct and what is criminal. In civil law the state protects your rights in its state courts.

When you depart from this world, the state regulates what disposition will be made of your property. It will tax you for state purposes, and rebate part of the yield to your local community for local improvements. If you like to hunt or fish, you carry a state license in most states. The state licenses your doctor, your dentist, and your nurse.

Through its state police or highway patrol your state controls traffic on major roads and enforces law and order in smaller communities. With its inspection services it safeguards public health. If you are a farmer, you often get a helping hand from your state agricultural service. Felons are incarcerated in state prisons. Thousands of patients are cared for in state hospitals.

By its welfare program the state looks after the unemployed, the aged, the indigent, and dependent children. Through its regulation of public utilities, such as electric and gas companies, and railroads operating entirely within one state, the state government exercises supervision over your daily life. In the field of recreation your state may provide state parks, beaches, playgrounds, and picnic areas.

All these functions follow the Constitution of the United States and its guarantees of "life, liberty, and the pursuit of happiness." Like other governments, states assume the duties of maintaining public order, providing for the security of their inhabitants, insuring equal rights among residents in the political, social, and economic fields, and offering each citizen the opportunity to develop his maximum usefulness.

Enforcing the Law

In most states the prohibitions listen in the Ten Commandments constitute the basic penal law. To these original crimes have been added a long list of other offenses which succeeding legislatures considered criminal. Penalties vary widely among the states, often influenced by public temper at the time the laws were enacted. An outbreak of armed violence, for example, would result in harsh laws and drastic penalties. Or again, depending on the public attitude, punishments might be softened in favor of a rehabilitation program for offenders.

In the field of law enforcement the state might be called the policy-making body which makes the laws. Local communities would constitute the operating body which tackles the job of enforcing them. The offender is usually arrested by a member of a local police force or a deputy from the country sheriff's office. A local prosecutor, called a district attorney or state's attorney, undertakes the prosecution. The felon is tried and, if convicted, punished, under laws made by the state.

For the most part, district attorneys are elected in their own counties. In some states the prosecutor is appointed by the governor or by the state attorney general. In almost all states, members of the local police, the constabulary, and the prosecutors are removable by the governor, after a hearing on charges, if they are found derelict in their duties.

Since local law-enforcement officials are responsible primarily to their own communities, the local standard of morals carries heavy weight with them. The moral climate of the community is likely to influence them in deciding which laws are to be enforced strictly and which ones can be quietly passed up. As the over-all agency, the state has the duty of enforcing a state-wide system of law enforcement. In performing this function, the governor may name a special prosecutor to investigate law enforcement in any county where he considers it defective.

When a new political party comes into power, appointments to "plum" jobs usually go to followers of the party. Recommendations on appointments come through the various county committees.

In New York all recommedations are thoroughly checked by the state police.

At a time when one of the appointments to be made was for

the job of coroner, a county politician recommended a doctor friend of his. The governor's office had an immediate check made on him and, much to their amazement, learned that the job-seeker was a veterinarian. When they checked back with the county politician, he said: "Well, yes, it's true, but how did you ever find out?" "We checked," was the answer. "Well, you can't blame me for trying," was his reply. "Nobody's ever checked before."

"Our rule of checking is now well established," continued the official. "They don't dare to send in names of those who are not properly qualified. Now counties send in good men and appoint them. As a result, we've attracted over the last eight years people who never before thought of politics as their career. The idea is beginning to catch on. If John Jones works at it, it must be okay."

In some communities the laws against gambling are enforced to the letter. In others, gambling is tolerated while the authorities crack down on other offenses. Some communities use their methods of enforcing traffic regulations as a means of putting local citizens under obligation to local political leaders through ticket fixing. At the same time they may let the touring motorist feel the full weight of their local laws. In still others, no citizen would ask a politician to fix his traffic ticket because the courts would not stand for any attempt at fixing.

In the field of law enforcement particularly, local sentiment affects the enforcement of state law. Law enforcement is always a matter of community morals. It never gets any higher than the community wants it to be. No one wants to live in a community where the police are oppressive, and most states have laws to protect their citizens against this. But if a community wants a high standard of law enforcement without oppression, the community can get just about what it orders.

The State and the Schools

It was little more than a century ago that state legislatures began requiring local communities to provide free schools. This step took a long time, even though the country's founders had recognized that literacy and education were essential to the proper functioning of a democracy.

From a small beginning, education has now become the No. 1 state function in terms of dollars spent. At first only free public schools were required. Now, in most states, high schools are necessary to meet the requirements of state law.

Some states go beyond primary and secondary education and require kindergartens, special bus transportation for handicapped children, and special schools for the mentally retarded, those with speech defects, and those with other physical handicaps.

Sometimes the states mandate by law the extent and variety of educational services beyond the financial capacity of the local community. This impasse is usually solved through a grant of state aid to the local agency. As a rule the state prefers this method to the alternative of widening the taxing power of its local subdivision. By using state grants instead, the state always retains the taxing power in its own hands.

All states exercise control over education. For many, education is the field of paramount interest. Usually the state sets a broad educational policy describing what is to be taught, the minimum professional standards for teachers, and the minimum performance by students which will warrant promotion, graduation, or entry into a higher institution of learning.

For the carrying-out of its broad directives the state relies upon local communities. It thus delegates not the power but only the function. The state wisely recognizes that school conditions may vary widely within its own borders; a one-room mountain schoolhouse in Tennessee, for example, would offer different problems than a city school in Nashville. So the state concludes that the local community knows best how its schools should be operated under minimum state standards.

Requirements Set by the State

Perhaps it is this habit of state government in assigning operating functions to its smaller communities that confuses the aver-

age observer. To clear up this confusion we should remember:
1. The sovereign power resides in the state. 2. The state exercises its power by setting a broad policy. 3. The state supervises the operation of its policy by the smaller communities.

In line with this, states prescribe the obligations of parents to send their children to school within certain specified ages. State law provides punishment for parents who disregard this obligation. The state requires local units to build schools and provide the funds to operate them. In addition to setting teachers' qualifications, the state may also set minimum salaries and retirement benefits for them.

The state prescribes the courses to be taught and the minimum content in these courses. These broad functions cover the fields of primary and secondary education.

In the field of higher education, the state sets minimum standards for admission to colleges or universities. It also sets the minimum requirements which students must meet to obtain degrees from these institutions.

While these controls may seem all-inclusive, the state permits its communities considerable latitude on the operating level. Parents in all states may enroll their children in private or parochial schools as well as in public schools, with one proviso: the private and parochial schools must meet or exceed the minimum state standards for the education of students.

The amounts which local governments must raise for schools by taxes are set by the state at a basic minimum. Under public pressure for higher standards, these minimums are usually exceeded. Similarly, the minimum pay standards for teachers are more often than not exceeded. State-prescribed contents of school courses are usually geared down to the poorest school district in the state. In colleges and universities the widest possible latitude is left to the individual administrative heads and faculty.

The State and Public Welfare

Public welfare ranks with education and law enforcement among the principal activities of state governments. Public welfare embraces not only care of the aged, indigent, and dependent children, but extends in a broad sense to hospitalization, medical research, public health, conservation of natural resources, unemployment insurance, and recreation.

Public assistance to those unable to help themselves has come a long way in the last fifty years as social thinking has become more advanced. "The poorhouse," the "old folks' home," and the "county poor farm" have pretty much disappeared from the picture.

Public assistance is aimed at keeping the home together wherever possible, in the belief that people work out their own problems best within their own family circles. The elderly parent is no longer shipped off to a state institution if there is any way to give him a comfortable life with his own family. The dependent child does not find himself in an orphanage if a foster parent can be found for him. Instead of segregation, the welfare program now aims at restoring the person in need of help to society at the earliest possible moment.

Dangers Confronted by the States

In retaining their sovereign powers, the states have had to weather severe storms at times. During the economic depression of the early 1930s many thinking individuals seriously questioned the need for the continuance of state governments in the forty-eight states. Wide unemployment and the business depression had dried up state tax revenues. The credit standing of stores was impaired, and many were forced to curtail their services. In near panic, they turned to Washington for help.

Meantime the main brunt of meeting the depression was being borne by local municipalities, using what help they could get from Washington. In New York City the "Bankers' Agreement" took what amounted to a chattel mortgage on the great metropolis. In return for loans, the bankers demanded and got first claim on the city's tax collections.

Against this general background, people seriously questioned whether the state governments should continue. They argued that the states represented a costly and unnecessary layer of government between the local and national levels. They also held that the sovereign powers could be divided up between the national government and the county or municipal governments. Under this setup, state responsibilities would be shifted either to a regional agency of the federal government, covering several states, or to municipalities where only the locality was involved.

They Weathered the Storm

Had this plausible-sounding idea prevailed, what would have been the result? The federal government was about the only solvent agency of government during the depression years. Cities and states alike were struggling to regain financial balance. Had the idea of state government been abandoned, the federal government would have moved in with its regional set-ups covering the nation. The net result would have been an overstrong federal government and the destruction of the balance-of-power theory written originally into the federal Constitution.

Fortunately the states weathered the economic storm. Now that they are flourishing financially, no one talks of abolishing them. They emerged from the depression with their sovereign powers intact, with state treasuries built up by high production and employment, and with a revived political leadership on the state level.

Today we, as citizens of our respective states, stand under the protection of strong state governments which affect our lives more vitally and directly than does any other level of government.

2   THE IMPORTANT ROLE OF STATE GOVERNMENT

In pre-Revolutionary days the original thirteen American colonies came under the sovereignty of the British Crown. When they broke away from Britain, proclaimed their independence and achieved it on the battlefield, they inherited their sovereignty from the Crown. Ever since, the states have exercised their sovereign powers, except for the powers they delegated specifically to the federal government.

The authority of the states to make laws on their own level is therefore established beyond question. Because of its geographical size, the state makes laws that affect far more people than are affected by local laws and ordinances. But each state makes laws concerning only its own residents, and state boundaries are usually observed. Only when an enterprise goes beyond state boundaries does the federal law come into play. So we see that transporting a stolen automobile across state lines is a federal offense and the regulation of interstate commerce is a federal function.

An analysis of state budgets for the year 1951 made by the Council of State Governments, a research and coordinating group functioning under the Conference of Governors, disclosed that 85 per cent of total outlays were for education, highways, and welfare. It revealed further that since the close of World War II states have been under heavy pressure from their citizens to increase and expand services. One measure of the way in which this demand has been met is the number of state employees. From 1946 to 1950 it rose from 726,000 to 1,033,000, a rise of 42 per cent, and it is still on the way up. The success of the states in meeting needs for services can probably be measured by the receding echoes of the demand for doing away with them.

From earliest days, states began to provide services for their inhabitants which the local communities were unable or unwilling to provide. With a primitive country awaiting development, most of these early services centered on such aids to commerce as canals, roads, and the general improvement of commercial facilities.

Roads and Transportation

In the beginning, state financing of road construction got under way long before the federal union was established. New roads could open up new areas to development. In addition, there were compelling military reasons for a good road system. As a matter of protection against hostile attacks by Indians, the states needed a fast means of moving troops and supplies to the frontiers.

After a rudimentary road system had been built, the states turned to developing their inland waterways as a cheap means of transportation. New York, with tremendous natural advantages, had one hundred and fifty miles of the Hudson River connecting New York City and Albany. From Albany northwest to Buffalo another three hundred miles of waterway stretched. By building the Erie Canal, New York State was connected from Buffalo to New York City by water. The canalboat speed of four miles an hour, horse-drawn, was considered quite swift in 1835.

Still later, the states encouraged private capital to build railroads by offering right-of-ways, grants of land, and other concessions to the builders.

Today motor-highway construction is a major concern in every one of the forty-eight states. Often it takes a larger share of state revenue than any other single activity. The total investment of the states in highway construction is undoubtedly greater than that in any other department.

Huge sums are spent annually in research to improve the safety and capacity of highways. Other enormous amounts are laid out for maintenance, to keep the highways open in all sorts of weather, and for police patrols to enforce traffic regulations. In recent years the states have been devoting increasing attention to the relief of traffic congestion within cities through construction of by-passes and through arterial routes. A great deal of progress has been made in this direction, but it has been offset by a sharp increase in the number of vehicles using the highways. Progress has also been made in increasing the safety of highways, but an enormous amount remains to be done. Highway accidents throughout the past ten years have caused as many casualties as World War II.

If use of the automobile increases in the future as is expected, highway construction, maintenance, and safety will be a difficult problem for many years to come. Thomas H. MacDonald, Commissioner of Public Roads in the United States Department of Commerce, has estimated that traffic over the highways will increase by 30 per cent between 1950 and 1960.

Highway transportation of freight is rising at a phenomenal rate. In 1936 it amounted to 28 billion ton-miles and rose to 58.7 billion at the outbreak of the war in 1941.

State Support of Education

Education has been a concern of state governments from their very beginnings. Today all forty-eight states attempt to make available at public expense a minimum of twelve years of schooling. Methods and standards vary widely, but a great many points of similarity exist. Variations appear to be the result of geographical, economic, and social differences in the states themselves. The proportion of school-age children to the total population varies widely.

New Mexico, South Carolina, and Mississippi have an average of 275 school-age children for each 1,000 of total population. California, Connecticut, New Jersey, New York, and Rhode Island have fewer than 175 per 1,000 population.

The income available for taxation per school child ranges from $10,000 in New York and Nevada to less than $3,000 in Arkansas and Mississippi. Of 140,000 schools in the forty-eight states, more than half have only one teacher. Of 22,000 high schools, more than 40 per cent have fewer than 100 students.

Not all states require local districts to provide the textbooks used in public schools. Some specify that books shall be provided at public expense only to students whose parents are unable to buy them. Three states—Louisiana, Mississippi, and New Mexico—require the furnishing at public expense of state-approved textbooks used in private and parochial as well as in public schools.

Constant Increase

Far more children are receiving educational opportunities, and of a higher standard, than was the case in 1900. But obviously a tremendous amount remains to be done, and most of the states are tackling the problem courageously.

In virtually every state, programs are under way to eliminate the substandard teacher and, where possible, to consolidate schools so as to eliminate the "little red schoolhouse."

Side by side with this campaign has been a drive to eliminate the Red teacher from the schoolhouse too. In most states an organized effort is being made to compensate for shortages in tax money for local schools by grants of state funds. Generally these grants have the purpose of equalizing educational opportunities. Standards of qualification for teachers have been raised in many states.

State-supported normal or teacher-training colleges for the training of teachers at public expense have been expanded. Minimum salary laws have been enacted, in an effort to induce the best qualified to remain in the profession. Costly research has been undertaken to develop better methods of teaching.

State library systems have been set up in some places. State support of colleges and universities has increased enormously, partly to offset declining income from gifts and endowments and partly to enable more children to obtain college and university training.

Out of total state expenditures for all purposes in 1948, amounting to $10.4 billion, $2.3 billion went to local districts for support of public schools and another $213 million was spent for state-supported colleges and universities. The figures have changed since, but the ratio is about the same.

State Role in Health and Welfare

Health and welfare constitute the third major field of state services. Their origins can be found in the early poor laws of Britain and the United States, but they have undergone so many changes that the resemblance between present and earlier services has all but vanished. The whole concept of governmental responsibility for the less fortunate in the community has been altered. The last vestige of the idea that idleness and lack of ability to support one's family or one's self

were due to laziness and stupidity was washed out in the suf-
ferings and misfortunes of the Great Depression of the 1930s.
Certainly it is no badge of honor to be the recipient of public
assistance today, but neither is it a mark of shame.

The greatest health service rendered by the states today involves the hospitalization and other care of the mentally ill and
mentally defective. The number of people requiring such treatment has risen steadily with the increasing complexity of modern industrial life. New York State today has a mental-hospital
population of 120,000 people, roughly one in 120 of the total
population. The proportion is not much different in the other
states. Total mental-hygiene expenditures by the forty-eight
states, including grants of federal funds, amounted to $2.5
billion in 1948, roughly the same amount that was spent for
education. States began entering the field about one hundred
years ago. At that time it was evident that few, if any, communities had enough patients to warrant setting up and operating the special facilities needed for the care of the insane. But
when all those needing treatment within a state were assembled, there was enough to justify one or more separate institutions.

At first, emphasis was on custodial care; now, in all states,
substantial expenditures are being made for preventive and
curative therapy.

Widespread Activity

In other health fields, state governments have stressed research
and epidemic controls. Some maintain special hospitals and
schools for the blind and other handicapped, for tuberculars
and cancer sufferers, or contribute to the support of such institutions run by local governments. But the main state effort has
been directed toward such things as large-scale campaigns for
finding cases of tuberculosis, location and treatment of ve-
nereal disease, abatement of stream pollution, discovery of
means for reducing dental decay, control of communicable
diseases, and the manufacture and stock-piling of serums useful in combating epidemics. States also insure the safety of
drinking-water supplies, the purity of milk sold in the fluid

state, and similar safeguards. Recently, in co-operation with the federal government, they have been assisting local communities in the planning and financing of local hospitals for general or special purposes and have attempted to raise the standards of nursing care.

During the depression years all states were forced to shoulder part of the cost of furnishing assistance to the needy. Before that time, welfare services were the exclusive responsibility of local governments and private charities, both operating under statutes enacted by the states in their sovereign capacities. Now state, federal, and local financing on public assistance appear to be inextricably intermixed. In addition a number of social-insurance programs have been set up under either federal or state control or under their joint administration. Federal, state, and local governments share, in varying proportions, the cost of furnishing relief to four classes of the indigent: the aged, the blind, dependent children, and the permanently disabled. State and local governments share the cost of providing relief to those in need who are outside these four classes, such as those who, although not disabled, cannot find work or those who, while not permanently disabled, are temporarily restrained from working by illness or accident.

Rhode Island, California, New Jersey, and New York have separate state-administered programs for providing benefit payments, temporarily, to those unable to work because of an accident or illness not connected with their employment. Most states have separate state-administered systems for providing benefit payments to those who become ill or meet accidents because of conditions connected with their employment.

Total governmental expenditures for welfare purposes are running over $10 billion a year, of which roughly $6.5 billion is supplied by the federal government and the balance by state and local governments.

The State's Part in Law Enforcement

Criminal statutes fall into three broad classifications: (1) offenses against the person; (2) offenses against property; (3)

offenses against society or government. The first group includes such crimes as assault and battery, mayhem, and murder. The second group pertains to such things as larceny, embezzlement, and forgery. The third group encompasses such things as state-tax evasion, usury, illegally keeping children out of school, and similar offenses. What constitutes a crime in any of the three classifications is decided for the most part by state legislatures. A few, but very few, acts which do not constitute a crime under state laws have been made federal offenses by act of Congress. In this category would be found espionage, smuggling, counterfeiting, and evasion of federal taxes. But, generally speaking, most acts which are federal crimes are also state crimes. Kidnaping and illicit sale of narcotic drugs are specific examples. Sometimes the difficulties of placing the scene of the crime within a particular jurisdiction make it easier to obtain federal instead of state convictions.

State governments, through their legislative processes, have very broad powers to decide what constitutes a crime and what does not. In New York it is a crime to shoot a black bear under one year old but all right to shoot him if he is older. In Georgia a few years ago a legislator proposed to make it a crime for anyone to sell lipsticks or other cosmetics within the state. His proposal was rejected, but it could have been adopted. Had it been, offenders would have been liable to fine or imprisonment or both. Most states have stringent laws against gambling, some of which are enforced and others of which are ignored. Until a few years ago it was legal to hold a professional baseball game in New York on Sunday after 1 P.M., but it was a penal offense to conduct a football game.

Judicial practice and crime, two fields that are closely related, are more often associated with state governments in the public mind than are other state functions. Probably this is because the average citizen is prone to think "There ought to be a law" any time he encounters conditions that offend his sense of propriety, fairness, or decency. When he thinks of laws and the lawmaking power he thinks more often of the State Legislature than of the federal Congress. Usually the thing that gives rise to the demand for a "law" is recognized as too trivial for congressional consideration, but not always.

The main purpose of laws governing judicial practice is to insure a fair and impartial trial, either in civil or criminal proceedings. One rule that is rigidly enforced in the courts everywhere bars the admission of "hearsay" evidence. Another rigidly enforced rule bars questions irrelevant to the trial issue. Whether a trial has been fair and impartial is frequently a matter of debate between opposing counsels. Each year various state appellate courts, and sometimes the United States Supreme Court, decide that the conditions required for a fair trial have not been met and reverse the findings of lower tribunals.

Controls and Licenses

State controls over economic opportunity take various forms and oftentimes are linked closely with regulation of health and sanitary standards, morals, and the use of potentially dangerous machinery. Laws regulating the number of hours that a wage earner may be employed in any day or week are justified by the duty of the state to protect the health of its citizens. Statutes forbidding the employment of women during the night hours in some occupations rest on the obligation to guard community morals. Establishment of state standards of sanitation and ventilation in factory buildings has an obvious relationship to health needs.

Licensing laws are being employed by the states with greater and greater frequency, in order to control economic activity. The list of occupations that cannot be entered upon until a license is obtained is growing. Those who require licenses either from the state or from a subdivision by virtue of state law include: accountants, physicians, teachers, plumbers, jockeys, osteopaths, dentists, race-horse trainers, barbers, beauticians, manicurists, surveyors, engineers, chauffeurs, weighmasters, psychologists, court stenographers, electricians, realestate salesmen, insurance adjusters, lawyers, and veterinarians. This list is by no means all-inclusive. There are dozens of other occupations which require a permit. In some states it is possible to engage in some listed activities without a license. Requirements and standards vary widely from state to state.

While the justification for licensing laws is usually health or safety needs, the human desire to restrict competition often plays a large part in the setting up of the licensing standards. In states where a license is required to practice barbering or manicuring it is a safe assumption that the impetus for the law came from existing barbers and manicurists who feared the economic effects of a sudden influx of new practitioners. Human nature being what it is, few people, whatever their profession, really welcome strong, heavy competition except when it is likely to be of profit to themselves.

The state's application of many of its regulations on conduct is indirect. The citizen who finds a summons for overtime parking pasted on his windshield thinks of the policeman on the beat, overlooking the source of the policeman's authority. The man denied a license as a plumber blames the members of a local board for turning him down. The waitress who must quit at midnight when tips are getting heavy, the man who cannot obtain a license to sell real estate, and others similarly affected generally place the responsibility for the curtailment of their activities anywhere but where it belongs: with the state government. Even though they may never realize it, they have been in touch with temporal sovereignty.

Additional State Services

Other state services fall under the following heads: (1) agriculture and conservation; (2) economic protection; (3) operation of a penal system; (4) planning and development.

In agriculture and conservation, state efforts are directed toward improving the fertility and yield of the soil. These efforts also include research and educational programs, assisting farmers to market their produce at the best prices obtainable, and guarding against the wasteful depletion of forests, game, and water resources.

In the field of economic protection the state acts to protect the individual against loss or denial of employment as a result of labor-management strife. This is where the state conciliation service steps in to settle industrial disputes. By periodic inspections of the books of banks and insurance companies, the state protects the wage earner against loss of his savings. It offers the investor a safeguard by banning the sale of "blue-sky" securities. By requiring safety devices on potentially dangerous machinery, it protects the worker against loss of life or limb. In many fields it provides technical schools where the worker can study to improve his earning capacity.

Operation of a penal system, generally described as "correction," involves incarcerating hardened offenders and offering rehabilitation opportunities to those less hardened.

States, like many private firms, compete with each other for business. This function involves the state's planning and development service for bringing new industry and employment into the state. State agencies often furnish advice, counsel, and sometimes financial aid to help a local community eliminate economic decay, wipe out its slums, and provide attractive new housing at low rent.

From the wide variety and scope of its activities, we can see that state government plays an important role in the pattern of American life.

3 HOW STATE GOVERNMENT FUNCTIONS

Since state government is big business, there is naturally keen competition among political powers to obtain the right to control and direct state activities.

This conflict gives incentive to political parties, factions, and individual politicians. While we have "a government of laws, not men," it remains true that men make the laws, other men enforce them, and still others in the judiciary decide whether they have been properly applied. Since men obtain the right to direct state government by reason of political victory at the polls, politics is the motivating force behind state government.

Lest this be misconstrued, let us say immediately that many professional politicians consider it "smart politics" to give the people honest and efficient government. For any officeholder who seeks re-election year after year, this is becoming the formula for success.

Political power derives from the ability to win elections or from the ability to control elections. As noted, a party will sometimes sweep in by offering a program of improvements that attracts public support. At other times the mere offering of a new candidate to replace the standard-bearer of a discredited and outmoded regime will accomplish the same purpose.

In states where the political parties have a close numerical balance it usually takes a reform program to win. In states where one political party is deeply entrenched the "new regime" approach often succeeds.

Political forces and political parties operating within states parallel those which operate in the nation. Their power in any single state will vary with the state's economic, social, and political factors. In some, rural agrarian forces, operating through one or both of the major parties, are dominant. In others, urban wage-earner and industrial influences predominate. In still others, the balance between rural and urban interests is so even that a relatively small, usually uncontrollable "floating center" is responsible for the ultimate decision.

Various Factors

A clear distinction must be drawn between political forces and political parties. The two are far from the same, although they sometimes appear to be. Under the American system, each of the two major parties, Democratic and Republican, represents a coalition of political forces. These include the organizations found in big cities, whose primary interest is usually municipal power and control; the county group, which has a similar interest in monopolizing offices and controlling contracts in rural areas; organized labor, which has alliances and representatives in both parties but usually is more closely identified with the large city organizations; farmers and those who retain "one foot in the soil," who generally have a loose alliance with the county political groups; and the financial interests, which include bankers, manufacturers, and retail merchants who want a favorable climate for the security of investments and for the earning of profits.

Contest for Power

Turning now to the political methods by which control of a state government is usually achieved, we find a constant struggle for power between the rural and the urban blocs.

In most states the rural agrarian group is virtually guaranteed control of one of the two houses of the state legislature, either by laws governing the selection of legislators, by some constitutional provision, or by simple failure to reapportion seats. This condition may be traced, historically, to the fear of "mob rule" entertained by early patriots or to a distrust of the reasoning capacity of urban residents felt by the same founding groups. In New York, Connecticut, and some other states it is the numerically larger branch of the legislature where the rural dominance is assured. In New Jersey and some other states it is the numerically smaller chamber where rural influences are in the ascendancy. Except for Nebraska, where agrarian interests have a natural predominance, all states have a two-chamber legislature, patterned in general after the United States Congress.

New York assures rural domination of the lower house of the legislature by constitutional provisions guaranteeing each county at least one representative, called an assemblyman, and prohibiting the award to any two adjoining counties of more than half the total. Of one hundred and fifty seats, New York City, with 55 per cent of the population, gets sixty-four. The remainder of the state, with 45 per cent of the population, gets eighty-six. Connecticut apportions seats in the lower house among its one hundred and sixty-nine towns on the basis not of population but of when they were incorporated. It bases the apportionment of senators on a population basis, as does New York. Thus New Haven County, with a population of 484,000, gets ten senators and forty-two representatives, while Litchfield County, with a population of 87,000, gets three senators and forty-three representatives. New Jersey, which just modernized its constitution in other respects, allows but one senator from each county, regardless of size. The principle is the same as that which awards each state, regardless of population, two seats in the United States Senate.

Most of the legislators from rural areas frequently bear a nominal allegiance to one political party, while a majority of those from the industrial cities belong to the other. Local differences result, however, in the election of some members of one party in territory where the other is dominant. Almost always there are some Democratic legislators from predominantly Republican rural areas in New York, for instance, and some Republicans from predominantly Democratic urban areas. The same is true of Ohio, Indiana, Illinois, and other states where a rural-urban legislative division is characteristic.

As in the federal Congress, legislators from predominantly agrarian areas tend to vote "country" on matters relating to agriculture, regardless of party, while congressmen from urban districts, regardless of party, vote "city." In states where an urban-rural conflict is up for decision, those from farming areas band together in opposition to those from cities. Where no urban-rural conflict is involved, the division may be along party lines or along economic lines. Because political forces rather than parties are the determining factor, the rural-urban division can be found in the one-party states of the South just as it is in the two-party states of the rest of the nation. The difference, without a distinction, is that the conflict is between factions instead of between parties.

Far-Reaching Effects

Control of the state legislature, or at least of one branch, is as important a goal for those who seek political power as is control of the executive department. The reason for this is that the sovereign power of the state can be exercised only by joint action of the legislature and the governor. Neither alone can wield its mighty sword. Once sovereign power has been invoked through enactment of a law, the governor, through the power to select and supervise those charged with its administration and enforcement, becomes more important. Even then the legislature retains influence through its control of appropriations. If the legislature refuses to authorize the employment of anyone to administer or enforce a law, violators are in no great peril of punishment.

One-man or one-group control of state legislatures happily is much less frequent today than formerly. Professor Allan Nevins, the noted historian, once observed that a primary function of a state political chairman was to act as broker for the legislature, trading legislative action for votes, power, and, on occasions, money. Today his function is more likely to be that of arbiter or umpire to referee disputes within the party and to keep it from flying to pieces.

The one power retained by the professional political leader is the privilege of picking his party's candidates for public office. If they win, he has a reasonable expectation that they will manifest their gratitude by seeking his advice on the filling of offices under their control and in the formulation of policy, an expectation in which he is seldom disappointed. Selection of candidates remains in the hands of the professional politician only because of the apathy and indifference of the electorate. In most states candidates for elective offices are chosen at party primaries in the late summer or early fall. Legally, all those who claim membership in the party are entitled to vote on the selection of these candidates. Actually, it is a rare occasion when as many as 10 per cent use this right.

Overlooked by the Voters

Control over nominations, particularly of candidates for the state legislature, is a major element in the strength of a political leader. Its value is notably enhanced by the tendency of so many voters to overlook legislative candidates entirely when they cast their ballots. In some states this is because ballots are overlong. Rival nominees for legislative office are listed near the end along with candidates for coroner and town highway superintendent. In other states large numbers of voters who believe themselves capable of picking a governor or President of the United States feel incompetent to make a choice for their own legislature. In New York in 1946, 300,000 who voted for governor or United States senator failed to vote for legislature candidates. In 1948, 200,000 of those who voted for President in New York were unrecorded for legislative offices. A similar situation prevails in virtually every state. On the average, at least 6 per cent of those who vote for the leading office on the ticket skip the contest for legislative seats. In states where the party division is close this is enough to shift control from one political organization to another if it were cast solidly for minority party candidates.

Party leader control over nominations is helped further by a lack of interest shown in the work of the legislature by many potential candidates. Demands made upon a legislator's time by groups interested in particular measures is frequently heavy. The prestige of the legislative office, partly due to unfamiliarity with its powers and prerogatives, is frequently low. Salaries, likewise, are generally low, sometimes deliberately kept that way to discourage the less affluent from seeking office. In many states legislative pay is less than the amount required for a room in a respectable hotel. The result is that in many communities nominations for legislative office frequently go begging. Is it any wonder that hastily considered, unworkable, and even plain foolish legislation sometimes finds its way into the statute books? The real marvel, it would seem, is that so few legislatures are under boss or special-interest domination.

Legislative Problems

Legislative—or, more precisely, sovereign—powers of a state are called into play by the enactment of a law. This means that a proposed law must receive the support of a majority of both branches of the legislature (except in Nebraska) and the approval of the governor (except in North Carolina, where he has no veto power). In rare instances a law is enacted by a legislative vote that overrides a gubernatorial veto. The power is inherent but seldom used. In consequence of the varying economic, social, and political interests represented within a legislature, measures of major importance usually must undergo a number of drastic changes between the proposal and the enactment stage to achieve the backing essential to final approval.

Hazards and hurdles faced by a new bill between the time it is first urged upon a legislature and the time it is added to existing statutes is well illustrated by the history of New York's "Sickness Compensation Act," which became operative in 1950. Although the solution reached in New York was somewhat different from that in other states, the legislative history of the measure had close parallels in Rhode Island, New Jersey, and California. It may yet be duplicated in Massachusetts, Connecticut, Pennsylvania, Michigan, and Illinois, which are struggling with the same problem, and possibly in other states. It took twelve years to enact the New York law.

In New York that twelve years stretched over six successive sessions of the legislature, each one of two years' duration. In the long struggle over the bill, numerous suggestions and countersuggestions were advanced and dismissed; the most powerful voices of labor and management were raised for and against it; similar proposals in other states were studied; and extensive debate was held in both houses of the New York legislature. Even in its adopted form, the law does not satisfy all elements. Subsequent years will doubtless bring modification and improvement after the results of this law are studied in operation.

Legislative procedure differs widely among the states. Some states, like California, require public hearings on all measures introduced. Others, like Massachusetts, require that every bill introduced be brought up for a vote. Many, like Ohio and

New York, give committees great latitude in deciding on the
form and content of legislation as well as on what measures
shall be taken up for consideration. Practice is more uniform.
Every legislator takes into account the desires of the more
potent political forces in his district and generally is guided
by what he believes the majority wants. The key to better
legislation is an electorate which takes a greater interest in
what is done and more care in always choosing men and
women of strong moral and intellectual fiber for the legislature
and other state offices.

4   THE PART YOU CAN PLAY

State government involves large numbers of men and vast
sums of money. In 1949 state and local government employees
numbered slightly more than four million and their total
monthly pay roll exceeded nine hundred million dollars. For
every 37.5 inhabitants, we have one state or local employee.

In 1890 state and local government revenue amounted to
only $562,000,000 annually. The latest figures show that it
has grown to nearly eighteen billion dollars each year, with
every prospect of increase as the population grows and production increases.

With these tremendous financial resources, state government also offers the individual a wide choice of employment.
Because of the diversity of its activities, the state has jobs
for game wardens, hospital dietitians and therapists, in teaching, library work, and a wide variety of jobs in law enforcement and public welfare. There is scarcely an activity maintained by private enterprise which is not duplicated by your
state government.

In recent years a higher caliber of employee has been flow-
ing into state service. Many state governments offer high-
level courses in public administration to qualify individuals
for better-paying jobs.

Special Training Advantages

As an example, New York State offers to college graduates a "graduate program in public administration" through its state university. In the state's words, the course is:

"Designed to strengthen the public service by providing an opportunity for employees of the state to broaden their experience in public administration and deepen their insight into public affairs. Classes are primarily intended to encourage the growth of administrative talent."

For the individual this is a wonderful thing. The employer—in this case the state—offers its workers a way up the ladder of success through greater responsibility. At one stroke this action abolishes the "dead-end" aspect of jobs which lead nowhere. Any interested person, in or out of government, may enroll for this sixteen-week course.

In addition to this formalized academic training, many states offer their employees "in-service" training right on their jobs. This training takes the employee one or more levels higher than the one he is currently occupying, develops his understanding, and trains him to assume more responsibility. Promotion and better pay accompany success in this type of training, which is really "learning by doing."

Lack of Interest

The size and complexity of state government discourage too many people who might contribute to its improvement and bring substantial benefits to their fellow citizens. Distaste for public service is not peculiar to state governments. It handicaps the federal and local governments as well. Most generally it stems from the popular association of public employment with politics and of politics with corruption.

Overlooked in the popular attitude is the obvious fact that public employees are, first of all, men and women. As stated before, they are probably no worse than any other group of human beings. Because they must perform so many of their functions in a goldfish-bowl atmosphere, their moral and ethical codes are higher than average. There is venality and corruption among them, of course, but in no greater proportion than is found in other occupations, and perhaps less.

What is also overlooked is that people generally are expecting more and more and better and better service from their governments. This public demand can be satisfied only as the people are willing, and able to pay for these advantages and find the workers needed. Even if there is no difficulty in getting "more," there is always the problem of getting those who are best qualified. This involves a better appreciation of how the individual can serve in government. Listen to what one New York State employee has to say:

What Others Do

"The opportunities in state government are great—and there is constant need for conscientious concern with legislation that is proposed . . . for some reason the proponents of evil never seem to sleep!

"I recall one legislator who was outstanding in his efforts. He fought constantly for good legislation. Yet while he was doing all the fighting in behalf of the people of his state—none of the people of good will came to applaud him—yet he was constantly harassed by the ragtag ends of the dissidents who always obstruct. It should have been a discouraging job for him—but his spirit never lessened.

"I remember the days when the Communists came by special train to obstruct legislation. State police were called to guard the Capitol and admit only those people who had business there. The Commies would parade annually and send a delegation to Albany demanding their right to be heard. They're the ones who know what their rights are and take full advantage of them. Once inside the Capitol, they would immediately disperse and go individually to the offices of senators and assemblymen to harangue and harass them. If only those who want good legislation would show as much interest!"

You Pay the Bill

One woman on a school board did her bit to bring home the fact that the taxpayer eventually pays the bill, even when he thinks he is putting it over on someone else. When several members attempted to include a swimming pool on the new school grounds, they said: "The state pays for it." She alone argued against it, asking them: "Who is the state?" Somewhat sheepishly one of them replied, "Well, I guess the people." "And who are the people?" she continued. "Oh, I suppose *we* are," was the only reply they could give. These members of the school board saw for the first time that the only money the state can pay out is what the taxpayer pays in. And therefore the luxury of a swimming pool would be possible only through the increased taxation that they, and others like them, would have to pay.

She Did It Singlehanded

Dorothea Lynde Dix gave an excellent example more than a century ago of how one individual can affect the course of state government. A writer of children's stories and devotional works, she paid a chance visit to a jail in East Cambridge, Massachusetts, at the age of thirty-nine. She found that the mentally ill were mingled together with felons and minor criminals, as was the common practice at the time. The conditions and treatment of the insane so aroused her indignation that she sat down and wrote a "Memorial" to the Bay State legislature.

"I come," she wrote, "to present the strong claims of suffering humanity. I come as the advocate of helpless, forgotten, insane and idiotic men and women, of beings wretched in our prisons and more wretched in our almshouses. I proceed, gentlemen, briefly to call your attention to the state of insane persons confined in this Commonwealth in cages, closets, cellars, stalls, pens: chained, naked, beaten with rods and lashed into obedience."

Her plea struck the conscience of the legislature and the

people. Massachusetts soon enlarged its state hospitals for the insane, but Miss Dix was not content. She visited eighteen other states to make a similar appeal. Eight states responded and established similar hospitals, and others, several of which, like Massachusetts, had had mental-hospital systems previously, humanized their methods of treatment.

Some idea of the benefits that flowed from Miss Dix's pleas can be formed from a few census figures. The 1840 Federal Census, taken the year before her visit to the East Cambridge jail, listed a total population of 17,000,000 and estimated the number of insane at 16,457 (which undoubtedly was low), of whom 2,561 were inmates of hospitals or other institutions. At the end of 1948, 556,625 were receiving treatment in mental hospitals (the population had increased to 140,000,000), of whom 84 per cent, or 469,000, were in state institutions. Moreover, treatment had progressed so far from early practices of restraints and chains that 473,318 were discharged that year as either cured or so improved as no longer to need hospital treatment.

Another Like Her

It may be argued that Miss Dix could be successful because the nation was smaller a hundred years ago and the people less distracted with other things such as war and Communism and atom bombs. But Mrs. James H. Killilea of Rye, New York, has demonstrated within the past five years that the argument won't hold water. Mrs. Killilea has three children, one of whom has cerebral palsy, an affliction that for a long time was associated erroneously with epilepsy or mental deficiency. She found that such children could be enabled to live useful, happier lives if given proper training but the cost of treatment was beyond the means of the average family.

So she began to visit and write to members of the New York Legislature, some of whom had never heard of the affliction. Her early efforts led to setting up a special committee to study the problem. It came back with a report recommending that state funds be used to train therapists for work

with spastics—as cerebral-palsy sufferers are generally known
—and that the state finance medical research into causes and
treatment and, further, that it set up institutions to give special treatment. These have all now been written into law.
Having succeeded in her home state, she is extending her
efforts to others, just as Miss Dix did a century ago.

All the Way Up

A man of many years of service in state government says he
is grateful for the wonderful years of experience that working
for the government has given him. While practicing law, he
handled civil and criminal cases for the defense. It was his
job to defend those being prosecuted by the government. In
the legislature he had the business of making the laws. An
assistant district attorney he had the privilege of enforcing
them, then as a federal judge the opportunity to judge them.
Finally, as president of the New York State Civil Service Commission, he was on the administrative side and worked tire-
lessly to improve the working conditions of state employees so
that careers in state government will appeal to people of high
purpose.

A Change in New Jersey

Arthur T. Vanderbilt, the present Chief Justice of New Jersey's Supreme Court, is another who has demonstrated what
one man with an idea and persistence can accomplish. As a
practicing lawyer, and later as dean of the New York University Law School, he was distressed by the emphasis placed
on procedure in the courts. It seemed to him that trials were
too frequently contests of skill between lawyers in which
justice to the parties involved was often an unnoticed casualty.

He obtained his opportunity to do something about it when
he was named a delegate to the convention that was created
to modernize New Jersey's antiquated State Constitution. As
a delegate he received no pay. The obstacles put in the path
of the sweeping reforms he advocated were enough to discourage a less valiant fighter. Lawyers reluctant to change a

system under which they prospered, and political interests who saw a danger that their influence in the courts would be reduced, made common cause.

But Dean Vanderbilt was able to explain the advantages of his reforms in terms that the average person could understand. The judiciary article—which combined a number of separate courts into a single tribunal, consigned to the scrap heap fine distinctions between pleadings, and made justice more certain and swift—was one of the most popular of the changes made in New Jersey's fundamental law. The American Judicature Society has called New Jersey's modernized court system the best in the nation. Naturally Mr. Vanderbilt was asked to head the state's highest court when it was finally set up.

Still Serving

A retired businessman, a widower, financially independent, felt he did not want to have his son and daughters burdened with him during his inactive years. He sat down to think over just where he could make the greatest contribution of his time. He felt that in spite of the forced retirement his company had given him, he still had many years in which "to do something for mankind."

He had become very concerned over the growing problem of the mentally ill in his state, and decided that perhaps in some small way he could help.

He hired out as a guard in one of the leading state mental institutions. His kindness, his philosophy of life, his self-sacrificing spirit have already benefited many patients there. He purchased Christmas trees and gifts for all from his own personal funds. His presence has not only aided the patients but has also been an inspiration to both the doctors and the rest of the staff at the hospital.

Everyone Can Help

State government offers a healthy, challenging climate for the employee with a new idea. Here's one example:

Violet Lifset is a stenographer in the Law Department of an eastern state. Violet studied her job carefully. Finally she thought she saw a way to improve it. She proposed a revised system for processing legal documents submitted by state agencies to the state attorney general for review. On trial, the new method showed that the streamlined filing and correspondence procedures saved up to 50 per cent of the time formerly required for stenographic and clerical work. This one step, small in itself, saves an average of ten hours each week. For her suggestion Miss Lifset got a one-hundred-dollar cash award and a commendation from her superiors.

Another case follows:

Four men, working together in a state health department laboratory, designed and built a battery of washers to cleanse small glass tubes used in their lab. Before they pooled their initiative and ingenuity, this work had to be performed by a single washer. The tubes that had to be washed each month numbered 188,000, making obvious what a money, time, and effort saver the battery of washers would be. This invention suggested another to them, so before they laid aside their thinking caps they came up with a new type automatic agitator for processing blood specimens. Their work brought them a four-hundred-dollar cash award and individual commendations which will aid them when they seek promotion.

Obviously, advances in state government result more often from the efforts of those engaged in it directly than from those who are outside of it. Those responsible for the administration of government are faced continually with problems demanding solutions. When an answer to a vexatious question is found in one state it usually forms a precedent for similar action in another where the problem may also have existed.

Each in His Own Way

Under Governor Alfred E. Smith, New York consolidated more than one hundred separate boards and commissions into eighteen state departments, each with a responsible head. Today this reorganization is generally rated as one of Governor Smith's major accomplishments.

Virginia did a notable job in similar reorganization. Other states were less spectacular, but many lasting and necessary reforms were achieved.

Another major contribution toward improving the efficiency of state government was made by Henry Cole, a state senator in Colorado. It consisted of establishment of the Council of State Government as a central clearinghouse for the exchange of information between the states on problems of common interest. This agency is now supported by appropriations from all of the states and some territories. It keeps the governors, legislators, and other officials in all the states informed of what the other states are doing. In effect it makes available to all the states the research and studies which any one of them undertakes in order to meet a particular problem. More recently the Council has been doing research of its own for all the states at the direction of the Governor's Conference, one of the components of the Council.

Millard F. Caldwell, a former governor of Florida, is responsible for a recent innovation in state education. He was confronted, as governor, with demands for enlarging and improving Florida's College of Forestry, for establishment of a State College of Medicine, and for other new technical schools. If all the demands were met, the expense would wreck the Florida budget. Moreover, the task of assembling competent faculties would be almost insuperable. Other southern states had the same problem. His solution was that the southern states pool their higher educational resources so that any student who wanted to attend a state-supported technical college in another state could do so on the same basis as residents of that state.

Out of this suggestion grew the Southern Regional Educational Compact, signed February 8, 1948. Fourteen southern states agreed to state-supported technical colleges within the region for all southerners who qualify, and to support these institutions jointly.

It Takes Time

Major reforms and improvements in state government are never overnight campaigns. Civil service was discussed by Calhoun and Clay for thirty years before Cleveland was able to get it written into law. It took Thurlow Weed, a master politician, twenty years to overcome the conservative opposition to abolishing imprisonment for debt (his father spent a great deal of time in a state debtors' prison). Sixteen years elapsed between the time unemployment insurance was first proposed in Massachusetts and the time Wisconsin became the first state to write it into law.

Nor are reforms and improvements a task for "summer soldiers." Not only must a natural resistance to change be overcome; it must be clearly demonstrated that there is a need and a real demand for the innovation. Since all change involves, in some measure, an alteration of established relationships, those whose influence is lessened can be counted upon to use all their strength to becloud, befog, and obscure the points at issue, if they do not dare a frontal attack. Their opposition must be countered by individuals willing to get behind the new idea and push.

Apart from employing his electoral franchise, the citizen has another weapon of great power. It is the right to help form an enlightened public opinion through discussion, writing letters, and joining organizations dedicated to the advancement of purposes in which he believes. The importance of these instruments is attested by the ingenuity and resourcefulness that left-wing groups have shown in forming a multiplicity of societies to pass a radical line and in bombarding legislators and public officials with letters.

Considering what an illusion of public demand has been able to achieve, it is interesting to speculate what great good would result if the average citizen would show as much concern for every branch of his government.

VII.   IT'S YOUR NATIONAL GOVERNMENT

VII. IT'S YOUR NATIONAL GOVERNMENT

1 THE HOPEFUL SIDE

Turning from state government to national government, I recall speaking last spring to government officials in Washington on making some motion pictures under Christopher auspices to portray public administration and the peacetime uses of atomic energy.

My visit to the nation's capital came at a time when Washington morale was very low. When a friend and I got into a cab at Washington's Union Square we got our first manifestation of that low public frame of mind. Instead of asking the usual "Where to?" the cabdriver, with weary cynicism, inquired: "Well, gentlemen, which investigation will it be?"

We chuckled at the driver's humor, recognizing that many visitors to the capital at that time were headed for one of the numerous investigations then in progress. In fact the competition for page-one headlines was pretty brisk. Washington had the continuing investigation into Communism of the House Committee on Un-American Activities; Senator Fulbright's Senate probe into the affairs of the Reconstruction Finance Corporation was on; the Kefauver Senate Crime Investigating Committee was just ending its public hearings before the television cameras, and a host of minor inquiries competed with these major probes.

Our first meeting brought us to the Department of Agriculture, a government agency that touches the lives of every man, woman, and child in the country. It's almost safe to say

that the research of this department will be represented at
your dinner table tonight no matter what you have for dinner, even if you dine on only bread and milk.

Before we started to talk, the official who received us called
in his assistant, and then I began to explain the purpose of
our visit. Neither of these gentlemen had more than a sketchy
idea of the work of the Christophers.

I said it was the Christopher idea to encourage more people
with a love of God and country to get into government. I said
that we planned to develop this idea—already spread in our
books—through a series of motion pictures. I told them that
these films would not be technical in any sense of the word.
We didn't propose to set ourselves up as experts on how government works or should work. We were concerned with
getting more good people to go into government service—we
were even more concerned with that than we were with getting bad pople out because we felt that our sins of omission
needed correcting more urgently than anything else.

"We should like to point out in these films," I continued,
"that while there are many good people in government, more
of high ideals are certainly needed—people who will be there
even at great personal sacrifice because they have a purpose,
because they are dedicated to the principles on which this
country was founded, because they have the same deep faith
in God that our Founding Fathers stated so forcefully in the
Declaration of Independence."

Double Advantage

The official behind the desk, a gray-haired man of quiet dignity, with years of public service behind him, was obviously
deeply moved—not by what I had said, particularly, but by
the thoughts the words had provoked in his own mind.

At first he merely said: "If the Christophers can bring more
God-fearing people with a purpose into government, they'll
be doing a wonderful thing."

Then his assistant, tall and youthful, added:

"If you can do anything to make people already in government feel that they're doing something worth while, you'll have accomplished a great deal too. Now, when you tell anybody outside you work for the government, they laugh and say, 'Oh, you're living off the government too!' "

It was then that the gray-haired veteran of government service, who had served under both Republican and Democratic administrations, said—in his quiet way—something that shocked me.

· "I come from a little town up in Vermont," he said, "and when I go home sometimes, I'm *ashamed* to say that I'm in the government."

This from the man facing me—a man of great ability and great patriotism—a man who obviously, with no trouble at all, could have risen to great heights in private industry. What a heinous thing that this man should feel *ashamed* to say that he was in the service of his country!

"That's the way people seem to feel," he said very quietly.

Again, it wasn't until later that the full implications of what this man had said struck me.

Who were the people who made this man feel ashamed? Well, they were ordinary people in a small town. They were like you and me, no better, no worse. They meant no harm. But they were doing what so many of us do—carping and complaining and criticizing and doing nothing themselves to make government better.

Then this thought hit me between the eyes: What if these people made this fine government official so ashamed, so fed up, so weary of taking it that he quit his job in government? Think what we would have lost—a good man doing a good job. Who knows what kind of man would have taken his place? But whoever took his place, we would have lost *him*. Could a score of Communists have done more to weaken our government than those who fail to distinguish the good from the bad?

Our next appointment in search of background material for the Christopher films on government took us into the rococo elegance of the old State Department Building, now housing the tremendously expanded administrative offices of the President.

In Terms of People

We met an official who had been a newspaper reporter. We found his interests so varied that our conference turned into the most fascinating glimpse into political science and practice that we had ever listened to.

We had told them that our interest was in people first of all. And so he talked of government in terms of people.

He explained the complex business by which a law is passed from the moment a bill is first dropped into "the hopper" until it reaches the desk of the President of the United States.

But this man "ad-libbed" it from start to finish—in terms of people. And he demonstrated eloquently our Christopher thesis that every person in government can help to make it better. He went from top to bottom, proving the point over and over again until he finally had placed the bill in the hands of a messenger boy.

Including the Messenger

"Now," he said, "for the moment, the fate of the bill is in the hands of the messenger. He can either deliver it promptly to the committee that is waiting for it or he can stop to watch a new building going up and then drop in a drugstore for a soda and perhaps he can waste so much time that the Committee will go on to something else—and the bill in the hands of the messenger will have to wait and, who knows, perhaps it will wait long enough to be put off again and maybe it will never get any farther than that."

And then the talk turned to the structure of the government, and again this government official reduced the full, complex story to down-to-earth, easy-to-understand, even colloquial terms. He traced the organization to the government from the White House down to the level of the smallest county.

Just in passing he tossed out fascinating details—as, for instance, the organization of counties in the state of Georgia, which has more of them—159—than any other state. He told us why this was so, how it came out in the days of the Reconstruction after the Civil War.

And I wondered why those who are doing an honest job in government are not more appreciated—why we don't build on them and get more like them? Probably it is because most of us tend to be so preoccupied with the evil that we do little to bring about the cure. We hurt ourselves more than we think by playing down the good, playing up the evil. Good people doing a good job usually don't make page-one headlines. It's often the other way around. The bad people make the headlines—just as they make the bad government.

Too many are content to shrug their shoulders and say, "Well, they're all a bunch of crooks in Washington. Nothing I can do about it. It's too much for me." The net result? However bad it may be, that attitude does nothing more than make it worse!

What if the man we were talking to adopted the attitude? What if he said, "Oh, why should I waste my time here. Why not get a job where I can take care of myself. Let somebody else worry about the public."

Well, we'd lose him and if we lost enough like him, our government would literally collapse and our enemies would take over without effort. Yes, lose enough of these good men—fail to provide more like them—and we lose everything including, quite likely, our own necks.

They Play an Important Role

Another day, during this visit to Washington, I had occasion to visit the Atomic Energy Commission, again to get a sort of briefing on the career possibilities in that fabulous field.

The Commission's offices are in a gleaming white building. In the files and the minds of the people who have their headquarters there doubtless there are locked secrets that will affect the whole course of history, the destiny of all mankind.

There is a marble counter in the lobby, and behind it sits a pleasant, intelligent girl receptionist. She is atomic energy's first line of defense.

On the wall behind her there is a sign reading: "The paramount objective is to assure the common defense and security. See Atomic Energy Act of 1947."

This girl part—and an important part—of the government's vast atomic-energy operation. Every visitor, no matter what his statute may be outside, must present himself before this young lady to state his business. He must be signed in and signed out by her. It's not difficult to grasp the importance of her job, and yet she has no more imposing title than that of receptionist.

Of course the young lady is backed up by other security restrictions. No one may enter the corridors without an identifying badge and an escort. Let any visitor put his badge in his pocket or wander too far from his escort and there will be prompt correction on the part of armed guards, who stand near the receptionist.

With High Purpose

In discussing the career possibilities in the atomic-energy field we talked with a young lawyer who had given up a bright future in private practice to take the job he held with the government.

The same was true of a former officer, graduate of the Naval Academy, brilliant and still young enough to take his pick of better-paying jobs. He had chosen to take less money and more opportunity to serve his country.

Another was a businessman who had come to Washington at some personal sacrifice but was happier than he had ever been, in the knowledge that he was doing a job that would help to change the world for the better.

In all of atomic energy today there are about seventy thousand people at work. If this great new force is ever fully developed for peacetime uses, more than a million will probably be needed—how many hundreds of thousands like the young man we had just seen?

And where are they to come from? You have part of that answer!

Where the Trouble Begins

On the way to the station in the taxicab there was time to glance at the headlines. They didn't make pleasant reading. Thinking of the several good people we had met in Washington, we saw that the State Department had just discharged four more of our representatives in the Far East for betrayal of their trust.

The Kefauver crime committee had just made the last of its revelations, no less depressing than the others showing the links between the underworld and politicians.

In the Senate, Senator Fulbright had gone on to suggest the formation of a "commission" to "draw forth meaning from the mass of data" revealed by his investigation.

Turning the pages of the newspaper, we found the following in an editorial commenting on the senator's suggestion for a commission on ethics:

"The corruption of our sense of values has not come overnight. The process has been a long and cynical one. This disintegration of public morality has been accompanied by impairment of our private sense of values. One need only glance at the degradation of old standards of family life, at the futile pursuit of material things in the name of happiness to see that this is so.

These conditions are not going to be remedied by any report. The cure must be generated in the hearts and consciences of men. Those in public life can do much by setting a worthy example, which many of them have not been doing. But in the last analysis the plain citizen must be his own healer. There will be real improvement in our public standards of morality when he decides he wants improvement and not before."

When will the average citizen decide? Time is running out.

Better Than Most Think

As it happened, it was a historic occasion at Union Station. President Vincent Auriol of France—the first French President ever to visit this country—was arriving, to be welcomed by President Truman.

I thought that this was reason enough for taking a later train and I went back and exchanged my ticket. I was glad I did.

The guns boomed out the twenty-one-gun salute of welcome, and President Auriol took his place in the car by the side of President Truman. The bands struck up and the big tanks began to roll on ahead. A thrill of pride seemed to run through the crowd around me.

As the parade moved down Pennsylvania Avenue, everyone in that crowd could have looked up at the dome of the Capitol across the way and thought:

"It's my government—my responsibility."

2   FIND OUT MORE ABOUT IT

Many authorities claim that a turning point in American history took place in 1933 when the United States formally recognized Soviet Russia.

Ever since that fateful move our country and the rest of the civilized world has suffered a serious decline.

Recognition by this country bestowed a world-wide prestige upon Communism that paved the way for their global program of death and destruction. More than any other single factor, this unfortunate approval by the United States is said to have made possible the enslavement of hundreds of millions of innocent persons as well as the undermining of our own country.

Many Americans are fearful that decisions are now being

made and trends developing in government that may fatally jeopardize the future of our nation. They are very much afraid that our country is being sold short by those in high places in government who, even though not malicious, may be making tragic mistakes from which we may never recover.

It is up to you, as a citizen and stockholder in America, to look into this and to separate the wheat from the chaff. It is not only your business. It is your holy duty to make sure that even in cases of doubt the best interests of all are safeguarded.

The problem as we constantly stress, is much larger than Communism. The one thing about Communists, however, is that they can be depended upon to do all in their power to cloud the issues, spread defeatism, confuse objectives, and weaken us in every way possible, so that all that remains for them is to step in and take over when the collapse they expect takes place.

Just how specific and determined they are is plainly evident in the pledge required of all new members of the Communist party in America. It reads as follows:

I now take my place in the ranks of the Communist Party, the party of the working class. I pledge myself to rally the masses to defend the Soviet Union, the land of the victorious Socialism. I pledge myself to remain at all times a vigilant and firm defender of the Leninist line of the party, the only line that insures the triumph of Soviet power in the United States.

A Serious Handicap

It has been found that Americans who have been fuzzyminded, cowardly, or actually traitorous often know little about the beginnings of their own country and system of government.

Unfortunately, this lack of knowledge seems to characterize many, if not most, of the citizens of our nation. Investigation after investigation reveals that college students in general know little about American history and the basic fundamentals of our concept of government. Why? Because often, neither in the home nor in the school, has the young person been taught much along these lines. Nobody meant any harm. It was more a matter of presuming that someone else had or would take care of that.

The fact remains that the youth of America today know precious little about the why and wherefore of their country.

Back to Beginnings

It would do much to revive the moral courage of everybody if all of us took the time and effort to look back and consider the problems of those who started the United States.

When we consider the origins of our national government, we must project it against its background of violent dissension in the thirteen colonies, conflicting sectional interests, and opposing schools of political thought.

After the Revolution almost four million Americans still considered the thirteen individual states as their governments. In 1781 the states had adopted Articles of Confederation on a voluntary basis as a sort of loose alliance. No federal court system had been established, the new country lacked a real national executive; and the Congress of those days was unable to enforce its laws, levy taxes, raise troops or compel the states to observe American treaties made with other nations. If you think conditions are desperate now, you should have lived then.

Plenty of Trouble

Armed rebellion against governmental authority was no novelty in the fledgling republic. Boundary disputes between states led to talk of war between them; there was no national regulation of trade or foreign commerce; and the individual states even started their own negotiations with foreign governments. Currency varied in value from state to state, with each state issuing its own. As an additional burden, a severe economic depression contributed to the general woe.

Curiously, it was a trade problem rather than a political problem which brought matters to a head. In 1785 the state of Maryland held sovereignty over the entire Potomac River, although Virginia, bordering the river, felt it was entitled to free navigation of the stream. To settle this dispute, a few representatives of Maryland and Virginia met with George Washington at Mount Vernon.

Preparation for the Constitution

From this small meeting of a few souls came the general demand for a larger conference. Called to assemble at Annapolis, Maryland, in 1786, this conference seemed doomed to failure when delegates from only five of the thirteen states showed up.

Alexander Hamilton, with his young fire and genius, saw an opportunity to make this small gathering serve a much larger purpose. He induced the Annapolis delegates to call upon all the states to send commissioners to a larger meeting in Philadelphia the following May to consider conditions in the United States. The convention call also specified that the delegates were to "devise such further provisions as shall seem to them necessary to render the Constitution of the Federal Government adequate to the exigencies of the Union."

Virginia promptly named Washington as its representative. Congress set a day in mid-May, 1787, for the convention to meet. All the states except Rhode Island chose convention delegates through their state legislatures. While the feeling for state sovereignty was still strong among them, a majority of the delegates were instructed to work for a strong national government. With Washington as a precedent, the other states felt compelled to send their finest spokesmen to Philadelphia.

Only Fifty-five in All

The gathering went to work with Washington, Benjamin Franklin, James Madison, Edmund Randolph, George Wythe, Robert Morris, Jared Ingersoll, James Wilson, and other noted Americans in attendance, fifty-five in all. With a sense of balance and proportion they reconciled the older concept of local power with the new idea of a strong national government.

As a result of their work, the new Constitution stated specifically the powers to be exercised by the federal government and assumed that all powers not so stated would continue to reside in the states. It may have been at about this time that a New Englander said: "New York will never amount to anything—too far from Boston."

We Owe It to a Few

If we think about it at all, most of us assume that the U. S. Constitution was here when the country began. The actual story of its origin should remind us that it was written by a small group of fifty-five individuals of great integrity and high purpose.

Each one of these individuals had to protect his own state, maintain his own sense of honor and decency, and keep his sense of proportion about the future of the country. And above all, each had to contribute his personal energies to the forward movement which resulted in the Constitution. Here again, in the very foundations of our government, we see that the emphasis falls upon personal interest, personal initiative, and personal ability.

The writing of the Constitution is a story of human struggle in a few hands; of disappointments, frustrations, and obstacles overcome; of a few Americans welded together by a common belief in sacrificing self for the best interests of their new nation. The challenge they faced and met was far weightier than any we have to meet today, because their problem was unique. *Nothing like the American Constitution had ever been seen in the world.*

From the Constitution evolved the concept of a balance of power between the three equal branches of government: the executive, the legislative, and the judicial powers. No one of these was ever to become too strong for the other two, and no two could combine to eliminate the third. Thus was the checks-and-balances idea carried into practice in American government. In 1789, after ratification, the new Constitution went into effect. With its amendments, it has been our basic law ever since that time.

Crystal Clear

Out of the welter of dissension just before the American Revolution came one clear statement of the fundamental rights of man. The founders of this country maintained that "all men" were equal in the sight of God and equal under the law. They also held that it is a "self-evident truth"—i.e., that no reasonable man would doubt—"that all men . . . are endowed by their Creator with certain inalienable rights"; and that word "inalienable" means that no agency short of death could alienate or take away their rights from them. Our highest courts have since held that no power on earth was strong enough to deprive any man of the rights he was born with. Even if the individual, through error, surrendered his rights voluntarily, they were restored to him by the courts.

Since these rights come from the Creator, no individual or organization can legitimately impair them. The early Americans in the exercise of their God-given rights saw the need for abolishing their older forms of government, and they did so legally. They substituted a new form designed to guarantee their rights to "life, liberty, and the pursuit of happiness."

Then and Now

The fundamental purpose of both the Declaration of Independence and the Constitution was to protect the God-given rights of the individual against infringement from any source. It took the bloody and bitter Revolution and near bankruptcy in the new nation to establish these rights. Yet, they are the very same rights which we blithely toss away today when we neglect to register, vote, or serve on juries.

The contrast between the passionate devotion to liberty shown by our forefathers and our own seeming indifference to liberty today should show us how far we have drifted from our original aims. Power over the government was purposely put in the hands of the people by the colonists who knew the errors of tyranny firsthand. Yet when the people fail to exercise their power, they place control in the hands of a very few who may place selfish interests above those of the nation.

When the great waves of immigration began in this country in 1848, the newcomers from abroad were quick to see the priceless boons of liberty and freedom. For the most part, they had lived their early lives under tyrannical governments, police oppression, and the constant fear of imprisonment for any or no reason. The native American, while still patriotic, lacked the sense of appreciation shown by the immigrant. To a large extent the same condition prevails today.

Just the Reverse

For a quick contrast, take a look at the organization of Hitler's Third Reich. If it were to be drawn on paper, its form would be a pyramid. At the apex stood the Fuehrer himself. Just below, on the next level, were his top subordinates, such as Goering, Goebbels, Hess, Himmler, and other high-ranking officials. Then the pyramid ran down to its base with the Nazi party block wardens occupying the lowest level.

Each individual in the pyramid was subordinate to the man above him and superior to the man below him. This was the organization of a police-state, designed to carry compliance by force from the lowest level to the highest. There was no freedom to question, to decline or to withdraw.

Under the American form of government, each individual is neither superior nor inferior, but equal to his neighbor. Power in government rises from the bottom, the grass roots, and flows to the top. Under Hitler, power originated with him and flowed downward, just the reverse of our system. Instead of exercising power by dictatorship, we exercise it by free election.

When we see a change is needed in our state government, we don't call for a revolution. We call for a constitutional convention, as New Jersey did recently, and bring our state constitutions into line with the needs of the people.

The very origin of the word "democracy" shows its derivation from the people, because the Greek word "demos" means "the people" and "cratos" signifies "rule."

Don't overlook, either, the significance of the word "republic." One of the best arguments for keeping in mind that America is a republic is that those who are out to wreck our country want to keep it out of your mind. They deliberately sidestep the fact that we *are* a republic. They have done an effective job of prostituting the word "democracy." They find it more difficult to confuse people about the meaning of republic and that is why they avoid it.

The word "republic" comes from the Latin *res publica,* meaning "public thing" or "affair." It is defined in the encyclopedia as a "state in which the supreme power rests in the people, or in officers elected by them, to whom the people have delegated powers sufficient to enable thm to perform the duties required of them."

Under our form of government each state retains its own sovereignty, except for the powers which it cedes to the national government for mutual advantage. Each citizen then lives under two bodies of law, one formulated by his national government and the other by his state government.

Without a strong national government this nation could not take its place in the family of nations, much less exercise the world leadership which it exercises today.

One Checks the Other

By dividing the governing power between state and nation, Americans make neither one all-powerful. Instead they hope to strike a happy balance in which the rights of the individual will always be paramount. Sectional feeling is also strong in various regions, but these sectional influences tend to cancel each other out.

The congressman, say, from a cattle-raising state soon finds when he gets to Washington that there is far more to national life than raising cattle. His native state's chief industry is important, to be sure, but his perspective widens as soon as he gets an opportunity to survey the national scene. Then he realizes that he must also consider the tremendous industrial development of the East, the agrarian problems of the Midwest, the fisheries of the Pacific Northwest, and many other problems which looked small when he was back home.

By its very nature, American democracy can never be a static form of government. As the need for new amendments to the Constitution develops, they are proposed, ratified, and adopted. Every decision of the U. S. Supreme Court, highest in the land, affects the daily living of Americans. Old laws are abolished, old concepts vanish. New laws are enacted, and modern concepts of government replace the old.

As population grows and industry expands, new problems arise and must be solved. Our economy must be sufficiently flexible to function at top speed in peace or war. The important thing for us is to freshen our knowledge of the origins of our government, then to decide our new problems according to the original basic principles. In the field of national government, that is our primary task.

3 PEOPLE MAKE THE GOVERNMENT

It was not by chance that the framers of our Constitution began with the phrase, "We the People." For, above everything else, it was their purpose to make this a government, as Lincoln later described it, "of the people, by the people, and for the people."

It was a matter of the utmost urgency that this be done, for under the old, weak, ineffectual Articles of Confederation the states had been brought to the brink of anarchy. Our national government was so impotent that it could not command respect abroad or obedience at home.

The Articles of Confederation had by-passed the people. The members of Congress were elected by the state legislatures, by whom they could be recalled at will. But now, under the Constitution, the members of the House were to be elected by the voters themselves.

Under the Articles the President was little more than the moderator of a debating society. Under the Constitution, he became, in truth, the President of the United States, with powers to execute the laws made by Congress throughout the land. Under the Articles there had been no permanent court to decide upon the validity of the laws or settle disputes between the states. Now, under the Constitution, a Supreme Court was established and federal courts were set up throughout the land for the protection of all the people.

But how does the original intention of the wise men who framed our Constitution operate today? Have we drifted off the course they charted for us? Do the people really make the government? Or is the voice of the people heard only at election time and ignored thereafter?

I put that question to a high career official in Washington just before this chapter was written. I was not asking about theories now; I wanted to know how it worked out in practice. I had come to this man because every bill enacted by the Congress eventually came to his desk.

"Let me answer you with a broad, general statement," said this official. "And I'll put it this way: No bill affecting the great mass of the people is enacted into law before it has in some way responded to the wishes of the public—of the people."

"How does it work?"

He thought a moment.

From Many Points of View

"All right," he said. "Let's take the present emergency. All the people were agreed on one point: we did face an emergency. The question was: How were we to deal with it? Now, human judgments are fallible. So we—the Congress, the executives, the people—hear all sides and try to strike a balance.

"Almost everyone was agreed that we must be prepared and that we had to meet what seemed to be the potential need. So we talked first of material things—billions of dollars for training-camp and military public-works construction, many more billions for weapons and equipment.

"Up to this point we had been dealing with inanimate things, and although the people had begun to make themselves heard, they had been talking about the larger issues.

"There was some opinion to the effect that since war is wrong, we should have no weapons at all. This was countered by the opposite view. Fire is destructive, the second view pointed out, but that's no reason for abolishing the fire department. The defense appropriation, said the second group, wasn't large enough."

Then the executive continued:

"We had agreed upon the need for the weapons. But what are the weapons? Planes, tanks, ships, guns . . . *uniforms and shoes and socks*. Who was to pull on the socks and step into the shoes?"

This was the crux of the question. manpower.

Our host in the government office continued: "The military said that the eighteen-year-olds made the best fighting men.

"Now came the great flood of reaction from the people. There was a great protest from the mothers of the nation, acting almost instinctively—as mothers will—to protect their boys against danger.

"But then the educators spoke up in protest. 'Don't take all the eighteen-year-olds!' they declared. 'In modern war you'll need trained technicians and scientists as much as you will need soldiers in the field—where are they going to come from?'

"Others said the age was wrong. 'Don't make it eighteen years, make it eighteen and one-half!'

"Still others questioned the period of service."

Reaction from the People

"And so by mail and telegram and personal contact, the people—reacting to a proposal that vitally affects every home in the land—made their feelings known to the President, to the Army, Navy, and Air Force, but most of all to their elected representatives. These difference of opinion and feeling became the ingredients of the debate in Congress, and before that debate was ended, every provision of the proposed legislation had felt the pulse of public opinion—of the people."

This was an example of the great mass of the people reacting—people exerting influence upon other people they had chosen as their representatives. But all along the line, there were people acting and reacting—nowhere in the process was there the push-botton functioning of a mechanism called government.

But the people are also stirred to action when they feel that their national government must perform a service for them that cannot be performed at any lower level.

The Japanese Beetle

Some years ago a farmer in New Jersey discovered a hard-shelled insect making a meal out of his prize grapevines. He looked around and saw that there were dozens of them—then hundreds of them.

He hurriedly consulted his neighbors. They had been invaded too by the Japanese beetle.

Nobody seemed to know what to do. The county agent didn't. So the problem was pushed up another level, to the state. By this time the Japanese beetle had, in fact, become a state-wide problem.

But—outside the state—New England wasn't particularly concerned. Certainly the Middle West wasn't. It was too bad for New Jersey, the outsiders agreed, but after all, it was New Jersey's problem and New Jersey would have to solve it.

New Jersey tried to do so, but without success. Then something happened. The Japanese beetle crossed the state line into New York. Some of them turned up in Connecticut. Then a lot of them rode a shipment of produce into Pennsylvania. Soon they were arriving by the thousands in the Middle West.

Here was an example of a problem become too big for the county and too big for any one state. And so the people of all

the states affected demanded that the people representing
them in Washington do something about the Japanese beetle.

Too Big to Handle

Of course the problem could not be solved by passing a law
against the beetle. But the national government did act. A
bill was introduced attaching a rider to an appropriation bill.
It was approved by Congress, and as a result the Department
of Agriculture began the research which made new methods
of dealing with the beetle available to the farmer. In brief,
the people—encountering a problem not possible to deal with
on town, county or state level—had called upon its representatives in national government to do something about it.

This was a small thing—or a large thing—depending upon
your viewpoint as a city dweller or as a tiller of the fields.
There are other more obvious situations when the people may
call upon their national government to act in their behalf—
situations which the Founding Fathers had no way of fore-
seeing and yet capable of being met within the framework of
the Constitution. The regulation of the airways and the building of national highways are examples.

Not only do the people directly influence all important
legislation, but the people are their own protection against
special interest legislation or legislation favoring one section
of the country against another.

A congressman may not always agree personally with the
aims of a bill he himself introduces. But if enough of his con-
stituents are behind it, he feels that it is his duty to take the
matter to the larger forum of Congress for decision.

Checks and Balances

A bill unduly favoring rural areas, for instance, might con-
ceivably win a majority in the House of Representatives, but
if it is unreasonably prejudicial to the people of the cities,
this fact will surely come to surface when the bill reaches
the Senate, where the members are more sensitive to the feelings of the city people.

If, however, a bill passes both houses and goes to the desk of the President, the people again have a last line of defense in the President's veto. Or, contrariwise, they have the power to overrule the veto of the Chief Executive if, in the opinion of the people's representatives, his reasons for a veto are unsound.

Thus ours is a government of checks and balances—in this respect, as in so many others, the best yet devised on earth.

Turned Down

Last year a bill providing for the promotion of veterans of World War II in the field service of the Post Office Department succeeded in getting through both the House of Representatives and the Senate. It was stopped finally by a veto of the President, who felt it was discriminatory legislation.

Opposition to the bill by a considerable portion of people both within and without the government had sufficient effect to secure the Presidential veto.

Under the terms of this bill, those in the postal service would receive pay increases of one hundred dollars for each year of military service on a pro-rata basis. They would also be given preference in promotion.

It was felt that there were four basic weaknesses in the bill:

1. It would allow credit for service in no way related to a civil service and would thus violate the long established principle of granting promotions or increases in pay on the basis of satisfactory performance.
2. It was limited to a small fraction of veterans working for federal government and to only one group of employees in the Post Office Department.
3. It sought particular benefits for a special group of veterans without reference to a real and distinctive need. Fewer than one hundred thousand of the more than fifteen million World War II veterans—of whom about nine hun-

dred thousand are in government service—would have received pay increases under this bill.

4. It would require an increase of twenty-four million dollars in 1951 (a total cost of over one hundred and sixty-three million dollars), when postal service throughout the nation was being curtailed in an attempt to reduce a postal deficit of over one half billion dollars a year.

This was another significant example illustrating how people make the government—how one group took lawful measures to see that a minority did not get what were regarded as special privileges. Those promoting the bill gave forceful arguments in its favor. But they failed to win enough support for it.

A Right to Be Heard

As I was leaving the government office where we had been talking about this subject, my official host walked with me to the corridor.

In the reception room there was a very old man waiting. He was laden with papers and he kept shuffling them and dropping them on the floor, muttering crossly as he bent over to pick them up.

Outside I asked the government man: "Who was the old gentleman with all the papers?"

"Oh," he smiled, "that's a nice old fellow who keeps coming up with new variations on the Townsend plan for old-age pensions. Apparently he's got a new one that he's sure will work."

"Does he ever get in to see anybody?" I asked.

The official nodded with some vehemence. "He always gets in to see somebody," he said firmly. "Why not? He's a taxpayer. He's got a right to be heard. After all, he's the people."

4 GET MORE LIKE THESE

In one important government agency in Washington, not long ago, a head file clerk did a service in saving a bit of the taxpayers' money that few of them would ever hear about. When he was first assigned to a particular department in which there was a huge volume of correspondence he had eight assistants. There was plenty of work for all of them. But having a keen desire to cut costs to the bone, he took it upon himself to make a study at night and over week ends in order to devise ways and means of simplifying the filing and thereby reducing the number of workers required.

When he had his plan completed he submitted it to the official in charge of the office. He recognized immediately that it was most practical and could effect a great saving. It was put into operation without delay. Under the new system the same amount of work was done by the head filer and two assistants. The other five were assigned to other departments where workers were needed.

If the average citizen had the time and opportunity to look into the functioning of federal government, he would see certain weaknesses, yes. But he would likewise be agreeably surprised and heartened by the public servants of high integrity and purpose who are doing as creditable a job as anyone could expect.

Unfortunately, the average citizen seldom hears of these. His attention is attracted much more to those who are inefficient, dishonest, or disloyal. In like manner, the general public is too infrequently reminded that the simplest way to overcome the damage done by the workers of evil is to increase the number of the workers of good. The more health is restored to the body politic, the less chance there is of its being afflicted by disease.

It is this positive constructive approach that the Christopher movement constantly stresses that could be well applied in strengthening federal government. Taking affirmative steps toward a hopeful solution invariably produces much better results than a mere negative attitude or faultfinding.

If nothing more was done than to multiply the good workers in government many times over, that one step in itself would constitute a major contribution to the strengthening of our nation. .

His Business Too

Back in the black days just after Pearl Harbor, in 1941, Washington sent a hurry call to a top executive of one of our largest corporations. He was urgently needed. This man was on his way to Washington by the next plane, and he stayed there in a grueling, heartbreaking job until victory was won. With the gratitude of the nation's leaders ringing in his ears, he went back to his peacetime career—this time as president of another great corporation. Not a man who knew him would deny the fact that he had done a superb job, and all wished him well in his new post. He had served his country well.

The executive devoted himself to his job and his family and his hobbies. If he was fortunate in his position, no one would challenge the fact that he had earned it.

Then, as we know, the storm clouds began to gather again. And eventually came another call from Washington. He was needed again in another great emergency. Again this man was on his way in a matter of hours.

A friend visiting him a little later at his Washington office observed that once more he was battling the man-killing job. "I won't take a minute," the friend said. "I just want to ask you one question. Why did you let them talk you into this thing *a second time?* You did it once! Why didn't you let somebody else do it this time?"

The executive smiled. "Well, Bill," he said, "we're in a jam again, and I felt it was my jam as much as it was anybody else's. I just didn't see how I could refuse."

"But doing this terrific job again is liable to kill you," the friend persisted.

"Well, what of it?" the executive replied.

Thirty Turned It Down

But a great many people *do* refuse.

There was the case of another top job in the defense setup. It was a tough job, but vital to the nation's security—maybe the nation's life. The calls went out from Washington—a lot of calls. Executive after executive pleaded that he couldn't be spared from his present job. But at long last the government found a man who was willing to drop everything and take on the job without thought of what it might cost him personally.

This man began to do the job to the best of his ability. But soon there were howls of protests from people affected by his decisions—and among the people howling the loudest were some of the very executives who had rejected the offer. Thirty of them had turned the job down. The man who accepted was the thirty-first asked to take it on!

A Fortunate Turnabout

And then there was the young man who entered government service with a true Christopher purpose, lost that sense of purpose and then found it again—just in time.

He had come out of the Army in 1946 and had begun to look around for some job in civilian life. Any job would do, but he hoped it would pay well. Then he ran across some friends who worked for the federal government. They talked to him about a government career. But they didn't speak of it as a "soft touch." They said it was an opportunity for him to serve his country in the trying days ahead. That appealed to our young friend. All enthusiasm, he went after a government job and got it. Not only that, but he appointed himself "A Committee of One" to induce other young people to enter government service with a purpose.

But then the young man's enthusiasm was put to a severe test. He ran into endless red tape, petty office politics, all the countless forms of "deadly dullness" that descend on any human endeavor that is without a deeper purpose than "just getting by."

Our young man decided to quit after four years. He put a few feelers out for a well-paying civilian job and had one lined up more quickly that he thought possible. Exultant, he started on a round of leave-taking—visiting his friends in the various government agencies.

Then it happened. Before he could say his first good-by he stood face to face with one of the friends he himself had persuaded to serve his country. This lad's enthusiasm had not waned—it was stronger than ever. The words of farewell stuck in our young friend's throat. He had come face to face with himself as he was before he had lost heart. He went back to his office and tore up his letter of resignation.

But he did say farewell a little later to all his fellow workers in Washington. He came into Christopher headquarters recently to say this one. He was going overseas to take up a new and important post at one of our embassies in Europe.

Everybody Counts

Of course not everyone can win an important job in an embassy overseas. *But everyone can do something.*

There was the girl, just out of college, who went after a job with the federal government in Washington and went after it with such dogged determination that she wouldn't take no for an answer—not even when they told her the only job open was that of messenger.

She became a messenger—to the bewilderment of her friends and even of the people to whom she delivered messages. Finally somebody asked her:

"What do you think *you're* proving?"

"I'm proving," the girl laughed, "that I can deliver messages faster than any girl in Washington!"

And what did *that* prove? Nothing much until another girl messenger was found to have deliberately mislaid an important document on China. The prompt delivery of this document would have been of real benefit to our government. Its delay would help no one in the world—except the Chinese Communists!

To Singapore

It's not always an easy decision to make—or perhaps it's never a really *easy* decision.

Two former newspaper reporters ran across each other outside the State Department. They hadn't seen each other for years and immediately began to compare notes. One told of how he had settled in New York as a free-lance writer.

"What's with you?" he asked the other.

The other former newspaperman pointed to the State Department. "Next Friday they're sending me out to Singapore."

"The State Department!" exclaimed his friend. "How did you ever get connected with the State Department?"

"Well," said the other, "a couple of years ago I got interested in doing something about things. I thought that just possibly the State Department might have some use for my training. So I filled out an application and sent it in. I watched the mailbox for several months, but nothing happened. So gradually I forgot about it. And then, by some coincidence, I suddenly got a big offer. It was the best job of my life. I grabbed it. We moved into a house that was fine for the kids—we even had two cars! Things were never better."

"Then why——"

"I got a letter from the State Department," he continued. "They could use me right away."

"I know—but you said you had the best job of your life!"

The new State Department man shook his head and grinned. "Sure," he said, "but there were a lot of good men for that job. Apparently there weren't as many for the job in Singapore or they wouldn't have gone two years back in the files. I figured they needed me—my wife and I talked it over. And here I am."

And, lucky for the rest of us, there he is—a good man representing his country in a place where our country needs all the good men it can find.

As a Donation

Here is another example of devotion to duty that is often overlooked. Tens of thousands, in a position to do so, are giving voluntary service to various government agencies. At the beginning of this year 85,119 persons were serving the federal government without pay. This is an increase of nearly 8,000 over the previous year.

More than 27,000 of these uncompensated workers are donating their time in the Veterans Administration hospitals. Another 37,641 individuals are serving without pay in the Selective Service System.

It would certainly be to the best interests of all if this desire to participate in the functioning of government even on a part-time basis, becames more popular and widespread.

They Are Protecting You

Few Americans know that during the past year nearly 580,000 aliens were deported, or nearly double that of the previous year. Ten years ago the number of aliens seeking illegal entry was only about 60,000 a year. The end of the war started a wave of those from foreign lands striving by every means to enter the United States, and the trend is still upward. Many of these are good people. Others are not.

The unsung heroes behind this enormous task of discovering, arresting, and deporting over half a million undesirable aliens during the past year were men that you will probably never meet. But they were thinking of you and working for you, often at great personal risk. They had one big objective in mind: your safety. They knew that the more they could bolster the internal security of the country, the more would they protect the best interests of all its citizens.

Getting more individuals into all sections of government with the devotion and thoroughness of the members of the Immigration and Naturalization Service, who achieved this feat, is a most worthy objective in which you can play a part.

An Encouraging Sign

A government executive—a career man of more than twenty years' service—said recently:

"People in government get discouraged every now and then.

Of course people everywhere get discouraged every now and then—but in government it seems to be easier to do so.

"I think it might be safe to say that if some of our best men in government forgot their *purpose* for any length of time, there would be a wholesale exodus from Washington.

"I know. It happened to me. It was at a time when everything seemed to go wrong. The red tape was never thicker, and the hand that passed the buck was infinitely quicker than the eye. I was fed up and had just about decided to write out my resignation. But then I thought I'd ask for a few days off and go back home and think it over.

"When I got home I took a walk down Main Street in my home town—a small Midwest community where everybody knew everybody else. Every few steps I ran into some old friend who wanted to know how things were in Washington —even before he wanted to know how *I* was.

"They seemed deeply concerned about the workings of their government. Some criticized and complained and made the old jokes about the hand in the public trough. But others seemed to be sincerely interested in the very job I was doing. I found myself talking, reassuring them, telling them about all the good men we had working for the country.

"Then one of them—an old doctor—said something that made me feel low enough to look a dachshund squarely in the eye:

" 'I know one thing,' he said. 'We've got one good man in Washington—keep up the good work, son.'

"Of course I never did write that letter of resignation. Instead I went back to Washington and tore into that job again.

"Now—whether I feel I need it or not—I make it a point to go back home and talk to the folks on Main Street. That's all that is necessary to remind me that my job is important as long as I do not lose sight of the purpose."

He Made a Good Choice

Like most other men in the service during World War II, a young air-force officer assigned to make motion pictures connected with the atomic-bomb tests had his own postwar future pretty well in mind.

He was primarily a writer. He had been a newspaper reporter, a radio writer, and he was determined to tackle Hollywood when he got out of uniform. He was young enough and talented enough to be assured of a job. As a matter of fact, he had a line on several even before he left the Army.

But after he had laid aside his uniform he began to think of what his experiences in the Army had taught him. He had learned a great deal about the destructiveness of the atomic bomb—now he began to think of its peacetime possibilities. The more he thought, the more he became convinced that he personally had to do something about it. Yet, on the other hand, there was Hollywood and the kind of writing job he had dreamed about.

He wrestled with his conscience for a long time. He always came to the same conclusion. Finally he sat down and wrote a letter to the atomic-energy commission in Washington. He told them what his experience had been in the Army and asked if they had any need for a man with his background.

The answer came by return mail. The commission had been searching for just such a man. He was needed urgently—could he report immediately?

He did, and he's there at this writing—turning out films that show the limitless peacetime possibilities of atomic energy. He's doing the work of three or four men—it's that kind of job —but he's happy in what he's doing because he has a purpose.

"I can go to Hollywood after we've got our present problems licked," he told a friend, "and if we don't lick our problems— well, there won't be a Hollywood anyway."

From One in Government

When a small item appeared in *Christopher News Notes* to the effect that this present volume was in preparation, it brought the following penetrating letter from a lawyer who had been in government service for nineteen years.

"I am very glad to see that such a book is being written

from the Christopher viewpoint," this legal expert wrote, "and I thought that out of my long experience in the government I might respectfully pass on a few suggestions."

Here are some of those suggestions—from a lawyer inside the government for almost a score of years:

1. Please emphasize that those who have had religious and moral instructions and who still play immoral politics are more reprehensible than those who have no religion. Likewise God must hold them much more accountable when they blast another person's reputation.

2. Encourage more interest in voting at primaries on the local level. Few national politicians "get that way" without starting in their own precinct. If the citizens on the local level choose the right people to represent them and watch them as they climb, we won't have gamblers running things later on.

3. Try to stop some of those well-meaning people who are only hurting themselves as well as everybody else by forever saying that federal government is so incompetent that God alone can help us. They are making it immeasurably harder for the many in government who are trying to do their duty to the best of their ability.

4. As I see it, a person in government has a moral obligation to place the interest of the nation ahead of party politics and personal friendship every step of the way.

5. The Christopher idea is a big boon to people in government as it gives the individual the inspiration to stick with what would be otherwise a deadening job. There is a terrific tendency to timidity and lack of imagination once one has reached an adequate income level.

6. Try to put over how important it is for the average person to study and analyze propaganda for and against various government programs and refrain from going off half-cocked.

7. You can't stress too often that good government involves much more than keeping Communists out. Too many who

have grown stale and undiscerning sing that song too often instead of doing something themselves to improve things.

In Many Ways

In this brief space it is impossible to recount numerous other instances, unknown to the average American, in which those intrusted with the administration of government are performing creditable service. They range from telephone girls to senators and representatives. Some have been elected or appointed to their offices, others have been selected through Civil Service. They are in many phases of important work. They may be scientists in the Department of Agriculture seeking better ways of insuring an adequate food supply for an ever-growing country and world. They may be local postmen who daily carry your mail. Again, they may be engaged in the placement of disabled veterans in jobs in which they can earn their own living. Or they may be lighthouse keepers upon whose vigilance the safety of thousands at sea depends.

Since it is *your* government, it is *your* business first of all to see that the good workers in government are not put in the same category with those who fail by neglect or corruption to live up to what is expected of them.

It is your business, likewise, to do whatever is in your power to guarantee the stability of the administration of your national government by getting more persons of competence and character to dedicate themselves to a career in federal government.

VIII. WHAT EVERYBODY SHOULD KNOW ABOUT CIVIL SERVICE

VIII. WHAT EVERYBODY SHOULD KNOW ABOUT CIVIL SERVICE

1 NO BETTER WAY HAS YET BEEN FOUND

At lunch one day in the Hotel Mayflower in Washington the conversation of four men turned to civil service. One man who had served long and well in a political field was very positive on the subject of civil service. "The whole thing ought to be abolished," he declared most emphatically.

The three other individuals held non-competitive appointive jobs in government service, and their remarks showed that they inclined to a similar view.

After several minutes, however, one of them modified his position a bit by saying, "Well, whatever defects it may have, no better way has yet been found to keep the wheels turning."

Because you, whoever you may be, are involved in the administration of the government as a citizen and taxpayer, you should be at least acquainted with the why and wherefore of civil service.

How It Began

During the early period of American government those in positions of authority were free to select their own staff and workers. They were good, bad, or indifferent, according to the standards of the one who appointed them and the political pressure brought to bear by those who had helped to elect him.

Under our first Presidents integrity and ability were prime requisites for appointment. Gradually, however, this method

279

of staffing the government ran into serious problems and obstacles. The political party that elected a President insisted on placing in office as many as possible of its members as a reward for service in a campaign. Before long, competence and character became secondary considerations. Complications were increased when a new political party came into power. It lost no time in removing everyone possible who belonged to the defeated party and replacing them with its own followers. In this way the personnel of government from top to bottom was in a constant state of change. Development of administrative programs that depended upon uninterrupted continuity for their proper development was practically impossible.

The best interests of government were more and more sidetracked. The chief concern became a contest between the "ins" and the "outs"—between the office holders and the office seekers. For all of this the public paid a high price.

Jefferson's Attitude

When Thomas Jefferson was elected President of the United States in 1800, there was a change of political party for the first time in the history of the country. Jefferson and his followers were convinced they had been deliberately kept out of government service during the two prior administration of the Federalists.

Jefferson resisted the insistence of his associates that he dismiss from public office all members of the defeated party. The new President sought to strike a balance between the two parties in regard to office holders and to avoid making any removals for political reasons. With this balance attained, Jefferson felt that he could "return with joy to that state of things when the only questions concerning a candidate shall be, Is he honest? Is he capable? Is he faithful to the Constitution?"

President Jefferson eventually found that his hope of distributing offices among followers of each party in proportion to their relative strength was impractical.

Another theory that he advocated for the administration of

government likewise failed to materialize. It was called the "Rotation Theory," which provided that all citizens, by holding some office in government for a period, would thus become more familiar with the principles and practices of government. It was an experiment tried with fair success in early New England townships as well as in the beginnings of local government in New York and Pennsylvania.

While this formula could be applied with practical results to government on the local level, it was quite another matter to attempt to apply it to federal government, small as it was in comparison to the giant of today. It was soon found out that no matter how frequently positions were vacated by this rotation theory it would be neither possible nor practical for everyone to have his turn.

During the War of 1812, President James Madison took a vigorous stand against appointment to office based solely on benefit of his own party. He gave the opposition a considerable share in both military and civilian appointments. This courageous stand brought about, as one observer put it, "the practical advantage of securing him united support in the crisis of the war, when defeat looked uncomfortably near, and large portions of American territory, including the capital, suffered invasion."

Under Andrew Jackson

When Andrew Jackson was elected President in the campaign of 1828, the practice of rewarding political friends greatly increased. With the best of intentions he regarded the patronage system not as an instrument of corruption, but "a logical conclusion of the principles of democracy." Having been accustomed to the elementary organization of a pioneer government, he feared that continuance in office might lead to dangerous bureaucracy and to an increasing attitude on the part of workers in government that the offices belonged to them.

The professional politicians, who rode into power under the immense popularity of Andrew Jackson, lost no time in building up political machines and using patronage to reward friends and punish enemies.

It is said that hordes of office seekers started descending upon Washington on the very day of Jackson's Inaugural in 1829. All of them clamored for appointments in every nook and cranny of federal service. The President was besieged by those seeking political favor. Likewise, all others in positions of influence in government were constantly pursued for appointments.

In 1832 Henry Clay made a vigorous speech in the Senate against the policy of dismissing those even in the lowest ranks of government because they happened to belong to a different political party. Here is a brief excerpt from that speech.

"It is a detestable system, drawn from the worst periods of the Roman Republic, and if it were to be perpetuated; if the offices, honors, and dignities of the people were to be put up to a scramble, to be decided by the result of every Presidential election, our Government and institutions, becoming intolerable, would finally end in a despotism as inexorable as that at Constantinople."

Harm to Morale

In later administrations the theory that "To the victor belong the spoils" gained more and more favor. It was not uncommon that those who sought office paid large sums to be assured of the appointment. As a result the administration of government itself suffered. The morale of the workers was seriously impaired. Those who worked with high purpose were frustrated in many ways, while the dishonest were seldom punished. Dismissals became so general that a sense of insecurity affected the majority in government work. No one could foresee who might be next. The fear extended so far that employees hesitated to express any opinion, even in private, less it be misinterpreted by those in positions of authority and cause their dismissal.

The election of Martin Van Buren to the presidency was

credited to the power of political machines. Soon after he came into office the storm broke. Samuel Swartwout, Collector of the Port of New York, had been reappointed despite the fact that during his first term in office there was a shortage of over $200,000 in his accounts. When things became too warm for him during Van Buren's administration he fled to Europe with over a million dollars in government funds.

Swartwout's default aroused the public. Investigations followed. It was soon discovered that abuse in public office affected unprecedented numbers. Bank failures that involved the loss of extensive federal funds resulted from the fact that government money had been deposited in banks selected for political reasons, rather than on the basis of sound finance. The panic of 1837 followed, bringing about an economic depression throughout the nation.

By this time the average citizen was beginning to see that his failure to show an intelligent and active interest in the running of his own government was in effect countenancing the corruption for which he, in the long run, had to foot the bill.

So you see it happened before—many times. If you are too busy to watch and know what's going on, disaster is liable to be the result. If you don't run your government, it will run you!

In running for re-election, Van Buren sought to improve working conditions among federal-service employees. It is interesting to note that by executive order he had the working day for all government mechanics and laborers shortened to ten hours.

Some Brought Their Beds

William H. Harrison defeated Van Buren, however, winning his bid for the presidency on his promise to reform conditions in government. It soon developed that the leaders of the triumphant Whig party, which had brought Harrison into office, had a different idea of reform than the public expected. To the party workers "reform" meant only one thing: a chance to get somebody else's job. One evidence of how quickly the scramble for office developed lies in the fact that thirty thousand office seekers swarmed into Washington on Inauguration Day itself. It is said that some of them even brought their bedding and prepared to sleep in the White House corridors, so determined were they to push their claims for government jobs.

For the next forty years there was little permanent improvement in the appointments of government workers on the basis of integrity and ability. In his first address to Congress in 1870, President James A. Garfield had attacked appointments based merely on political influence. In his party platform he had indorsed appointments on competitive examination. After he became President he selected as Postmaster General Thomas L. James, who had been postmaster of New York City. It was one of the few instances up to this time in which a cabinet post had been filled by the designation of one from within government service. James had been most successful in effecting administrative reform in the New York Post Office.

Fatal Reaction

In a very few months Garfield was to pay with his life over a patronage dispute. Senator Roscoe A. Conkling, who headed the group which brought about the nomination of Chester A. Arthur as vice-president, strove to have the prize of the Collectorship of the Port of New York given to one of their supporters. Garfield insisted, hovever, in designating his own candidate. The pros and cons over this appointment stirred up considerable resentment. One obscure office seeker, Charles A. Guiteau, took it upon himself to seek revenge. He found out that President Garfield was to take a train from the Washington railroad station on the morning of July 2, 1881. Guiteau managed to slip up behind the President and shot him twice in the back.

For three months President Garfield hovered between life and death. When he finally passed away, impatience at the conduct of government affairs suddenly broke into open indignation.

Finally, in response to public demand, Congress passed the Civil Service Act. It was signed by President Arthur on January 16, 1883. Its one objective was to regulate and improve the lot of the worker in federal government. The U. S. Civil Service Commission was established by this act as the central personnel agency for the federal merit system, which has operated for over half a century under the provisions of the act. It was drafted by Dorman B. Eaton and introduced in Congress by Senator George H. Pendleton. Features of the act are:

1. Open competitive examinations.
2. Provisions for the extension of the competitive service by the President of the United States.
3. The prohibition of political activity.

Only 10 Per Cent Then

In 1883 only 10 per cent of the executive civil service was within the jurisdiction of the act. In 1951, 93 per cent of the positions in the executive civil service are included.

Between 1883 and the present time numerous improvements have accompanied the growth of civil service. In the beginning of 1949 a committee headed by former President Herbert Hoover, which we will refer to in more detail in the next chapter, proposed several recommendations for the improvement of personnel management in federal government. One proposal made by this committee calling for a reorganization of the administrative setup of the United States Civil Service Commission was put into effect during the same year. Congress has enacted legislation which provided for a revision of federal pay schedules. Government employees received nominal increases in their salaries as a result. In all revisions of federal pay scales, the tendency has been to give the largest proportional increases to workers in the lower grades.

Neither More nor Less

The new chairman of the U. S. Civil Service Commission, Mr. Robert Ramspeck, gave his stand on the compensation of those employed by government when he stated in a speech at the National Press Club in Washington, D.C., on April 25, 1951: "I believe that government workers should have the same pay, the same working conditions, and the same benefits that fair employers in private industry offer their workers. I do not believe that government employees should have more—or less."

Since government today affects the lives of every one of us in a vital way, it is important that each and all show an individual and personal responsibility in knowing both the strength and weakness of all sections of our government.

Particular concern should be devoted to the welfare of the personnel who make up government service. Every effort should be made to see that the best type of citizen is encouraged to dedicate himself to a career of this type. The better fitted such persons are in both character and competence, the better off the public will be.

A mistake that many of us make is to expect first-class government at second-class rates. Not only do we discourage better-quality people from going into government service but we also find fault with nearly everybody in it and make the tragic error of lumping the good with the bad, even though the corrupt and inefficient are a minority. We tend also to begrudge the government worker the same financial security that most of us enjoy. For some strange reason we expect him to give a dollar's worth of service and get only fifty cents' worth of pay in return.

The Other Side

Those who oppose civil service claim that its adherents overplay themselves in labeling everything as the "spoils system" which does not come under competitive classified civil service; that the system encourages a lot of loafers whose one big ambition is to get on the government pay roll and stay there; that it deadens individual initiative and gradually makes automatons out of the majority of workers; that one trying to render a notable service for government is handicapped by having no choice in the selection of those who will work with him or under him but must often put up with the impractical and incompetent type forced upon him by civil service. The argument usually runs like this:

"Civil service is becoming a safe harbor for incompetents who can't hold jobs elsewhere and who can't be fired here."

"The examination argument covers too much, therefore proves too little. Joe may get by now. But what is he going to be like ten years from now? He may turn out to be a dead beat. But nobody can fire Joe or remove him from a department at any time as long as he keeps just one step ahead of outright dismissal."

"Security is okay to a certain point. But too often it begets mediocrity, lack of imagination and no other interest except the pay check."

"Pensions are all very well. But it's my money that's paying for them. And I don't get any pension."

"Sick leaves are abused. Too many are taken regularly along with vacations to the amount allowed each year. And no boss can protest."

"Promotions are to a large extent based on the number of people supervised. The advantage therefore is to hire as many people as possible, and to stretch instead of clip the red tape."

The Christopher Position

There is little doubt that civil service is here to stay. Consequently, the best-qualified people should get into it in order to improve it and correct abuses.

It is up to you to find out the pros and cons of civil service. That's your business too! In this chapter we present its history, some pertinent facts about it, and some of the objections and answers usually given.

The Advocates' Reply

The advocates of civil service, in reply, constantly point out that when political patronage is the determining factor in filling government jobs there is little chance of developing that essential continuity for the proper performance of government work. They maintain that those who depend on politicians are swept in and out of office with every change of the political breeze; that at best hiring is haphazard and it's only by exception that the best qualified are selected; that unnecessary jobs are frequently created to satisfy those who claim a right to jobs because they have supported the political party; that time and energy which should be devoted to the running of government is sidetracked to the getting of votes and the furtherance of the interests of the political party; that because politics rather than good government is the chief issue there is a tendency to spend rather than save the taxpayers' money.

Those who favor civil service give us an example that under civil service a mail clerk or a postman must pass a competitive examination before he is hired, whereas to be a postmaster in a big city the most important thing is to receive the endorsement of the local political leader of the party in power; that when positions are added to the civil-service system large numbers in the employ of government are dropped because they fail in the examination that all must take to measure up to the standards required for civil-service status. They cite examples such as the following to prove their point:

"In the federal government, the percentage of failures ranges between 12 per cent and 25 per cent.

"In Michigan, 1,225 of the 17,000 employees failed the qualifying examinations given during the first year of civil service, and 518 were demoted to lower positions.

"In Akron, when examinations were given affecting 164 positions, 36 per cent of the incumbent employees failed to keep their jobs. Some of these were demoted to positions for which they could qualify."

The Letter and the Spirit

Back in 1906, President Theodore Roosevelt made an observation about civil service that seems worthy of consideration at this time. He stated: "While of course it is true that the mere observance of the civil service law can never result in a thoroughly efficient administration of any office, yet I am inclined more and more to feel that the observance in letter and spirit of the civil service law is the first requisite in obtaining clean, decent, efficient government service in any branch or bureau of the Government."

As mayor of New York, the late Fiorello H. La Guardia made a slightly more pungent comment. He said:

"There is no Democratic way of disposing of garbage, and no Republican way of cleaning the streets."

Since civil service affects the lives of so many who represent us in the administration of government, it is to our own advantage, as well as that of our country, to familiarize ourselves with its policies and to distinguish between its accomplishments and its deficiencies.

The better management of government that we get, the safer it is and the more money the taxpayers save. Constant effort should be made to seek more efficient methods at lower cost. Close attention should be paid to see to it that no sections of government are oversupplied with personnel and that employees are dropped from the public pay roll who are not needed, who are not hard workers, not trustworthy, or who are more interested in holding on to their jobs than they are in promoting the public good.

Efficient civil service can do much to achieve this goal.

2   CIVIL SERVICE AFFECTS YOUR LOCALITY

Political precedent was broken sharply and dramatically some years ago in New York City in the case of a career public servant who had spent most of his life as a conscientious, hard-working civil servant, with no political influence whatsoever.

Starting at the bottom and working his way up, this man had finally reached the post of chief clerk of the Docks Department, the highest departmental job under civil service. Year after year he had shouldered the duty of counseling and advising new commissioners as they came in over him with no qualifications except political pull. He saw that the life of the harbor was New York's lifeblood and was quite content to play his small part in developing the port.

One day the commissioner of docks was suddenly forced to resign under questionable circumstances. The department itself was put under investigation. For months it ran along without a head, with only the chief clerk supervising its affairs. Meantime it became evident that this department needed a commissioner in whom the public could have confidence.

Under these circumstances, the chief clerk was called over to City Hall for a routine city board meeting of the same kind he had attended hundreds of times. On a knotty problem, he had the answers at his fingertips, as usual. Suddenly the mayor asked:

"John, how long have you been with this department?"

"Twenty-five years, your honor," the chief clerk replied.

"How would you like to be commissioner?" asked the mayor.

Flushed with embarrassment, the chief clerk could only mumble that he would like to serve as his department's head.

Half an hour later he took the oath of office. Through succeeding changes in city administrations he held his post with increasing distinction. Never was there a breath of scandal about his work, and never in its history did the department run more smoothly. The chief clerk's name was John McKenzie.

While this case is exceptional, it is mentioned here because it illustrates one important point: conscientiousness, ability, and hard work do play a large part in securing promotion to more responsible positions. Few, of course, wind up as commissioners, but many can advance to posts where their influence for good may be more widely exerted. Goodness and honesty *do* pay as often as crime does *not!*

In a complete classification, each job in those categories is not only specified but the duties and qualifications are enumerated as well.

How Positions Are Filled

There are usually a number of jobs in the non-competitive class which are filled directly by the departments concerned. The department itself selects the employees, who must meet the minimum requirements for the job.

For information on competitive examinations, prospective candidates can obtain copies of former examinations at various libraries and bookstores throughout the city.

When examinations for job openings are to be held, it is recommended that candidates consult civil-service publications, to be found in most large centers. If a city does not have such publications, it would be advisable to consult the local newspapers, which often run announcements of civil-service information.

Announcements that the civil service commission is accepting applications for examinations are usually published during the second or third week of the month, and the examination itself is held about two weeks after the final notification. The only exceptions are when announcements are kept on a continuous basis until enough people apply for the position vacant to warrant a competitive examination.

Through Examination

Most positions are filled on a competitive basis, by means of written, oral, and physical examinations. Those with the highest grades are given preference on the civil-service list. Veterans who make a passing mark receive veterans' preference, and in some cities they have five points added to their score. Disabled veterans receive an additional ten points. A veteran can use his preference only once. There are a number of positions in the laboring class which are filled in the order of priority, with the first arrivals getting the available jobs.

To be considered for a job in municipal civil service one must apply to the proper office in the city administration and there register for notification of examination for the type of position desired. As a rule, a notice of the examinations in question will be mailed on request.

Where qualifications for each position are clearly defined, it should not be too difficult to determine if you can meet the essential requirements.

As for the examinations themselves, personnel officers usually prepare them and see that they are well advertised through city newspapers, schools, and clubs. Usually an applicant for employment must describe education, experience, and general data regarding physical facts and conditions. Then a formal written test is given to show the ability of the applicant to do the particular work.

This test may also measure the general intelligence of the applicant with a view to later promotion. Where the written test is definitely required, it is usually preceded or followed by an oral interview. In this interview such things as physical characteristics, manner, habits, and appearance are evaluated.

For the Protection of All

Different cities have different methods of compiling and announcing the results of civil-service examinations. New York City, for example is most prompt and efficient in this respect. Those who take the examinations, which begin at ten-thirty in the morning, may see the answers to the questions in the afternoon paper. This does not mean that there is a possibility of "leaks" through the various newspaper offices, for the very good reason that the examinations are not released to the press until after eleven o'clock of the morning of the test. Since the examination rooms are locked to prevent outside interference, there is no chance of the applicants being "briefed" during the session. In addition, each applicant's paper is identified by a code symbol only.

"Exempt" Class of Positions

The "exempt" class of civil service is set aside for those people who are appointed to confidential positions, serving as deputies to commissioners, judges, and other high officials. They can be appointed to the jobs without meeting any special qualifications. Such appointments are limited to the number of jobs actually allotted to their respective departments. For any appointment over and above the allotted number, the candidate must meet the civil service commission's minimum requirements.

A Final Word

Getting people of high principles into the various branches of government, no matter in what capacity, will certainly be a step in the right direction. But it won't do the whole job. Once in civil service, individuals of sound purpose must work to fulfill their objective: that of providing the most efficient, honest government possible. They will have to assume personal responsibility to work for the good of all their fellow citizens. Good government does not come about by wishful thinking. It has to be achieved.

The relationship of the civil-service worker to government is similar to that of the worker in a plant to his employer. In the case of government, when you come right down to it every citizen in America is the civil servant's employer. Hence his responsibility is to each and every one of his fellow Americans. Just as the employee in a factory or office is charged with rendering a fair day's work for a fair day's wages, so the civil servant must give the people who employ him honest, loyal service for the confidence and trust they place in him.

By the same token, the public, as the actual employer of government workers, has an obligation to see that the latter receive a just compensation and have suitable working conditions.

To keep this double objective ever in mind requires the cooperation of every person in these United States, both inside government and out. Where the people take a genuine interest in how their affairs are administered, high standards can be maintained, because civil service is thus kept under the close scrutiny of the community.

Often civic clubs, political organizations, and other groups of public-minded men and women take practical steps to insure the efficiency of their city governments, as well as government on the higher levels.

Civil service can do no more than give the public an opportunity to obtain high-grade city employees. It will not automatically produce honesty and efficiency. Vigilance on the part of citizens, individually and in groups, is a first requirement for the proper functioning of civil service in city, state, and nation.

3 THE ROLE OF CIVIL SERVICE IN YOUR STATE

A young man just out of military service recently took a state civil-service examination for no other reason than "idle curiosity." He certainly did not take it to get a job, because he had already started his own advertising agency. While he was not making a fortune, he was making a go of it. "I just wanted to see what kind of questions they asked," he explained, "and see if I could pass."

Much to his surprise, he passed with such a high score that he was soon notified he had been appointed to a state civil-service position. For reasons he was unable to explain, even to himself, he decided to accept, though with the mental reservation not to stay in the job too long.

That was his original plan, but in the succeeding months it was to undergo a marked change. "As time went on," this young man related, "I found myself becoming more and more interested in this job than in anything I had done in advertising. I realized that I had a very intriguing position and that the whole philosophy behind the central board on which I was serving had tremendous economic and political ramifications. I was in a position to serve the best interests of everybody."

Today this same young man holds a most important job in

state government. Admittedly, his purpose to serve the common good came a little late, considering his original intention. Still the fact remains that his story does serve as a reminder. It reveals the increased personal satisfaction that comes from shifting from a mere "making a living" approach to one of serving the public good. Those who strive to enrich the lives of others enrich their own as a result.

Another man whose particular specialty is personnel work gave up his job in a West Coast department store not too long ago. He went into the same type of work in his state government because he was convinced of the greater good he could do there. Moreover, he intends to stay in governmental work, even though his new post means a slight reduction in pay. He realizes that through his presence in the vast sphere of civil service he may be able to make some little contribution toward maintenance of sound administration. In personnel work, especially, he had endless opportunities to see that only loyal, efficient Americans are employed.

Long and Honorable Service

A third man, at present the assistant administrative director of civil service in one of the Midwest states, is another example of what patience, perseverance, and devotion to duty can accomplish in government work. Almost thirty years ago he first started in civil service, beginning as a secretary in the office of the civil service commission.

In the intervening years he advanced steadily to positions of greater responsibility, transferring to the Department of Education in the process and then moving back to the civil service commission once again. Finally he took and passed the state examination for his present high post. Since his appointment he has performed his duties so well that he has been lauded by high government officials and has been publicly honored on several occasions.

Our American system depends on strong state government. If state governments are weak or inefficient they may be squeezed between an overstrong national government and their own powerful city political machines. When this happens the normal balance of power between national, state, and local government is destroyed.

In recent years we see a trend toward placing more and more state employees under civil service. For example, last year, out of 650,000 state employees in the United States, 374,000, or 58 per cent, were under civil-service laws. This figure does not approach the 93 per cent under civil service in federal jobs—nor even a proportionately high percentage in some city government positions—but it does represent a great increase in recent years.

At present at least eighteen states have comprehensive civil-service laws covering all state departments. Fourteen more states have civil-service laws covering some employees.

Present trends definitely indicate a further increase of civil-service laws in all of the states. Most authorities agree that in a few years practically every state department may be covered by civil-service regulations.

State Civil-Service Divisions

By and large, civil service in the states follows the general pattern of the departments of the federal government. Most states have a civil-service commission consisting of one to four members appointed by the governor or the governor and state senate. All commissions have an executive officer and a staff. Often there are several divisions, such as the administration division, the examination division, and the classification division. These three divisions analyze jobs, requirements, training, salaries, promotions, and publicity.

The staffs of these divisions break down and classify all state services so that qualified persons may be more easily found to do the work efficiently. A great variety of jobs, therefore, are listed in almost all states. The following partial list will give you some idea of the type of service required in state government:

Administration
Agriculture
Attorney General
Auditor
Banking
Conservation
  Forestry
  Fish
  Game
Corporation and Taxation
Education
Industrial Commission
Insurance
Military

Public Health
Public Safety
Public Welfare
Public Utilities
Registry
  Motorcars
  Property
  Vital Statistics
State Aid and Pensions
State Library
Supreme Court
Tax Appeal Board
Treasurer

Of Interest to College Graduates

From this listing it should be obvious that there are enough job classifications to interest almost anyone disposed to serve the public. However, for those now in college many states list specific openings for students upon graduation. Some of these openings are:

Senior Engineering Aide
Senior Draftsman
Social Worker
Junior Economist
Junior Statistician
Senior Laboratory Technician
Junior Personnel Technician
Library Assistant
Junior Librarian
Assistant Game Research
Investigator
Resident Psychiatrist

Occupational Therapist
Factory Inspector
Industrial Investigator
Junior Tax Examiner
Law Assistant
Staff Nurse
Physical Therapy Technician
Public Health Nurse
Junior Research Aide
Publicity Aide
Dietitian
Institution Teacher

Positions in civil service are of two main types: classified and unclassified. The classified positions are those filled by competitive examinations and those where technical qualifications are not so high. The unclassified jobs include both the highest policy-making jobs and the laborer where no examination is required, and where, incidentally, the greatest abuses can and often do take place.

Getting a Job

The usual steps leading to a permanent position in your state civil-service system center around the competitive examination. The following is suggested procedure:

1. You can learn about the examinations in many ways. The ordinary sources are newspapers, radio announcements, schools, or colleges, libraries, post offices, state employment services, and the Department of Civil Service.
2. You decide what examination interests you.
3. You procure an application blank either by writing to the State Civil Service Department or the State Employment Service, specifying which examinations you wish to take.
4. You file your application, having filled it out carefully and accurately. Have it notarized and include the examination fee when you mail it to the Civil Service Department.
5. If you meet the basic qualifications and your application is accepted, you can take the examination proper at the civil-service center nearest your home. Here there may be an oral interview and a physical test.
6. If you pass, your name will be placed on the eligible list, which is sent to the appointing officer, who may, in turn, select one of the three highest names on the list.
7. If appointed, you will have to serve a period of probation for observation as to your fitness.
8. If found satisfactory, then you will have a permanent place in the civil-service system of your state.
9. Using your first job as a springboard, you may work up the ladder through later promotion examinations.

Jobs Most in Demand

The jobs most in demand in state civil service are parallel to those in every branch of government, including the federal. We refer to the classification of stenographers and typists.

The qualifications for these positions are fairly well standardized in most of the states. Salaries for these positions are not uniform throughout the country. Average yearly pay is about $2,100.

Encouraging Sign

It is encouraging to note an increasing interest in civil-service jobs.

Colleges and universities all over the country recognize this trend and have set up courses geared to train for public service. This is a hopeful development. It is certain that neither the enthusiasm of young students nor the foresightedness of their educators would have materialized had they not been sure that government was a meritorious career.

Advantages of Civil Service

So far we have purposely stressed the qualifications for civil service, the steps to be taken to secure an appointment, and the need for sound-thinking, high-principled men and women in this vital sphere of influence.

Desire to serve the common good should be the first consideration for one contemplating a civil-service career, of course. But there will be certain reasonable advantages which will accrue to the successful applicant. For example, most civil-service jobs guarantee:

1. Assignment and promotion on merit.
2. Good salaries with regular periodic increases until the top salary for the grade is reached. Then the employee may take a promotion test for the next higher grade.
3. Job security. State services have to continue even during depressions.

4. Retirement benefits, plus vacation and sick leaves comparable to those granted in private industry.

Over and above all personal advantages, however, the state employee in civil service should be stimulated by a sense of service. He should feel that whatever ability God has entrusted to him can be used to strengthen our American system of government which guards our liberties and is dedicated to the welfare of all its citizens.

4 CIVIL SERVICE CONTROLS MOST FEDERAL JOBS

On the evil of selfish job seekers, a famous American once explained that he felt like a man "so busy letting rooms at one end of his house that he had no time left to put out the fire blazing and destroying at the other end."

President Abraham Lincoln made that observation. More than eighty years later his thought was echoed by a United States senator who said: "I am tempted to resign because I am deluged night and day by people who want endorsements for jobs. I just don't have the time for that sort of thing."

As we have seen earlier, it took a long and bitter fight to get the merit principle in civil service established at all. This nation was more than one hundred years old when the Civil Service Act was passed by Congress in 1833. Since its establishment, civil service has developed and widened to the point where it now offers almost any type of employment.

By adoption of the merit principle, supporters of civil service maintain that they can relieve any elected official from President to congressman from the chore of patronage worries. The opponents of civil service hold that this is oversimplifying a big problem.

The story is told of a political leader in Brooklyn who had given one of his supporters a juicy political job. The unsuccessful applicants were jealous and envious of the lucky one. But one day the job holder fell seriously ill, and late one night he succumbed. One of his competitors dashed to the phone on hearing the news and called the political leader out of bed.

"Smith just died," the competitor said. "What about the job?"

"I'm a political leader," the boss replied. "What you need is an undertaker!"

Grim as it is, this tale reflects the heavy pressure that the political job-seeker can exert. Civil service has its strength, and its weakness as well. It has been criticized on the ground that it tends to freeze incompetents into public employment so tightly that they can never be dislodged.

For Better Service

Federal civil service encourages government employees to take an active, personal interest in better government. In Washington not long ago, gathering data for this book from the U. S. Civil Service headquarters, I saw a large poster saying that any employee might suggest any step to improve its functioning.

"It might be a proposal for providing better public service; for speeding up an operation; for cutting red tape; for conserving supplies; for improving working conditions or morale; in fact, anything that could strengthen or improve any aspect of the Civil Service Commission's work," it said.

As inducements the Commission offered cash awards ranging from ten dollars to one thousand dollars, within-grade promotions, and Honor Award Certificates. One official I questioned said there was nothing new or unusual about the inducements. They had been established years ago as part of the Commission's effort to encourage a more personal participation in good government by its employees. By pooling the individual contributions, the net effect would be a smoother and more efficient government.

Two Divisions

Civil service generally is divided into two broad classifications. One is the classified civil service and the second is the exempt classification. In the classified, jobs are filled by those who succeed in passing competitive examinations open to all who can meet the conditions.

Many officials elected or appointed to office maintain that they can bring in more efficient assistants from private business than Civil Service can provide.

What the Civil Service Commission Does

The United States Civil Service Commission has some *ten* principal activities. They are, in order:

1. Providing examinations to test the aptitude of applicants for positions in the competitive service, and establishing qualification standards for promotion, reinstatement, and transfer.
2. Providing the appointing officers in various federal agencies with the best available personnel to fill whatever positions are vacant.
3. Administering the Veterans' Preference Act of 1944 which grants preference to certain classes of persons because of military service.
4. Conducting investigations pertaining to the enforcement of civil-service laws and the Civil Service Rules.
5. Administering, through the Loyalty Review Board, statutory and Executive-order provisions relating to loyalty of federal employees.
6. Administering the Classification Act of 1949 which provides for the classification of positions according to duties and responsibilities.
7. Administering a performance-rating system for federal workers.
8. Maintaining service records of employees in the executive civil service and in the government of the District of Columbia.
9. Administering statutory provisions and civil-service regulations restricting political activity by federal employees in the competitive service, and by certain state and local

employees participating in certain federally financed activities.

10. Administering the Civil Service Retirement Act.

Two Million Under Civil Service

In January 1951 employees in federal civil-service positions numbered some two million men and women.

These two million occupy positions ranging literally from "a" to "z"; from accountant and auditor, aeronautical engineer and architect to zoologist and zoologist's assistant. Federal employees work in offices, laboratories, machine shops, and hospitals all over the United States. They deliver the mail, staff government offices, make weapons for our armed forces, take care of disabled veterans, inspect foods and drugs to see that they are pure, they improve the quality of fruits, vegetables and other agricultural products, they maintain our national parks, forecast the weather, they perform research in the fields of electronics, radio, and related fields.

From even such a partial listing of the variety of positions in federal employment it is obvious that all federal service is by no means confined to Washington and the surrounding area. Actually, only one tenth of the employees of the government work in our nation's capital and the territory surrounding the District of Columbia. The other nine tenths work in other parts of the United States and in various sections of the world.

Competitive and Exempted Positions

Positions in the federal executive civil service are either "competitive" or "exempted." "Competitive" means just what the word implies. Citizens compete against one another in examinations prescribed by the U. S. Civil Service Commission. "Exempted" covers those positions which because of their confidential or policy-making character should logically be exempted from competitive examinations. Such exemption places the burden of appointment directly in the hands of authorities in the various federal agencies concerned—not on the Civil Service Commission itself.

In the continental United States, approximately 92 per cent of the positions in the federal executive civil service are competitive. The remaining 8 per cent are exempted and application for such exempted employment should be made to the agency in which employment is desired. Time and effort will be wasted if application for such positions is made to the U. S. Civil Service Commission itself.

Competitive Jobs

The Civil Service Commission accepts applications for all kinds of competitive jobs only when there are federal jobs to be filled, and when this situation comes about it issues what is known as an examination "announcement." This "announcement" gives all the necessary information—what education or experience you must have before your application is accepted, whether a written test is required, where the jobs are, what the duties consist of, what the pay is, and so on.

The easiest way for most people to keep posted on civil service developments is to inquire at their local post offices. An employee of every first-class and second-class post office, except in cities where civil-service regional offices are located, works part time for the Civil Service Commission. He is called a local secretary, and it is his job to give out civil-service information, applications, and copies of announcements.

If a person lives in a city where there is a regional office of the Civil Service Commission, it is suggested that he go to that office for information. For those interested, the regional office listings are as follows:

FIRST REGION: Post Office and Courthouse Building, Boston 9, Mass.: Maine, New Hampshire, Vermont, Massachusetts, Rhode Island, and Connecticut.
SECOND REGION: Federal Building, Christopher Street, New York 14, N.Y.: New York, and New Jersey.
THIRD REGION: Customhouse, Second and Chestnut Streets, Philadelphia 6, Pa.: Pennsylvania, and Delaware.
FOURTH REGION: Temporary "R" Building, Fourth Street and

Jefferson Drive SW, Washington 25, D.C.: Maryland, Virginia, West Virginia, North Carolina, and the District of Columbia.

FIFTH REGION: New Post Office Building, Atlanta 3, Ga.: South Carolina, Georgia, Alabama, Florida, Tennessee, Puerto Rico, and the Virgin Islands.

SIXTH REGION: Post Office and Courthouse Building, Cincinnati 2, Ohio.: Ohio, Indiana, and Kentucky.

SEVENTH REGION: New Post Office Building, Chicago 7, Ill.: Wisconsin, Michigan, and Illinois.

EIGHTH REGION: Post Office and Customhouse Building, St. Paul 1, Minn.: Minnesota, North Dakota, South Dakota, Nebraska, and Iowa.

NINTH REGION: New Federal Building, St. Louis 1, Mo.: Kansas, Missouri, Oklahoma, and Arkansas.

TENTH REGION: Federal Office Building, 610 South Street, New Orleans 12, La.: Mississippi, Louisiana, and Board of United States Civil Service Examiners, Balboa Heights, C.Z.

ELEVENTH REGION: 302 Federal Office Building, First Avenue and Madison Street, Seattle 4, Wash.: Montana, Oregon, Idaho, Washington, and Territory of Alaska.

TWELFTH REGION: 129 Appraisers Building, 630 Sansome Street, San Francisco 11, Calif.: California, Nevada, Arizona, and Territory of Hawaii.

THIRTEENTH REGION: New Customhouse Building, Denver 2, Colo.: Colorado, New Mexico, Utah, and Wyoming.

FOURTEENTH REGION: 210 South Harwood Street, Dallas 1, Tex.: Texas.

General Requirements

Nearly every position in federal civil service calls for some special qualifications, and these qualifications are announced when specific examinations come up for certain classes of jobs. These qualifications are not always of great scope, some are very elementary, and complete details may be secured by writing or visiting the regional offices of the U. S. Civil Service listed above.

There are, however, certain general requirements which every applicant must meet. Are you in good physical condition? The announcement will tell whether applications will be accepted from people with disabilities.

Are you a veteran? Some examinations are open only to people with veteran preference.

How old are you? Many examinations have age limits.

A Word about Veteran Preference

Veterans have advantages over non-veterans in getting a government job. Honorably discharged veterans get five extra points on their examinations. Ten extra points are given to disabled veterans or their wives, the widows of veterans, and the widowed or divorced mothers of veterans who lost their lives while in the armed forces or who were totally disabled while on active duty.

Veterans have other advantages which are listed in full in the pamphlet *Veteran Preference in Federal Employment,* which may be secured by writing to the Civil Service Commission in Washington or to any of the regional offices already mentioned.

Oath of Office

Every government employee must swear to support and defend the Constitution of the United States, that he is not a Communist or Fascist, and that he does not advocate or belong to any organization that advocates the overthrow of the government of the United States by force or violence. An inquiry into the employee's loyalty will be started at the time of application.

The employee will also be asked to swear that he did not pay or offer to pay any money or anything of value to get his appointment. Anyone who purchases or sells a public office is subject to fine or imprisonment or both.

This matter of oath of loyalty and proof of loyalty to one's country should be welcomed by every patriotic citizen. And it is no infringement on anyone's liberties. No one can force people with confused or subversive ideas from thinking that way. But, such people have no right to a place on the federal pay roll. It is a point that you and every other citizen should remember well.

Many Types Needed

There is a wide range of openings in federal civil service for those with varying qualifications. A large proportion of those employed in government agencies are clerks, typists, stenographers, secretaries, office machine operators, guards, security officers, and the like. These positions can be filled by either men or women.

There is a constant turnover among government employees, due to sickness, death, retirement, shifting of place of residence and transfer to nongovernmental work. Only recently the Civil Service Commission informed a House Appropriations subcommittee that over 600,000 new employees will be needed in the fiscal year, 1951-52, to replace workers leaving federal employment. Half a million more workers must therefore be employed to care for defense and other emergency requirements.

Whether one is in a high position or low in civil service he has an opportunity to fulfill a responsibility that can benefit his nation and contribute to the well-being of all its citizens. The more his work is motivated by such a high sense of purpose, the more apt is he to see a new and important meaning in the most menial and monotonous tasks.

It is difficult in the humdrum of routine work for a civil-service worker to keep ever before him a perspective that is high and noble. But the more he does, the more meaningful will his whole outlook become and the better he will serve his country.

IX.   THE SOURCE OF AMERICAN STRENGTH

IX. THE SOURCE OF AMERICAN STRENGTH

1   THIS NATION UNDER GOD

Each week at Christopher headquarters we receive thousands of letters from many parts of the world. One from a marine in war-torn Korea several months ago was particularly heart-warming. It sums up so much of the Christopher thesis that we feel we should reprint most of it here. The letter reads:

"Your book, *You Can Change the World*, did wonders for my morale. Believe me when I say I have prayed often since I have been in Korea for guidance and I have found comfort in the fact that my prayers have been answered. A man in the field has faith in himself when he knows that he is being led by a Force greater than all the might of the enemy combined.

"When our division was trapped in the North a few weeks ago I found that the men in my platoon had all said a prayer for our "buddies." One of the men mentioned that he had prayed the previous night for the safe passage of the men trapped and to my surprise many of the other men had done the same thing. It is history now, but the withdrawal of the troops in that sector was a great feat. I know in my heart that there was a Supreme Commander in charge of that operation and it was a success.

"During the past five months I have had the opportunity to see and talk to people who have lived under the heel of the Kremlin and I only wish I could express to the people at home the impression it left on me.

"How any man or woman in America could even consider joining a party that advocates the overthrow of our government is beyond me. I wish also that all the people in the United States could come to Korea and see the results of the Communist doctrine. I'm sure our way of life would be insured in America forever.

"I am not a flag waver, but I feel that what I'm doing here as a marine is the right thing to do at present. But I feel that isn't enough. . . . If if were possible to tell every American what I think and my reaction to the things I have witnessed in Korea and how important it is for all the people at home to take an interest, a real live interest in their government, I would say I have completed at least one task. What's happening over here must never happen in our country and as you so vividly point out that unless we do something about it, it can happen in the U.S."

A Challenge to All

There is an important lesson for all of us in this young marine's eloquent testimony to the Source of his strength. As an American fighting to save his country, he points out in one sentence what is the driving force of those down through the ages who have been willing to sacrifice themselves for the love of others. It would be well for all, especially those who dedicate themselves to any branch of public service, to keep ever before them the ringing challenge of one sentence in particular:

"A man in the field has faith in himself when he knows that he is being led by a Force greater than all the might of the enemy combined."

Strangely enough, *the Communists know this too*. They realize that the most effective way to make anyone lose faith in himself is to deprive him of faith in Almighty God. From long experience, all the totalitarians know that once the divine cause of freedom is eliminated, the effects automatically disappear. Destroy the roots and the branches eventually wither.

If there were no reason why we should be *for* God, the mere fact that the Communists are so much against Him and want to eliminate all trace of His truth from every sphere of life is a strong argument that there must be some intimate connection between God and the basic freedoms that all of us cherish. Obviously they recognized even more clearly than do the people who enjoy those liberties the fact that the body languishes and dies once the heart is seriously affected.

This explains why there is no letup in the Communists' continual war against everything connected with religion. When the Communists set to the task of enslaving a country, the Church is always the first target for ridicule, undermining, and eventual extermination.

Not the Only Threat

In all this necessary emphasis on the threat of the godless totalitarians to our God-given freedom, however, it should not be thought that they are the only threat to our freedom.

All traces of Communism could vanish in thin air and the much greater weakness would still remain: namely, that more and more Americans are losing sight of the fact that their liberty is rooted in a divine origin. They are actually abandoning the spiritual force that accounts more than anything else for the greatness of America.

The most serious problem confronting our country today is that *"this nation under God,"* as Abraham Lincoln envisioned it, is fast becoming *"this nation without God."*

Although we still inscribe *"In God We Trust"* on our American coins, we are failing more and more to inscribe it on American hearts.

An increasing number of voices are being heard throughout the length and breadth of our land bemoaning the general moral breakdown that is taking place under our very noses. They all sound the same warning, that something has gone wrong.

Unfortunately, most of those who express sincere dismay have given no thought to what a sound solution might be. It's the old human weakness; people don't want to be ill, but they don't want to take the medicine that makes them better, either.

As it says in the *Imitation of Christ*, they want peace, but not the things that make for peace.

Increasing secularism among Americans provoked a comment in 1947 from the Catholic Bishops of the United States. In discussing the attitude of many Americans toward God, the Bishops said:

"For the most part they do not deny God. On *formal* occasions they may even mention His Name. Not all of them would subscribe to the statement that all moral values derive from merely human conventions. But they fail to bring an awareness of their responsibility to God into their thought and action as individuals and members of society. This, in essence, is what we mean by secularism."

Depends on Us Too

But freedom, although God-given, depends on us too. It is a fragile gift entrusted to us, which we must preserve and fortify.

Freedom is not for the lazy. It demands character, will, and dedication. It requires decisions, self-respect, and self-reliance. A man must guard and love his freedom as he loves his home, his children, with a love that doesn't count sacrifices and constant effort.

A Survey by the Y.M.C.A.

Murray G. Ross, in a recent survey sponsored by the YMCA, disclosed that most young people in the United States have had little contact with religion and therefore religion was not "a directing, compelling force in life." Perhaps the most deadly effect of this godless philosophy upon them is that it stifles their allegiance to anything outside of self; it smothers the initiative and imagination that have so long been identified with American youth.

Mr. Ross said that approximately three quarters of the young people he questioned "do not feel that their individual lives are very important in the larger scheme of things. . . .

Few share deeply in the life of a group dedicated, and actively devoted to the highest goals of mankind."

The depressing effect that a society without God has on the stamina of future citizens is also emphasized by D. E. Fay Campbell, executive directior of the Commission on Christian Higher Education of the National Council of the Churches of Christ. He expressed amazement at "what has happened to the morals of American youth of college age. The 1951 undergraduate seems to have lost his grip on the future. He is concerned only with what may happen to him today."

Last year two British Protestant leaders declared that millions in their midst are losing their faith. Dr. M. E. Aubrey, head of the Baptists in Great Britain, said that *a vast proportion of the population worships nothing at all.*" Right Reverend R. D. Whitehorn, moderator of the Presbyterian Church of England, said that an *"enormously magnified factor in the modern environment"* is a revulsion against religion.

A partial yet most significant explanation of this condition is found in a book published in London a few years ago. Its title is *How Heathen Is Britain?* It was written by B. G. Sandhurst.

In the very beginning of his book, the author makes this statement of fact:*"Nearly half the young men leaving our public and secondary schools are almost pagan . . . are starting life in ignorance of their nature, their purpose and their destiny."*

Mr. Sandhurst points out in a most conclusive manner, however, that while most of this number "denied they were anything more than animals," at the same time there was a definite desire on the part of even the most skeptical among them to know more about religion. They were really groping for some authentic leadership to rescue them from the disillusionment that follows in the wake of no faith at all or in the worship of false gods.

These young people, "sheep without a shepherd," were gradually realizing that when God is eliminated from the lives of men, men invariably turn to the state as a substitute for God. They replace a vital sense of dependence on God and

self with frustrating and often enslaving dependence on the
Almighty State.

A Hopeful Sign

There is a value in these warnings. In fact, there is even a
note of hope. They reveal that the average person is not anti-
God or anti-religious. He simply has been conditioned by education and literature, as well as by government, to a godless or
secularist attitude.

The situation confronting us is serious, but can be changed
for the better once enough stalwarts are found to lead America
back to its Source of strength. Once a spark is lit it can burst
into a flame. This is a challenging and inspiring objective for
any God-loving, true American.

Those who have the courage to tackle this big job must be
willing to pay the price, and it may be a very dear one, of
hardship, misunderstanding, lower pay, sacrifice of personal
ambitions. But the more they realize that the destiny of hundreds of millions in our country and over the world depends on
how valiantly and how quickly they act, the more inspired and
determined they will be.

Fortunately it is not necessary to resort to any radical
changes or innovations to repair the damage. What is required
is to restore to public consciousness the cornerstone of American life, which, as our Founding Fathers repeatedly said, is
God Almighty. All changes or reforms that may be needed in
our country must always be solidly grounded on this foundation.

If the men who launched America on its road to greatness
thought it important enough to underline with so much emphasis our dependence on the Almighty, it certainly should be-
hoove those who are blessed by the freedom and bounty of
America to be as resolute.

On November 6, 1950, the President publicly affirmed that
"our concept of freedom has deep religious roots," that our
government is anchored in the truth that God is the ultimate
Source of all our rights and liberties.

Can enough persons be found to reintegrate into every branch of government this basic American belief that the purpose of government is to secure the God-given rights of all?

It Can Be Done

Without a moment's hesitation we say it can be done! And furthermore that it *must* be done—without delay—if we are to survive as a free nation.

All right-thinking people in America should find deep satisfaction in the realization that a number of those in government service work quietly and conscientiously, every day, to revive the letter and the spirit of the law in various government branches.

We think of one man who occupies a very high and responsible position in Washington. He prays before each major project that he will be blessed by God in acting for the best interests of the country and for all the citizens he represents. Because he is constantly aware that he must one day render an account of his stewardship to God, he is scrupulously honest and strives to avoid every trace of inefficiency and favoritism.

A young college student in Portland, Oregon, explained why she turned down offers of better jobs to take a minor post in the State Department.

"I took the State Department job because I felt it offered me an unusual opportunity to meet my obligation to God and my country," she said.

A senior in Manhattan College who picked up the Christopher idea that a person may live an apostolic life and accomplish great good in a government career decided immediately after graduation to start at the bottom and work his way up. He began in a minor capacity in the local government of a small Long Island town. He has already had a promotion that gives him a wider range of influence. To fit himself better for his future obligations in the field of public service, he is attending night classes in government administration.

A young lady entrusted with secret files in a federal agency in Washington said frankly: "The one thing above everything else that keeps me honest with my country is that I am first of all honest with my God."

A Deep Consolation

Seven years ago a lawyer in the Midwest gave up a lucrative practice to do what he felt was his duty. He has always been a man of deep spiritual convictions and has led a very religious life. He felt a special obligation, therefore, to work for the common good of all and not merely for his own private advantage. He became a Judge of the Circuit Court. His record on that bench has been an enviable one. Difficulties confronting him have been many, but there has always been the deep consoling satisfaction of knowing he has had the privilege, through his work, of solving many problems for his fellow man and therefore of leaving the world a bit the better for his being in it.

These are only a few of countless cases showing what Christopher-minded people can do. It is heartening and refreshing to know that so many are willing and anxious to work and even suffer that it continue to be "this nation under God" and thus prevent the catastrophe that would befall all of us if it should ever become "this nation without God."

All that remains to insure this happy result is to multiply many times over those who are dedicated to save America, rather than to destroy it.

To reduce it still further, it will be decided by a few million within the United States who realize that government is their business and who are willing to take whatever steps are necessary to see that all phases of government are staffed by God-loving rather than God-hating or God-less workers.

2 PROTECT OUR MATERIAL BLESSINGS

A young American who attended a Communist training school in Moscow in the mid-thirties reports that the school stressed that Communists feel they have two major obstacles in their efforts to dominate the United States. The first is religion, which gives mankind faith and hope in a Supreme Authority above all states. The second is the savings of the American middle class. With these two factors eliminated, Communists believe their goal of world domination would be much nearer realization.

The American readily understood Communist opposition to religion because religion reminds everyone not only of his social obligations but also that one of the primary functions of the state is to preserve the fundamental rights he receives from God and God alone. In the Declaration of Independence and the Constitution the derivation of these rights from the Almighty is clearly and specifically stated.

On the subject of savings, the student's grasp of his lesson was not so quick. He was somewhat astonished to learn that elimination of middle-class savings ranked as the No. 2 impediment in the minds of his Soviet teachers. Upon reflection, he saw that savings were a bulwark against the economic adversity on which Communism thrives. To the downtrodden, the "What have I got to lose?" argument carries strong appeal. They can easily be persuaded that Communism is no worse than their present state, and might be better. The man with even moderate possessions does not swallow the propaganda quite so easily.

Two Important Assets

From the American point of view, this country has two stout bulwarks against the Communist threat as we have stated in the preceding section. Religion gives Americans a moral and spiritual bulwark against the false ideology of the Reds.

Some measure of material possessions gives them a cushion against the hard knocks of poverty.

The type of American most feared by the Communists, then, is the type which recognizes the need for the practice of religion as well as a basic minimum of material security.

Unfortunately, for the Communists, this type predominates

in the United States, though here again the problem is not automatically solved. Even if Communism were a problem of the distant past, the task of making our economy sound, with fair treatment to all our citizens, would still require the wholehearted co-operation of you and every other citizen and taxpayer.

While there are more than a few defects in our economic system which should be corrected, and positive reforms are needed, yet most Americans enjoy a standard of living considerably higher than the average person in the rest of the world. Recent statistics show that total earnings and income of everyone over the earth is about four hundred and fifty billion dollars.

Almost half of that sum, however, goes to one hundred and fifty million Americans. The other half goes to the nearly twenty-three hundred million who inhabit the rest of the globe. In India, for instance, the average individual income is only fifty-four dollars a year. Almighty God has certainly blessed the United States with a productive capacity and material assets far exceeding that of any other country.

What Others Think

So blessed is the United States with material possessions that countless thousands living abroad would leap at the opportunity to come here and lead the life of the poorest American. The Soviet leaders, in their determination to reduce all mankind to slavery for the state, are intent on abolishing at all mankind to slavery for the state, are intent on abolishing at all costs the high American living standard. If they had their way, the United States would be reduced to the poverty and starvation that afflicts most of mankind today. Communists strive mightily to keep even the knowledge of American prosperity from the peoples they hold in bondage. To take an example:

Soviet authorities arranged for the showing in Russia of the film *Grapes of Wrath*, which realistically depicted the plight of American farmers reduced to poverty by dust storms which destroyed their crops. To the Soviet mind, Russian audiences would view the film with great satisfaction, realizing that the average Russian was far better off than such destitute Americans. The reaction, however, was quite different. Athanase G. Politis, Greek Ambassador to the United States, reported:

"The audiences were staggered by the sight of migrant farmers traveling from job to job in automobiles piled high with furniture which the average Soviet citizen did not hope to possess even in his wildest dreams."

American government is the biggest business in the world today. It is well for all of us to be ever aware that American government, federal, state, and local, is the largest customer of all other forms of American enterprise.

The spending policies of our government therefore have both domestic and international reactions. Those policies affect you as an individual. And, with increased taxes, government spending will affect you more in the future than it has in the past. It is for you to do your part in seeing that all such spending is done wisely.

The Position of the Individual

Now where do we as individuals stand in relation to this broad picture? While the United States is a country of great wealth, individual Americans are not possessors of great wealth.

Only 18 per cent of Americans earned five thousand dollars or more in 1948. Those who earned between $2,000 and $4,000 in that year accounted for 38.6 per cent of all wage earners. These are the individuals who pay the bulk of the taxes, because they are the only group numerically strong enough to shoulder the load. The poor pay through hidden taxes and double taxes more than they realize. The extremely poor cannot pay taxes, and the very rich are comparatively few. If you're looking for millionaires, remember that only 2½ per cent of all Americans earned $10,000 or over in 1948.

Now let's take a look at savings of all types. Here we see a downward trend since 1944. But unfortunately for the

Soviet ambition, all the people of this county saved almost thirty-five billions of dollars in 1948. A record of seventeen billion dollars in life insurance is now carried on American children under fifteen years of age. With that amount of money in savings accounts, insurance, securities, and the like, the savings of the American people seem a long way from "liquidation." Today, thank God, most Americans can be included in the middle class. The larger this group grows, the better for all.

Pillar of the Social Order

Only recently the Holy See warned Spaniards against the dangers of "inflation" and "excessive taxes," which, it pointed out, kill the "spirit of saving" and thus prevent the formation of a strong middle class. This warning was given through Monsignor J. B. Montini, substitute Secretary of State.

Referring to the middle class as a large and varied one, he also included in his statement the following which is well worthy of note: "Its members come from industry and farms, trades and business, they are clerical workers and career people. They represent a great part of the population with characteristics of their own and whose social influence deserves special attention.

"The proper characteristic of this class is economic independence by means of which it is possible for it to attain social stability and the production of wealth, thus bringing about a harmonious balance between personal work and private property.

"Through his own efforts and work, the middle-class man preserves his autonomy and dignity, without having to beg for his living.

"By means of private assets he attains a wholesome and just distribution of property which thus retains a character of responsibility without falling into forms of corporate collectivism and preserves its true function as a pillar of the social order."

As Things Stand

Much remains to be done however to raise the level of a few million families who are still on a subsistence basis. Constant effort must be shown to provide a living family wage. Other adjustments are likewise necessary for the economic welfare of those who are not receiving a just return for their labor.

But let us recognize the over-all picture at the same time. While there are defects to be rectified, yet the average American has certain advantages. There are tremendous natural resources in various stages of development, and a huge productive machine which gives him employment at high wages. In more instances than not, he can take good care of his family and himself.

Why, then, should he worry about how wisely the government spends or whether our resources are sufficiently protected? Because he is a stockholder in that government. And because, as we mentioned earlier, that government is the biggest business in the world. In the next fiscal year it will be over seventy-one billion dollars.

When government becomes that big, a certain group in the population adopts the attitude: "The government owes me a living." It is well illustrated by a new privately printed handbook with one hundred detailed pages showing what the individual can get out of his government. The emphasis is all on what the government should do for the individual. A certain amount of that is good. But unfortunately little or no mention is made of what the individual should do for his government.

All of us are stockholders in the government and some of us justify our status by our contribution to it. Every farmer and gardener knows that you have to get nourishment into the soil before you can take good crops out of it. In this sense the stockholders are good farmers and good gardeners. Those who are interested only in what they can get out of government are the parasites in our society, the "weeds" which sap the nourishment from our "soil."

Dangers from Within

The Communists hope that we will spend ourselves into bankruptcy. And naturally they would like to do all they can to speed up the process. By every means, fair and foul, they would like to upset the economic applecart. Therefore it is obviously to their advantage to get those careless with government funds, even though they be anti-Communistic, into the spending end of government.

This process recalls the attitude of Willie Sutton, a notorious bank robber. A reporter once asked Willie why he robbed only banks.

"That's where the money is," Willie replied.

The majority of the people holding the purse strings of American government on every level are as good as the average citizen—not any better, not any worse. Their responsibility, however, is much greater. Mistakes in spending and overexpansion have wrecked some of the best-run businesses.

While public welfare is a holy duty, it should not go to the extreme of supporting those who are fully capable of supporting themselves. The citizen pays for every government service he receives. If he does not pay for it personally, other citizens like him pay for it. Government in itself has no inexhaustible bank account. It derives its income solely from its citizens, *for it has no other source of funds but your earnings.*

In the case of one family on relief, the father drew fifty dollars a month for blindness which he said prevented him from working even though it did not interfere with his marksmanship as a hunter. His wife received $114 monthly for dependent children. Her mother was on an old-age pension of fifty dollars, making the family income $214 every month. Two of the "dependent children" turned out to be able-bodied men. Neither would take a job for fear that their employment might remove their mother from the relief rolls.

This is an exception, to be sure. But it's an example of the abuse that can take place.

Find Out the Facts

A few months ago a taxpayer wrote his congressman complaining about the "tremendous increase in costs of the operations of the various federal departments since 1940." He felt that something was wrong. The reply sent to him was an eye opener. He readily saw from the facts sent him that he had oversimplified the problem and jumped to a conclusion. He had imagined that it would be a simple matter to slash costs here and there. To his amazement he learned that 89 per cent of the 1952 budget would be applied to the following three areas of expense:

1. NATIONAL SECURITY. Defense measures here and overseas, precipitated by the world emergency, call for an outlay of fifty-two and one half billion dollars, as against one and one half billion dollars in 1940.

2. VETERANS SERVICES AND BENEFITS, which are determined by the number of those who served in the armed forces, and who chose to avail themselves of rights and benefits granted in basic law, would use up another five billion dollars, in contrast to ½ billion dollars in 1940. (There are at present 3,168,000 compensation and pension cases, 1 million veterans in education and training, an average daily patient load in veterans hospitals and homes of 138,-000 and nearly five million veterans receiving out-patient examinations and treatments.)

3. INTEREST ON DEBT. This is a continuing cost that has arisen almost entirely from past wars in which the country has engaged. Outlay for interest alone now amounts to nearly six billion dollars, whereas in 1940 the total expense on interest was slightly over one billion dollars. This interest on the debt is paid to those individuals and groups who own United States government bonds or who have in any way made loans to the government.

The above three items, therefore, account for a little over sixty-three billion dollars of the seventy-one and one half billion total budget for 1952. This means that only one ninth, or slightly more than eight billion dollars, is devoted to all remaining government projects and programs. But even a 10-per-cent saving in this eight billion dollars would amount to almost a billion dollars.

Economizing is not the only factor to be considered. Even more it is determining how to spend the right amount for the right thing. There are large and pressing needs to be faced as well as fixed charges we have to meet. Each of them should be constantly studied for possible readjustments.

Even with the most cautious and well-intentioned planning, serious and possibly irreparable mistakes can be made in the field of economy. All the more reason then why this particular matter of government spending should be of deep concern for one and all. Failing to balance our budget can be a real threat to our economic stability.

Don't ever take the attitude there is nothing you can do about it, that you are too small to count. Time and time again one person, making his voice heard, has been able to bring about a more efficient apportionment of funds in city, state, and federal government and not infrequently to cause those who are administering public funds to curtail unnecessary expenses.

Extremes must be avoided, of course. The country can be wrecked not only by those who would consciously or unconsciously spend us into disaster, but also by those who lose a sense of proportion and expose us to catastrophe by insisting on unreasonable economies.

If carried too far, penny-wise and pound-foolish economy could cripple our program for national defense. It could seriously hamper the legitimate expenditure for social benefits that the nation is under obligation to provide for its people. Overemphasis on saving could also block and possibly undermine the development of our natural resources and expansion of our economic system. A happy balance between saving and spending is the ideal that all should constantly strive to attain. But here is never an excuse for waste.

Still another danger can come from those who misunderstand or give their own interpretations to matters of public concern without being fully versed in all the essential details regarding them. For instance, when public hearings were being held in New York City regarding the raising of the fare on the city-owned subways from five to ten cents, one woman insisted on taking the stand. Once there, she vigorously demanded that all subway rides be free.

An important service can be rendered, however, by those who made reasonable protests.

The man who was presiding over the hearings asked her how she ever arrived at the conclusion. Without a moment's hesitation she blurted out: "Why not? After all, it's a free country!"

You Pay the Taxes

A private tax and business law organization in Chicago figured out recently that a twenty-nine-year-old man, now earning $4,300 a year, can look forward to paying throughout the years a minimum of $34,700 in taxes by the time he is sixty-five. It is up to you to decide whether your taxes are too much or too little. You are the taxpayer. You have a financial stake in the country. For better or for worse, it is your business.

In approaching the problem, you can apply the same sense of proportion and economy that you use in your home, shop, factory, office, in buying a suit of clothes or taking a vacation. No matter how urgent the need or how much you desire it, you know you should not spend any more than you have or at least avoid going into a debt that you cannot carry.

You would do well always to keep in mind the derivation of the word "economy." It comes from the Greek word "*oikonomia.*" The first part of it, "*oiko,*" means "house," and the second half, "*nomia,*" signifies "putting in order." In short, the more you try to put the same order into government spending that you insist on in your own home, the better off the country and everybody in it is likely to be.

It's Your Pocketbook

Literally, none of us can afford to be indifferent toward government spending. The money comes out of our pockets just as surely as the butcher's bill or the milkman's weekly collection. Some of our taxes, like the income tax, are clearly visible. Others, like the tax on your car, your television set, and your wife's handbag are not so apparent. It is important to remember that these hidden taxes that we notice the least are the ones we pay the most—everyday of the year. They show up just the same in the government tax collections at the end of the year. And it is your pocket they come from. That is reason enough for you to be concerned.

As Americans, we have no excuse for failing to have the best government in the world. It was founded upon Divine Truth, and we pay more for it than any people ever paid for government. *God does not long bless those who are negligent or wasteful.* As a government supported by workers each doing his rightful share, we could be unsurpassed.

Protect That Heritage

We have Providence to thank for the immense natural resources of America. We also have a great debt to our forefathers. As God-fearing and hard-working individuals, they bequeathed us a precious heritage. But they left us a far greater gift—an emphasis on moral standards by which most Americans live.

They had a sense of dependence on God and a destiny beyond the grave. They were conscious that "not by bread alone" does man live. The things of the spirit came first. At the same time, a certain amount of physical well-being is essential for the spirit. Man is a combination of body and soul.

From our pioneer ancestors we received this heritage. What have we done with it? Have we sought to maintain and increase it? Or have we through carelessness or indifference dissipated it?

It is difficult to visualize the early Americans taking a complacent attitude toward the black marketeer, for example.

Much more readily can we imagine them dealing swiftly with anyone who sought to victimize the public for his personal gain.

More Than Money

Perhaps because America has so many physical advantages, we are in constant danger of becoming too avaricious as well as too materialistic. The primary emphasis in our national life more and more seems to fall upon the acquisition of money; lots of money, acquired in a hurry.

One government worker who held a key post in the purchase of war supplies became shocked at the callousness of a few who were profiteering at the taxpayers' expense. Ignoring the personal trouble it would cause him, he decided to take a stand against the profiteering.

When an order for critical materials came through at a price 60 per cent above the market figure and involving an outlay of one million dollars he refused to sign the requisition. Trouble began immediately. His department head, who to judge from his actions was implicated in the deal, wasted no time in trying to get him removed from his post. The government worker, however, fought back. To the surprise of everyone, he made it stick and the requisition remained unsigned. It cost him nothing more than his signature. To the taxpayers it meant a saving of $600,000 on just one order.

While there are many people in government who are working hard to bring about economies, there also seems to be a constant tendency in the opposite direction. Only recently Senator Paul H. Douglas, Democrat of Illinois, took notice of this and recommended a drastic means of cutting the high cost of government, saying: "We should reduce the number of Government employees . . . We should reduce the present five and one-fifth weeks of vacation for governmental employees and the three-weeks-a-year sick leave . . . We should cut out extras such as expensive automobiles . . . There is one Undersecretary who has a car for himself, uses one for his wife and one for his kids when they come home from school for a vacation."

It is of the utmost importance that those with a sound economic sense exert every bit of influence they can in the realm of public affairs. In these times particularly every such person is vitally needed.

A girl who was an efficiency expert in a large New York corporation gave up her job and went to Washington. Unfortunately she withdrew too soon from a spot where she could have performed an important public service. After giving up her job she complained bitterly about waste and inefficiency. "Why should anyone ever want to work for the government? It's the most frustrating experience I've ever had . . . and I certainly wouldn't encourage anyone else to try it," she told a group of several girls, some of whom were ready to make application for similar jobs in government.

Any way you look at it, this girl could have done a great service by remaining in government. If things are as bad as she claims, all the more reason for her to stay in and make them better. Even one good person withdrawing from a bad situation only makes it worse. "The absent are always wrong."

It was bad enough that she herself left, but even more serious that she discouraged other would-be workers who were well qualified to bring about savings in government.

Providentially, another girl from the same group returned on a visit from her job in Washington. When confronted with the "frustrating" part of working for the government, she replied, "Well, it is true that there are lots of things that don't run as smoothly as they should. There's plenty of red tape and a certain amount of waste. But that's why I'm staying. I want to do something about it. Just like the Christophers say 'Purpose makes the difference.' I never even think of it as frustrating. I'm just thinking of all the good that can be done if we get a lot of people in there working to better our government. While I thought I was making a big sacrifice when I left my former job, I can honestly say that my job with the government is the most fascinating work I've ever known because I am in a position to fight for the best interests of everybody. And it's only the beginning!"

The more people who are fired with love of God and country and who have a healthy respect for economical efficiency get into the running of government, the safer the country will be.

To Summarize

As individuals we have two big legacies, one of moral wealth and one of material wealth. Our enemies seek to destroy us by destroying those two inheritances. Shall we aid our enemies with our own indifference and apathy to what our government does? This is obviously not the answer. You can help supply the right answer. As an individual citizen you should seek to strengthen the moral and economic foundations of your government. You can do much to encourage the spiritual and material stability that it must have in order to endure.

3   BETTER MEN MAKE BETTER GOVERNMENT

Those who would change the world for the better have these factors in common: faith in God, faith in their fellow men, and faith in themselves. The three are interlocked, and one cannot prevail without the other. Many Americans have mislaid their faith in themselves, in their ability to surmount the obstacles of everyday living. The individual's faith in himself and others derives from his faith in God and his belief that a Higher Power will assist him in time of need.

Perhaps the greatest weakness in America today is lack of faith. Those who believe in nothing outside themselves seldom do much even for themselves. They easily drift into agnosticism and atheism. The unfortunate result of this trend is lack of purpose and lack of hope. Confusion, frustration and cynicism is too often the consequence.

Mr. Otto E. Koegel, general counsel for 20th-Century Fox Films, made an interesting observation on this in a talk he gave at the American University in Washington, D. C., on February 23, 1950. He said: "Atheism is philosophical illiteracy. It shows an utter inadequacy itself to solve the problems of the world and life . . .

"It limps terribly in its own account of things, talking fluently about science but failing miserably to formulate a theory of life and morals.

"Any strength it has lies in its criticism of faith rather than in any positive recommendation of its own unfaith.

"Atheists are a maze of contradictions.

"While believing they are free, they are not free; believing themselves responsible, they are not.

"They assume the possibility of logical thought processes and deny the assumption as totally unfounded."

A government investigator told us that the majority of those who succumbed to the half-truths of Communism in America during the last twenty-five years were people who had no basic religious beliefs of their own or who had strayed away from a faith in God.

Together with this breakdown in faith, another strange trend has developed. Those who hate God are showing great vision and untiring zeal in reaching to the far ends of the earth with that hatred. On the other hand, those who believe in Him are more and more thinking only of themselves, their own personal convenience and the little world in which they live.

In Denver recently two young men made decisions of the kind that weaken America instead of strengthening it.

One was a young lawyer of unusual character and ability. He was offered an important post in the State Department. It gave him the opportunity to make a valuable and much-needed contribution to his country's welfare. After thinking the offer over casually, he decided against accepting it.

"First of all," he told a friend, "it would mean moving to Washington. Then it means leaving my old friends and making new ones. Third, it would mean a slight cut in income, and I don't feel I can afford it."

All three reasons went directly to his personal convenience.

Not one word did he utter about the chance offered him to serve his country when the nation needed his services.

The second young man was of a wealthy family. A friend of his told us about this individual's shift to Communism. Despite the latter's American background he had become devoted to Communism while in college. In his case the cause of advancing Communism proved more compelling than his own self-regard. As part of his development as a Communist, he had broken away from religion years before. Here is his reasoning:

"I believe in Communism and I want to do something about it. That's why I turned down a business opportunity in Denver with fine prospects and decided to enter a teachers' college. As a teacher, I felt I would have a wide opportunity to impart my ideas on government to young students. The students in turn will put these ideas into practice."

A Weakness the World Over

Here we have two young men both residents of the same city, who chose opposite courses. The loyal American, offered an opportunity to strengthen his nation, declined it. The Communist made his own opportunity, at personal sacrifice, to advance the cause he believed in.

Governments all over the world are being weakened by the work of these two types. Those with real capacity for improvement remain on the side lines, doing nothing. Those least fitted to play an active part in American life get themselves into positions of influence where they can spread their poison.

Once a sufficient number of people realize that the future of their country is at stake we will have a better atmosphere. Once these people realize that they personally and individually, can do something about betterment, we will see an improvement.

Maywood, New Jersey, is a small community in the rolling countryside just west of the Palisades. In a recent primary election only 354 of its 3,413 eligible voters went to the polls.

That means that roughly 90 per cent of the registered voters abandoned their franchise to the 10 per cent who actually voted. This 10 per cent decided the election. In figures, 178 voters, one more than half the total voters, were in a position to affect the lives of 3,413.

On the face of it, this shows a dangerous trend toward minority rule in a democracy where the majority is supposed to rule. Those who voted in Maywood were chiefly members of political parties with special interests. Those who stayed away were for the most part loyal and responsible people who "just couldn't be bothered."

Bigger Responsiblities Ahead

Judging from the 1950 census, this country will grow at the rate of 25,000,000 every ten years. We are now a country of 150,697,361 souls. By 1960 the population should increase to 175,000,000. This prospective growth should remind us that our present duties and responsiblities will be multipied in the future with every year of growth. If we fail to discharge our responsiblities toward present duty, who will look out for the 25,000,000 future Americans?

Government on the local, city, county, state, and national levels stands as our biggest business today. The number of public employees in all branches of government now runs above six and on half million persons. In federal government alone, civilian employees number more than 2,400,000. *Roughly one American in every twenty-three holds a government post of some sort.* In pay, government employees receive about nineteen and one half billion dollars a year or some one and one half billion dollars each month.

The number of civilians in government employ has shown a phenomenal growth in the last twenty years with the build-up of the armed forces and the extension of health and welfare benefits. Is the number too large? It's *your* business to find out. It's *your* country.

With the growth of population, we must expect an expansion of government services as well. How much is too much should be your concern and that of every other citizen.

It is to your interest also to see that the best type of worker is found in every level of government. To be a vital force for good government, the employee must feel a deep sense of responsibility to God and his fellow man. He needs the sense of dedication to a vocation which distinguishes the parent, a religious leader, a teacher, or any other figure who molds the destiny of others.

Always There

God has implanted in all men's hearts and souls a bit of missionary desire to serve others as well as self. Though many go through life without discovering that fact, the desire to serve is always there waiting to be put to work. Because that is true, we may cherish the hope that even the most apathetic may be spurred into useful activity. The desire to serve has no age limits. It is found in all the ages of man.

District Attorney Miles F. McDonald of Brooklyn, who exposed a sinister alliance between gamblers and some policemen, received a "Knickerbocker Award" from New York City's Fusion party for his good work. At the presentation dinner he heard another award recipient call for a "higher code of ethics" for people in government. In accepting the award the Brooklyn prosecutor said:

"It is a sad commentary on the state of public affairs when a man like me gets an award for doing no more than the duty he has sworn to do.

"Ninety-five per cent, or maybe 99 per cent of the people in public life are performing faithful service to the nation each day of their lives. Their work is not the conspicuous kind that gets a public award, but they are the unsung heroes of government.

"We have a code. Our code is the Ten Commandments, which apply just as much in public life as in private life. It is a very simple code. But it works."

Obstacles to Be Faced

Rudolph Halley, former counsel to the Kefauver Senate Crime Investigating Committee, was another award winner. He told the diners what one man could do in government.

"Before our investigation," he said, "the public believed that the stories about criminals in politics were fiction. We spent $250,000 and one year's time proving that those stories were fact, not fiction.

"But before we could begin, Senator Kefauver had to fight almost alone on the floor of the Senate for his belief that the proof could be shown. He had a long, uphill struggle, until finally he prevailed."

District Attorney Frank S. Hogan of New York, whom we have mentioned earlier in connection with the basketball scandals, was another award winner. Let's listen to him:

"The individuals who head any group establish the moral tone of that group. That applies to the family, the army, a school system, a political party, or any other group.

"Law enforcement suffers from the unwillingness of people to come in with evidence of a crime. Somehow the word 'informer' has come to be identified with the word 'snoop' or 'bluenose.'

"If we do not want our laws enforced, why employ policemen, prosecutors, and the courts to enforce them? If we do want them enforced, let the members of the public play their part by coming forward with evidence of crime. The very persons who complain most loudly of graft and corruption do nothing about it, even when they have direct evidence against the grafters. Apathy, fear, and self-interest are the enemies of law enforcement.

"You can help. Our basic laws cannot be enforced without your help. It is a primary duty of citizenship to come forward with evidence of those crimes which attack the foundations of our society. Without your help, these crimes will never be eradicated."

Lincoln's Inspiration

Opportunity for great service did not come to Abraham Lincoln until he was forty-five. Then he tackled a task that would have broken the heart of a lesser man. His country torn by regional strife and on the brink of war, he would have failed without an inner purpose greater than himself. Lincoln's utterances show his abiding faith in divine guidance, and it was from that conviction that he drew the inspiration to continue against almost insurmountable obstacles.

Perhaps the greatest tribute to him came from his enemies in the South, who mourned his death even more than his friends in the North.

From President down to the lowliest clerk, any position in government service is a position of trust. That is true whether the office is village alderman, city policeman, file clerk in the Atomic Eenergy Commission, or membership in the United States Senate. The public expects each of its servants to make public service his first consideration, with the proper compensation warranted by the job a secondary consideration. Reversing the order results in a dangerous situation.

Task 1: To Deepen the Sense of Purpose
in Government Workers

First and most important is the task of developing a higher sense of purpose in those who serve us in every section of government.

Many workers are beset by the lack of vision and sense of purpose that afflicts most of us, but we feel many of them could easily be roused. Much government work is divided into compartments, so that one individual handles the same type of work each day. This assembly-line routine tends to stifle individual thought and initiative to the point where the work becomes mechanical.

At that point it is up to the worker himself to find his own release from boredom. One of the best releases is to find where his work originates before it comes to him, then to follow it on up to the top. Once he sees how his own small part works as a factor in a major operation, his work will take on new interest and new challenge.

From this it is an easy step to broaden his usefulness on a higher level and derive the inner satisfaction of accomplishment which comes with achievement. But it is impossible to climb the ladder unless we see where the next rung is. We must see it first, before reaching for it.

Unless the individual employee has an inner purpose, he may, through neglect and indifference, fall into an attitude which is dangerous because of its lack of purpose.

A one-time Communist spy courier testified in the Alger Hiss trial that most of the secret information he obtained from Washington did not come from Communist party members. Rather, it came from presumably loyal employees who saw no harm in giving it to him. With their dull and deadened sense of values, they said:

"Well, what difference can it make if I do give him the information?"

These givers of secret information honestly did not mean to betray their country. If put to the test, most of them would be as loyal as the most patriotic American. It was their fuzzy thinking that betrayed them, and probably a "fed-up" feeling with their daily jobs had much to do with it. They were incapable of seeking out an opportunity for service to their country. Instead they took the opportunity to do it a disservice. In this connection we can say once more:

"People who stand for nothing fall for anything."

This weakness in many people goes all the way back to Original Sin. Danger and excitement carry their appeals even if the end is wicked. Tedium and boredom are our prisons, and each human being tries to escape them. For those who were fooled by Communists, the sin is not that they sought excitement to replace boredom. Their fault is that they failed to see opportunities for excitement and exuberance in working for their own country and doing a patriotic job well.

Take the case of David Greenglass, a young ex-army sergeant who stole atomic-bomb secrets from his post in Los Alamos for the Soviet Union. Greenglass was an average young man in appearance, not much different from most young men. After spying for Soviet Russia successfully for years, he was caught. Before his associates were tried he decided to testify as a government witness against them. When he described how he worked on just one small part of the atom bomb, a defense lawyer suggested:

"But that was just a little thing, wasn't it?"

"Sure," Greenglass agreed. "But a lot of 'little things' go into something big." The "big thing" was the atom bomb.

With a lovely young wife and two small children, Greenglass was sentenced to fifteen years in prison. He is paying a heavy price for his loyalty because it came to him very late.

The little things and the little people do make a difference. Purpose is the quality that makes the difference. If you start today to know where you're going and why, you become a different person immediately. Your life takes on new significance which percolates down to the smallest things you do. Why learn it the hard way—the Greenglass way—when the road of high purpose lies open before you?

What is the primary qualification for joining the Federal Bureau of Investigation as a special agent? Schooling? Yes, partly. Training as a lawyer or as an accountant? Useful, but still not the controlling factor. Youth, intelligence, physical stamina? All good, but secondary. The No. 1 qualification is character.

These special agents are moderately paid, hard-working, unacclaimed individuals often compelled to face extreme danger. They see little of their families because their hours of duty vary from day to day. Even when they complete a case, the individual agents seldom get any recognition outside their own agency. Most of the time they work alone and each man is on his own.

"Why do they do it?" you ask.

They do it for the most part because they know they are performing a great public service. It is this inner purpose which animates them and overrides considerations of personal comfort.

Devotion to duty, scrupulous honesty, loyalty, humanity, responsibility, and fair dealing with all are qualities which could well be encouraged in every section of government.

Task 2: To Guide into Government Those with High Purpose

With its rapid employee turnover, government needs a constant flow of replacements. Of what type and caliber are these people to be? It is to the general interest to see that they are of the best obtainable. Where will we find them?—in families, churches, and schools.

Government itself seeks the best individuals for its service. If it cannot find them, of necessity it falls back on the second best or third best. With an employee turnover of about 10 per cent monthly, government loses up to sixty-five thousand employees each month and must replace them with sixty-five thousand newcomers.

Families, schools, and churches would do well to guide their best products toward government as a career. Much work in this direction is already being done, but more is needed. In 1950 the State Department was forced to resort to newspaper advertising to recruit people for well-paid foreign-service jobs from $4,600 to $10,000 a year, plus living allowances abroad. Fifteen possible fields of service were listed for those between twenty-one and forty-five. After four weeks most of the jobs were still unfilled. This example in itself shows how many of us neglect the opportunities to live useful lives in government service.

Colleges and universities now offer technical training in public administration, but technique is not enough. The well-qualified public servant will have in addition a humanity based on his love of God and country. Government is essentially a human enterprise, since it deals primarily with people. Those who administer it must therefore have a love of humanity as part of their basic equipment.

Task 3: To Eliminate Those Harmful to Good Government

We believe your main effort should be bent toward encouraging higher purpose in those already in government and developing it in prospective government employees. If these steps can be accomplished, the elmination of people harmful to government will be almost automatic.

People harmful to government may be deliberately so, because of a prior allegiance to communism, or haphazardly so because of incompetence or indifference. In either case the welfare of the great mass of one hundred and fifty million Americans must be the paramount consideration.

We must protect the innocent government employee against smears and unfair treatment. Great caution should be taken lest harm be done to the wrong person. But where a question of loyalty is involved, there must be no pussyfooting. Loyalty is an absolute quality, either black or white. There is no such thing as "divided loyalty." Unless government employees can pass a loyalty test without question, there should be no place in government for them. The welfare and safety of one hundred and fifty million Americans demands that as an absolute minimum.

America can suffer quite as much from the fuzzy-minded, the extravagant, the wasteful and the indifferent employee as it can from the disloyal employee. Our own national interest demands that we replace such types with intelligent, diligent, and competent individuals.

To sum up, we can get better men in government by encouraging a deeper sense of high purpose among government employees; by guiding into government those who by character and background are best fitted for it; and lastly by using every legitimate effort to eliminate parasites and subversives from the public pay roll.

4 HOPE FOR THE FUTURE

We have already seen how in our most vital elections a relatively small number of votes can "make the difference." Those who vote on one side or the other, of course, play their part in the outcome. But the crucial vote, the deciding vote, is usually cast by a small group of voters.

In our quest for better government, success can also be achieved by a relatively few persons. If only a small additional percentage of Americans can be convinced that good government is worth fighting for, they alone will be sufficient to add the strength it needs and thereby eradicate the weak spots. In reaching this conclusion we have tried to keep a sense of proportion which considers all aspects.

The need for a sense of proportion is well illustrated in the tale of the two tramps.

These two vagabonds were trudging along a dusty country road one hot day when one of them suddenly spied what looked like a bottle of wine at the roadside. Apparently it had been left there by a group of picnickers who had forgotten to take it along. Parched with thirst, the first tramp didn't waste a moment. His eyes alight with expectation, he made a dive for the bottle. When he lifted it, his joy turned quickly to disappointment. Turning to his companion, he said: "Wouldn't you know! It's half empty!"

The second tramp was not a bit taken aback. He was more realistic. His philosophy was to take things as they were and not as someone might think they should be. As he uncorked the bottle he said to his friend: "Yeah. But it's half full too!"

The first tramp smiled again!

Do Something

In times of national crisis we many become more impatient than ever with any evidence of ineptness by our government. This is understandable, because a national emergency tends to stretch our patience to the breaking point. But at such times it is more important than ever to keep our heads and our sense of balance.

In the Army, infantry platoon leaders are trained under pressure corresponding to the pressure they may expect to find on the battlefield. The cardinal rule in a tight situation is: "Do something!"

The Army reasons that some form of "doing" is better than none at all.

Develop Your Capacity

It is in the same spirit that we should develop our attitude toward government. We may justifiably have no patience with the "do-nothing" employee or official. But merely complaining accomplishes little if anything. Doing something about it, however little, is far more constructive—and hopeful.

Numerous statesmen of long experience have said that the American people, once they understand a situation, can be counted on to solve it. We are a great nation, possessed of enormous power in peacetime production. Yet, in sudden emergency, this production can be tripled or quadrupled quickly. In large part this power to expand quickly comes down to the individual who is willing to devote more of his time and effort to the work.

We know we have this power, because we used it toward victory in World War II. After the war we lapsed back into "business as usual" life. But the reserve power for quick expansion is still within us. Each individual can devote more of his time and effort to better government just as he devoted it to better production.

First, we must see clearly that the big problem ahead is to develop the capacity of people already in government, and secondly, to attract to government more people of demonstrated or potential ability. Far back of these two aims, but still important, is the continuing need to use every fair means to eliminate undesirables from the public pay rolls in all communities.

We need to renew our faith in God, faith in ourselves, and

faith in others. We need to realize all over again the priceless advantages of American citizenship and the duties and obligations that go with it.

The Price of Freedom

A young musician who plays on radio and television programs was recently summoned for jury duty. The call came at a bad time for him, because as a free-lance he had just lined up several lucrative engagements. On his jury he found some utility-company employees whose firms paid their regular salaries while they served on the jury. Unlike the musician, their income was guaranteed.

"Serving on this jury is probably going to cost me a nice job on a regular television program," the young musician said. "I can pick up some odd jobs at night, but I still have to be in the courtroom at nine-thirty every morning. But the law says each man accused is entitled to a trial by a jury. That's why I don't feel that I should try to get out of jury duty. If I were on trial myself, I would want every right the law provides for me."

Here is a case that involved personal sacrifice for the sake of upholding an American democratic principle. Far too many of us have permitted defeatism and a cynical attitude to dull our minds. In some circles it is considered "reactionary" to be loyal, "old-fashioned" to be patriotic, and "quaint" to uphold a decent moral code.

Fortunately for the welfare of our country, the great majority of Americans still believe in loyalty, patriotism, and honesty, however little they may put these qualities into practice.

Tribute Indeed

Only recently a newspaperman describing the reactions of American soldiers newly arrived in Korea said:

"They weren't here long before they came to the conclusion that our government, with all its defects, is about the best government anyone could have."

Another tribute to the part that America is privileged by

God to play in the world of today came in the haunting plea of a poor, tired old woman on the island of Malta.

Last year as we were about to sail from Malta to Naples she came up to a group of us on the dock and said, "You Americans have been generous in sending us food and many other things. But all we ask of you is peace. That can be America's biggest contribution to the world."

If you had been there and heard her as we did, your heart would have gone out to her and the millions like her everywhere. There she was standing on the edge of that tiny island, which in the first two years of World War II had been bombed thirty-five hundred times—an average of almost five bombings a day! Yet she didn't ask for the luxuries or the everyday comforts as we understand them. All she wanted was peace. She still stands out in my mind as the symbol of countless hundreds of millions of helpless people who are looking almost in vain for someone to lead them. To bring peace to even one such person would be a privilege.

Another evidence of faith in the role that the United States can play was seen in the bequest made a few months ago to the government. A Greek emigrant left five thousand dollars in saving bonds to the United States Government in gratitude for what this country had done for him. This appreciative donor, Matheos E. Aligizakis, came to this country from Crete about forty years ago. He earned most of the money operating a candy store in New London, Connecticut, and saved it dollar by dollar.

All of us are likewise indebted, under God, to our nation. One of the best ways for each of us to show his gratitude is to play a personal role in strengthening our government now and for the future. There will be great hope for our country and our world if you—and enough like you—take the time and trouble to do this.

Points to Check on

To show our appreciation in a practical manner it would be well for all of us frequently to include the following in our *examination of conscience:*

1. To what extent am I participating in the betterment of my government?

2. Do I hold up service in government as an honorable occupation to which the best citizens should aspire or do I use every opportunity to belittle and ridicule those who undertake a career in government?

3. Do I indiscriminately brand everyone in goverment as a "grafter" or a "crook" and thus slander those who are doing as honest and efficient a job as most others who earn their living outside of government?

4. Am I constantly harping on defects in government and seldom if ever drawing attention to the service it renders each and all of us?

5. Do I merely sit on the side lines with a "let George do it" attitude or am I constantly striving to take a hand in the preservation and development of the God-given liberties which it is my business to protect?

6. Do I expect others to provide first-class government at a smaller salary than I myself would take for the same job?

7. Do I make the bad mistake of labeling every forward move in correcting social abuses as Communism, Fascism, or Socialism, or do I distinguish intelligently and objectively between infringement of goverment upon the individual and normal public service?

8. Do I run the risk of oversimplifying delicate and complicated problems of government by jumping to hasty conclusions that solve nothing and do little more than muddy the waters further?

9. Do I make it a practice to disagree without getting disagreeable when discussing weaknesses and difficulties of government?

10. Do I become so preoccupied with the little issues that I miss the big ones?

11. Am I so wrapped up in my own interests that I overlook what is best for the country and everybody in it?

12. Do I make the unfortunate mistake of waiting for the perfect person to fill a government job and therefore run

the risk of letting it go to the worst because the ideal never appears?

13. Do I put the objectives of a political party, a business, or an organization before the best interests of the country?

14. Do I take a special delight in stirring up trouble or in making a bad situation worse, when I should be using my time and energy to bring conflicting interests together?

This habit of examining your own position can contribute much to purifying your motives and to stimulating you to a keener sense of personal and individual responsibility.

The more conscious you are that you are important and that you have a mission to perform, the more likely you are to plunge into the mainstream of life instead of withdrawing to the backwaters, there to wait hopelessly for the world to fall on top of you.

It's Your World

You not only have a stake in the future but you can do much to shape that future for yourself and for everybody else. In a very real sense, *you* can change the world. For as America goes during the next five or ten years, so probably will go the world.

It is a breath-taking challenge. It is a great time to be alive —to participate, even in the smallest way, in the fashioning of a future that can bring the love and truth of Christ to America and the world—to play a part in helping not only Americans but all mankind for our time and for eternity.

The very desire and attempt to enrich the lives of others will make your life the richer, for "it is a more blessed thing to give rather than to receive" (Acts 20:35).

It's Your Job

Now, specifically, what can *you* do for *your* government? You should shoulder the obligations of an individual citizen. Unless *you* do your part, you and your fellow Americans suffer.

What are the duties and obligations of good citizenship? For clarity, we will list them briefly.

1. First and most important, you have a duty to register and vote in elections on all levels from local to national.
2. You have a duty to keep yourself informed on happenings in government so that you may vote intelligently on men and issues.
3. You have a duty to serve on a grand jury or a trial jury if called for service. You should not place your personal convenience above your obligation to uphold the jury system and the principle of a fair and open trial for all persons accused of crime.
4. In wartime you may be called to the colors. You have a duty to serve, since America can draw its armed strength only from its own population.
5. You have a personal obligation to see that all branches of your government—local, state, and national—are staffed by the best Americans, whether they are elected, appointed, or retained by Civil Service. Even if you cannot dedicate your own life to public service, you can help others to undertake this important responsiblity. Be sure to work in some capacity in some part of your local, state, or national government at some period of your life. This will do much to give you a sense of belonging.
6. You have an obligation to count your blessings as an American citizen, and a duty to do more than complain and criticize: to act toward correcting what you believe to be evils in government.

The Sum of Good Government

Yes, government is *your* business. Beyond that, it is your privilege to protect and fortify it for the benefit of countless others. Remember, your children and your children's children will benefit or suffer by your actions today.

In his inaugural address in Washington, D.C., on March 4, 1801, Thomas Jefferson gave what he regarded as "the sum of good government." You should refer to it frequently, as should all Americans interested in renewing the source of American strength.

They would do well to ponder long over his statement that Americans were "enlightened by a benign religion, professed indeed and practiced in various forms, yet all of them inculcating honesty, truth, temperance, gratitude, and the love of man; acknowledging and adoring an over-ruling Providence, which by all its dispensations proves that it delights in the happiness of man here and his greater happiness hereafter; with all these blessings, what more is necessary to make us a happy and proseprous people?"

Jefferson felt that this admonition was necessary, for he immediately continued with this pointed reminder; "Still one thing more, fellow citizens—— A wise and frugal government, which shall restrain men from injuring one another, which shall leave them otherwise free to regulate their own pursuits of industry and improvement, and shall not take from the mouth of labor the bread it has earned—— This is the sum of good government."

Learn It and Live It

For a present-day description of "the sum of good government," we can think of nothing more accurate and simple than the oath of loyalty to the United States which we have quoted earlier. It bears repetition, for it is only a few lines long. Americans can do two things in relation to this oath. For themselves, they can memorize it and live according to it. For others, they can demand that each officeholder who takes it must live up to it. Here it is:

"I do solemnly swear that I will support and defend the Constitution of the United States against all enemies, foreign and domestic; that I will bear true faith and allegiance to the same; and that I take this obligation freely, without any mental reservation, or purpose of evasion: So help me God."

In these few words we have the key to godlike and decent living as members of the greatest government on earth, the American form of democratic government.

APPENDIX

1 THE DECLARATION OF INDEPENDENCE

In Congress, July 4, 1776
THE UNANIMOUS DECLARATION
OF THE THIRTEEN
UNITED STATES OF AMERICA

When in the Course of human events, it becomes necessary for one people to dissolve the political bands which have connected them with another, and to assume among the powers of the earth, the separate and equal station to which the Laws of Nature and of Nature's God entitle them, a decent respect to the opinions of mankind requires that they should declare the causes which impel them to the separation.

We hold these truths to be self-evident, that all men are created equal, that they are endowed by their Creator with certain unalienable Rights, that among these are Life, Liberty and the pursuit of Happiness.—That to secure these rights,

*PUBLISHER'S NOTE With the exception of the section headings and footnotes to the Constitution, which were added for the reader's convenience, we have adhered to the original text of the documents, preserving the original spelling and capitalization.

We wish to thank the Library of Congress for permission to use the section headings and footnotes from its publication, *The Constitution of the United States.*

Governments are instituted among Men, deriving their just powers from the consent of the governed.—That whenever any Form of Government becomes destructive of these ends, it is the Right of the People to alter or to abolish it, and to institute new government, laying its foundation on such principles and organizing its powers in such form, as to them shall seem most likely to effect their Safety and Happiness. Prudence, indeed, will dictate that Governments long established should not be changed for light and transient causes; and accordingly all experience hath shewn, that mankind are more disposed to suffer, while evils are sufferable, than to right themselves by abolishing the forms to which they are accustomed. But when a long train of abuses and usurpations, pursuing invariably the same Object evinces a design to reduce them under absolute Despotism, it is their right, it is their duty, to throw off such Government, and to provide new Guards for their future security.—Such has been the patient sufferance of these Colonies; and such is now the necessity which constrains them to alter their former Systems of Government. The history of the present King of Great Britain is a history of repeated injuries and usurpations, all having in direct object the establishment of an absolute Tyranny over these States. To prove this, let Facts be submitted to a candid world.

He has refused his Assent to Laws, the most wholesome and necessary for the public good.

He has forbidden his Governors to pass Laws of immediate and pressing importance, unless suspended in their operation till his Assent should be obtained; and when so suspended, he has utterly neglected to attend to them.

He has refused to pass other Laws for the accommodation of large districts of people, unless those people would relinquish the right of Representation in the Legislature, a right inestimable to them and formidable to tyrants only.

He has called together legislative bodies at places unusual, uncomfortable, and distant from the depository of their public

Records, for the sole purpose of fatiguing them into compliance with his measures.

He has dissolved Representative Houses repeatedly, for opposing with manly firmness his invasions on the rights of the people.

He has refused for a long time, after such dissolutions, to cause others to be elected; whereby the Legislative powers, incapable of Annihilation, have returned to the People at large for their exercise; the State remaining in the meantime exposed to all the dangers of invasion from without, and convulsions within.

He has endeavored to prevent the population of these States; for that purpose obstructing the Laws for Naturalization of Foreigners; refusing to pass others to encourage their migrations hither, and raising the conditions of new Appropriations of Lands.

He has obstructed the Administration of Justice, by refusing his Assent to Laws for establishing Judiciary powers.

He has made Judges dependent on his Will alone, for the tenure of their offices, and the amount and payment of their salaries.

He has erected a multitude of New Offices, and sent hither swarms of Officers to harrass our people, and eat out their substance.

He has kept among us, in times of peace, Standing Armies without the Consent of our legislatures.

He has affected to render the Military independent of and superior to the Civil power.

He has combined with others to subject us to a jurisdiction foreign to our constitution and unacknowledged by our laws, giving his Assent to their Acts of pretended Legislation:—For quartering large bodies of armed troops among us:—For protecting them, by a mock Trial, from punishment for any Murders which they should commit on the Inhabitants of these States:—For cutting off our Trade with all parts of the world: —For imposing Taxes on us without our Consent:—For depriving us in many cases, of the benefits of Trial by Jury:—

For transporting us beyond Seas to be tried for pretended offenses:—For abolishing the free System of English Laws in a neighbouring Province, establishing therein an Arbitrary government, and enlarging its Boundaries so as to render it at once an example and fit instrument for introducing the same absolute rule into these Colonies:—For taking away our Charters, abolishing our most valuable Laws, and altering fundamentally the Forms of our Governments:—For suspending our own Legislatures and declaring themselves invested with power to legislate for us in all cases whatsoever.

He has abdicated Government here, by declaring us out of his Protection and waging War against us.

He has plundered our seas, ravished our Coasts, burnt our towns, and destroyed the lives of our people.

He is at this time transporting large Armies of foreign Mercenaries to compleat the works of death, desolation and tyranny, already begun with circumstances of Cruelty and perfidy scarcely paralleled in the most barbarous ages, and totally unworthy the Head of a civilized nation.

He has constrained our fellow Citizens taken Captive on the high Seas to bear Arms against their Country, to become the executioners of their friends and Brethren, or to fall themselves by their Hands.

He has excited domestic insurrections amongst us, and has endeavoured to bring on the inhabitants of our frontiers, the merciless Indian Savages, whose known rule of warfare, is an undistinguished destruction of all ages, sexes and conditions. In every stage of these Oppressions We have Petitioned for Redress in the most humble terms: Our repeated Petitions have been answered only by repeated injury. A Prince, whose character is thus marked by every act which may define a Tyrant, is unfit to be the ruler of a free people. Nor have We been wanting in attentions to our British brethren. We have warned them from time to time of attempts by their legislature to extend an unwarrantable jurisdiction over us. We have reminded them of the circumstances of our emigration and settlement here. We have appealed to their native justice and magnanimity, and we have conjured them by the ties of our common kindred to disavow these usurpations, which, would inevitably interrupt our connections and correspondence. They too have been deaf to the voice of justice and of consanguinity. We must, therefore, acquiesce in the necessity, which denounces our Separation, and hold them, as we hold the rest of mankind, Enemies in War, in Peace Friends.

We, therefore, the Representatives of the United States of America, in General Congress, Assembled, appealing to the Supreme Judge of the world for the rectitude of our intentions do, in the Name, and by authority of the good People of these Colonies, solemnly publish and declare, That these United Colonies are, and of Right ought to be, Free and Independent States; that they are Absolved from all Allegiance to the British Crown, and that all political connection between them and the State of Great Britain, is and ought to be totally dissolved; and that as Free and Independent States, they have full Power to levy War, conclude Peace, contract Alliances, establish Commerce, and do all other Acts and Things which Independent States may of right do. And for the support of this Declaration, with a firm reliance on the protection of divine Povidence, we mutually pledge to each other our Lives, our Fortunes and our sacred Honor.

NEW HAMPSHIRE

Josiah Bartlett
Wm. Whipple
Matthew Thornton

MASSACHUSETTS

John Hancock
Saml. Adams
John Adams
Robt. Treat Paine
Elbridge Gerry

RHODE ISLAND

Step. Hopkins
William Ellery
Fras. Hopkinson
John Hart
Abra. Clark

VIRGINIA

George Wythe
Richard Henry Lee
Th. Jefferson

Benja. Harrison
Thos. Nelson, jr.
Francis Lightfoot Lee
Carter Braxton

SOUTH CAROLINA

Edward Rutledge
Thos. Heyward, Junr.
Thomas Lynch, Junr.
Arthur Middleton

MARYLAND

Samuel Chase
Wm. Paca
Thos. Stone
Charles Carroll of
    Carrollton

CONNECTICUT

Roger Sherman
Sam'el Huntington
Wm. Williams
Oliver Wolcott

NEW YORK

Wm. Floyd
Phil. Livingston
Frans. Lewis
Lewis Morris

GEORGIA

Button Gwinnett
Lyman Hall
Geo. Walton

PENNSYLVANIA

Robt. Morris
Benjamin Rush
Benja. Franklin
John Morton
Geo. Clymer
Jas. Smith
Geo. Taylor
James Wilson
Geo. Ross

NORTH CAROLINA

Wm. Hooper
Joseph Hewes
John Penn

DELAWARE

Cæsar Rodney
Geo. Read
Tho. M'Kean

NEW JERSEY

Richd. Stockton
Jno. Witherspoon

The signatures are arranged according to states, not in the
order in which they appeared on the original document.

2 THE CONSTITUTION OF THE UNITED STATES OF AMERICA

Preamble

We the People of the United States, in Order to form a more perfect Union, establish Justice, insure domestic Tranquility, provide for the common defence, promote the general Welfare, and secure the Blessings of Liberty to ourselves and our Posterity, do ordain and establish this Constitution for the United States of America.

ARTICLE I

SECTION 1.*Legislative Powers* All legislative Powers herein granted shall be vested in a Congress of the United States, which shall consist of a Senate and House of Representatives.

SECTION 2 *House of Representatives, How Constituted, Power of Impeachment* The House of Representatives shall be composed of Members chosen every second Year by the People of the several States, and the Electors in each State shall have the Qualifications requisite for Electors of the most numerous Branch of the State Legislature.

No Person shall be a Representative who shall not have attained to the Age of twenty five Years, and been seven Years a Citizen of the United States, and who shall not, when elected, be an Inhabitant of that State in which he shall be chosen.

Representatives and direct Taxes shall be apportioned among the several States which may be included within this Union, according to their respective Numbers, which shall be determined by adding to the whole Number of free Persons, including those bound to Service for a Term of Years, and excluding Indians not taxed, three fifths of all other Persons.[1] The actual Enumeration shall be made within three Years after the first Meeting of the Congress of the United States,

[1]*Modified by Amendment XIV, Section 2.*

and within every subsequent Term of ten Years, in such Manner as they shall by Law direct. The Number of Representatives shall not exceed one for every thirty Thousand, but each State shall have at Least one Representative; and until such enumeration shall be made, the State of New Hampshire shall be entitled to chuse three, Massachusetts eight, Rhode-Island and Providence Plantations one, Connecticut five, New-York six, New Jersey four, Pennsylvania eight, Delaware one, Maryland six, Virginia ten, North Carolina five, South Carolina five, and Georgia three.

When vacancies happen in the Representation from any State, the Executive Authority thereof shall issue Writs of Election to fill such Vacancies.

The House of Representatives shall chuse their Speaker and other Officers; and shall have the sole Power of Impeachment.

SECTION 3 *The Senate, How Constituted, Impeachment Trials* The Senate of the United States shall be composed of two Senators from each State, chosen by the Legislature thereof, for six Years; and each Senator shall have one Vote.

Immediately after they shall be assembled in Consequence of the first Election, they shall be divided as equally as may be into three Classes. The Seats of the Senators of the first Class shall be vacated at the Expiration of the second Year, of the second Class at the Expiration of the fourth Year, and of the third Class at the Expiration of the sixth Year, so that one third may be chosen every second Year; and if Vacancies happen by Resignation, or otherwise, during the Recess of the Legislature of any State, the Executive thereof may make temporary Appointments until the next Meeting of the Legislature, which shall then fill such Vacancies.[2]

No Person shall be a Senator who shall not have attained to the Age of thirty Years, and been nine Years a Citizen of

[2]*Provisions changed by Amendment XVII.*

the United States, and who shall not, when elected, be an Inhabitant of that State for which he shall be chosen.

The Vice President of the United States shall be President of the Senate, but shall have no Vote, unless they be equally divided.

The Senate shall chuse their other Officers, and also a President pro tempore, in the Absence of the Vice President, or when he shall exercise the Office of President of the United States.

The Senate shall have the sole Power to try all Impeachments. When sitting for that Purpose, they shall be on Oath or Affirmation. When the President of the United States is tried the Chief Justice shall preside: And no Person shall be convicted without the Concurrence of two thirds of the Members present.

Judgment in Cases of Impeachment shall not extend further than to removal from Office, and disqualification to hold and enjoy any Office of honor, Trust or Profit under the United States: but the Party convicted shall nevertheless be liable and subject to Indictment, Trial, Judgment and Punishment, according to law.

SECTION 4 *Election of Senators and Representatives* The Times, Places and Manner of holding Elections for Senators and Representatives, shall be prescribed in each State by the Legislature thereof; but the Congress may at any time by Law make or alter such Regulations, except as to the Places of chusing Senators.

The Congress shall assemble at least once in every Year, and such Meeting shall be on the first Monday in December, unless they shall by Law appoint a different Day.[3]

SECTION 5 *Quorum, Journals, Meetings, Adjournments* Each House shall be the Judge of the Elections, Returns and Qualifications of its own Members, and a Majority of each shall

[3]*Provision changed by Amendment XX, Section 2.*

constitute a Quorum to do Business; but a smaller Number may adjourn from day to day, and may be authorized to compel the Attendance of absent Members, in such Manner, and under such Penalties as each House may provide.

Each House may determine the Rules of its Proceedings, punish its Members for disorderly Behaviour, and, with the Concurrence of two thirds, expel a Member.

Each House shall keep a Journal of its Proceedings, and from time to time publish the same, excepting such Parts as may in their Judgment require Secrecy; and the Yeas and Nays of the Members of either House on any question shall, at the Desire of one fifth of those Present, be entered on the Journal.

Neither House, during the Session of Congress, shall, without the Consent of the other, adjourn for more than three days, not to any other Place than that in which the two Houses shall be sitting.

SECTION 6 *Compensation, Privileges, Disabilities* The Senators and Representatives shall receive, a Compensation for their Services, to be ascertained by Law, and paid out of the Treasury of the United States. They shall in all Cases, except Treason, Felony and Breach of the Peace, be privileged from Arrest during their Attendance at the Session of their respective Houses, and in going to and returning from the same; and for any Speech or Debate in either House, they shall not be questioned in any other Place.

No Senator or Representative shall, during the Time for which he was elected, be appointed to any civil Office under the Authority of the United States, which shall have been created, or the Emoluments whereof shall have been encreased during such time; and no Person holding any Office under the United States, shall be a Member of either House during his Continuance in Office.

SECTION 7 *Procedure in Passing Bills and Resolutions* All Bills for raising Revenue shall originate in the House of Representatives; but the Senate may propose or concur with Amendments as on other Bills.

Every Bill which shall have passed the House of Representatives and the Senate, shall, before it become a Law, be presented to the President of the United States; If he approve he shall sign it, but if not he shall return it, with his Objections to that House in which it shall have originated, who shall enter the Objections at large on their Journal, and proceed to reconsider it. If after such Reconsideration two thirds of that House shall agree to pass the Bill, it shall be sent, together with the Objections, to the other House, by which it shall likewise be reconsidered, and if approved by two thirds of that House, it shall become a Law. But in all such Cases the Votes of both Houses shall be determined by yeas and Nays, and the Names of the Persons voting for and against the Bill shall be entered on the Journal of each House respectively. If any Bill shall not be returned by the President within ten Days (Sundays excepted) after it shall have been presented to him, the Same shall be a Law, in like Manner as if he had signed it, unless the Congress by their Adjournment prevent its Return, in which Case it shall not be a Law.

Every Order, Resolution, or Vote to which the Concurrence of the Senate and House of Representatives may be necessary (except on a question of Adjournment) shall be presented to the President of the United States; and before the Same shall take Effect, shall be approved by him, or being disapproved by him, shall be repassed by two thirds of the Senate and House of Representatives, according to the Rules and Limitations prescribed in the Case of a Bill.

SECTION 8 *Powers of Congress* The Congress shall have Power To lay and collect Taxes, Duties, Imposts and Excises, to pay the Debts and provide for the common Defence and general Welfare of the United States; but all Duties, Imposts and Excises shall be uniform throughout the United States;

To borrow Money on the credit of the United States;

To regulate Commerce with foreign Nations, and among the several States, and with the Indian Tribes;

To establish an uniform Rule of Naturalization, and uniform Laws on the subject of Bankruptcies throughout the United States;

To coin Money, regulate the Value thereof, and of foreign Coin, and fix the Standard of Weights and Measures;

To provide for the Punishment of counterfeiting the Securities and current Coin of the United States;

To establish Post Offices and post Roads;

To promote the Progress of Science and useful Arts, by securing for limited Times to Authors and Inventors the exclusive Right to their respective Writings and Discoveries;

To constitute Tribunals inferior to the supreme Court;

To define and punish Piracies and Felonies committed on the high Seas, and Offences against the Law of Nations;

To declare War, grant Letters of Marque and Reprisal, and make Rules concerning Captures on Land and Water;

To raise and support Armies, but no Appropriation of Money to that Use shall be for a longer Term than two Years;

To provide and maintain a Navy;

To make Rules for the Government and Regulation of the land and naval Forces;

To provide for calling forth the Militia to execute the Laws of the Union, suppress Insurrections and repel Invasions;

To provide for organizing, arming, and disciplining, the Militia, and for governing such Part of them as may be employed in the Service of the United States, reserving to the States respectively, the Appointment of the Officers, and the Authority of training the Militia according to the discipline prescribed by Congress;

To exercise exclusive Legislation in all Cases whatsoever, over such District (not exceeding ten Miles square) as may, by Cession of particular States, and the Acceptance of Congress, become the Seat of the Government of the United States, and to exercise like Authority over all Places purchased by the Consent of the Legislature of the State in which the

Same shall be, for the Erection of Forts, Magazines, Arsenals, dock-Yards, and other needful Buildings;—And

To make all Laws which shall be necessary and proper for carrying into Execution the foregoing Powers, and all other Powers vested by this Constitution in the Government of the United States, or in any Departmental or Officer thereof.

SECTION 9 *Limitations upon Powers of Congress* The Migration or Importation of such Persons as any of the States now existing shall think proper to admit, shall not be prohibited by the Congress prior to the Year one thousand eight hundred and eight, but a Tax or duty may be imposed on such Importation, not exceeding ten dollars for each Person.

The Privilege of the Writ of Habeas Corpus shall not be suspended, unless when in Cases of Rebellion or Invasion the public Safety may require it.

No Bill of Attainder or ex post facto Law shall be passed.

No Capitation, or other direct, Tax shall be laid, unless in Proportion to the Census or Enumeration herein before directed to be taken.

No Tax or Duty shall be laid on Articles exported from any State. No Preference shall be given by any Regulation of Commerce or Revenue to the Ports of one State over those of another nor shall Vessels bound to, or from, one State, be obliged to enter, clear, or pay Duties in another.

No Money shall be drawn from the Treasury, but in Consequence of Appropriations made by Law; and a regular Statement and Account of the Receipts and Expenditures of all public Money shall be published from time to time.

No Title of Nobility shall be granted by the United States: And no Person holding any Office of Profit or Trust under them, shall, without the Consent of the Congress, accept of any present, Emolument, Office, or Title, of any kind whatever, from any King, Prince, or foreign State.

SECTION 10 *Restrictions upon Powers of States* No State shall enter into any Treaty, Alliance, or Confederation; grant

Letters of Marque and Reprisal; coin Money; emit Bills of Credit; make any Thing but gold and silver Coin a Tender in Payment of Debts; pass any Bill of Attainder, ex post facto Law, or Law impairing the Obligation of Contracts, or grant any Title of Nobility.

No State shall, without the Consent of the Congress, lay any Imposts or Duties on Imports or Exports, except what may be absolutely necessary for executing its inspection Laws: and the net Produce of all Duties and Imposts, laid by any State on Imports or Exports, shall be for the Use of the Treasury of the United States; and all such Laws shall be subject to the Revision and Controul of the Congress.

No State shall, without the Consent of Congress, lay any Duty of Tonnage, keep Troops, or Ships of War in time of Peace, enter into any Agreement or Compact with another State, or with a foreign Power, or engage in War, unless actually invaded, or in such imminent Danger as will not admit of delay.

ARTICLE II

SECTION 1 *Executive Power, Election, Qualifications of the President* The executive Power shall be vested in a President of the United States of America. He shall hold his Office during the Term of four Years, and, together with the Vice President, chosen for the same Term, be elected, as follows

Each State shall appoint, in such Manner as the Legislature thereof may direct, a Number of Electors, equal to the whole Number of Senators and Representatives to which the State may be entitled in the Congress: but no Senator or Representative, or Person holding an Office of Trust or Profit under the United States, shall be appointed an Elector.

The Electors shall meet in their respective States, and vote by Ballot for two Persons, of whom one at least shall not be an Inhabitant of the same State with themselves. And they shall make a List of all the Persons voted for, and of the Number of Votes for each; which List they shall sign and certify, and transmit sealed to the Seat of the Government of the United States, directed to the President of the Senate. The President of the Senate shall, in the Presence of the Senate and House of Representatives, open all the Certificates, and the Votes shall then be counted. The Person having the greatest Number of Votes shall be the President, if such Number be a Majority of the whole Number of Electors appointed; and if there be more than one who have such Majority, and have an equal Number of Votes, then the House of Representatives shall immediately chuse by Ballot one of them for President; and if no Person have a Majority, then from the five highest on the List the said House shall in like Manner chuse the President. But in chusing the President, the Votes shall be taken by States, the Representation from each State having one Vote; A quorum for this Purpose shall consist of a Member or Members from two thirds of the States, and a Majority of all the States shall be necessary to a Choice. In every Case, after the Choice of the President, the Person having the greatest Number of Votes of the Electors shall be the Vice President. But if there should remain two or more who have equal Votes, the Senate shall chuse from them by Ballot the Vice President.[4]

The Congress may determine the Time of chusing the Electors, and the Day on which they shall give their Votes; which Day shall be the same throughout the United States.

No Person except a natural born Citizen, or a Citizen of the United States, at the time of the Adoption of this Constitution, shall be eligible to the Office of President; neither shall any Person be eligible to that Office who shall not have attained to the Age of thirty five years, and been fourteen Years a Resident within the United States.

In Case of the Removal of the President from Office, or of his Death, Resignation, or Inability to discharge the Powers and Duties of the said Office, the Same shall devolve on the Vice President, and the Congress may by Law provide for the Case of Removal, Death, Resignation or Inability, both of the

[4]*Provisions superseded by Amendment XII.*

President and Vice President, declaring what Officer shall then act as President, and such Officer shall act accordingly, until the Disability be removed, or a President shall be elected.

The President shall, at stated Times, receive for his Services, a Compensation, which shall neither be increased nor diminished during the Period for which he shall have been elected, and he shall not receive within that Period any other Emolument from the United States, or any of them.

Before he enter on the Execution of his Office, he shall take the following Oath or Affirmation:—"I do solemnly swear (or affirm) that I will faithfully execute the Office of President of the United States, and will to the best of my Ability, preserve, protect and defend the Constitution of the United States."

SECTION 2 *Powers of the President*   The President shall be Commander in Chief of the Army and Navy of the United States, and of the Militia of the several States, when called into the actual Service of the United States; he may require the Opinion, in writing, of the principal Officer in each of the executive Departments, upon any Subject relating to the Duties of their respective Offices, and he shall have Power to grant Reprieves and Pardons for Offences against the United States, except in Cases of Impeachment.

He shall have Power, by and with the Advice and Consent of the Senate, to make Treaties, provided two thirds of the Senators present concur; and he shall nominate, and by and with the Advice and Consent of the Senate, shall appoint Ambassadors, other public Ministers and Consuls, Judges of the supreme Court, and all other Officers of the United States, whose Appointments are not herein otherwise provided for, and which shall be established by Law: but the Congress may by Law vest the Appointment of such inferior Officers, as they think proper in the President alone, in the Courts of Law, or in the Heads of Departments.

The President shall have Power to fill up all Vacancies that may happen during the Recess of the Senate, by granting

Commissions which shall expire at the End of their next Session.

SECTION 3 *Powers and Duties of the President* He shall from time to time give to the Congress Information of the State of the Union, and recommend to their Consideration such Measures as he shall judge necessary and expedient; he may, on extraordinary Occasions, convene both Houses, or either of them, and in Case of Disagreement between them, with Respect to the Time of Adjournment, he may adjourn them to such Time as he shall think proper; he shall receive Ambassadors and other public Ministers; he shall take Care that the Laws be faithfully executed, and shall Commission all the Officers of the United States.

SECTION 4 *Impeachment* The President, Vice President and all civil Officers of the United States, shall be removed from Office on Impeachment for, and Conviction of, Treason, Bribery, or other high Crimes and Misdemeanors.

ARTICLE III

SECTION 1 *Judicial Power, Tenure of Office* The judicial Power of the United States, shall be vested in one supreme Court, and in such inferior Courts as the Congress may from time to time ordain and establish. The Judges, both of the supreme and inferior Courts, shall hold their Offices during good Behaviour, and shall, at stated Times, receive for their Services, a Compensation, which shall not be diminished during their Continuance in Office.

SECTION 2 *Jurisdiction* The judicial Power shall extend to all Cases, in Law and Equity, arising under this Constitution, the Laws of the United States, and Treaties made, or which shall be made, under their Authority;—to all Cases affecting Ambassadors, other public Ministers and Consuls;—to all Cases of admiralty and maritime Jurisdiction;—to Controversies to which the United States shall be a Party;—to Controversies between two or more States;—between a State and Citizens of another State;—between Citizens of different States,—between Citizens of the same State claiming Lands under Grants of different States, and between a State, or the Citizens thereof, and foreign States, Citizens or Subjects.[5]

In all Cases affecting Ambassadors, other public Ministers and Consuls, and those in which a State shall be Party, the supreme Court shall have original Jurisdiction. In all the other Cases before mentioned, the supreme Court shall have appellate Jurisdiction, both as to Law and Fact, with such Exceptions, and under such Regulations as the Congress shall make.

The Trial of all Crimes, except in Cases of Impeachment, shall be by Jury; and such Trial shall be held in the State where the said Crimes shall have been committed; but when not committed within any State, the Trial shall be at such Place or Places as the Congress may by Law have directed.

SECTION 3 *Treason, Proof and Punishment* Treason against the United States, shall consist only in levying War against them, or in adhering to their Enemies, giving them Aid and Comfort. No Person shall be convicted of Treason unless on the Testimony of two Witnesses to the same overt Act, or on Confession in open Court.

The Congress shall have Power to declare the Punishment of Treason, but no Attainder of Treason shall work Corruption of Blood, or Forfeiture except during the Life of the Person attained.

ARTICLE IV

SECTION 1 *Faith and Credit among States* Full Faith and Credit shall be given in each State to the public Acts, Records, and judicial Proceedings of every other State. And the Congress may by general Laws prescribe the Manner in which such Acts, Records and Proceedings shall be proved, and the Effect thereof.

[5]*Clause changed by Amendment XI.*

SECTION 2 *Privileges and Immunities, Fugitives* The Citizens of each State shall be entitled to all Privileges and Immunities of Citizens in the several States.

A Person charged in any State with Treason, Felony, or other Crime, who shall flee from Justice, and be found in another State, shall on Demand of the executive Authority of the State from which he fled, be delivered up, to be removed to the State having Jurisdiction of the Crime.

No Person held to Service or Labour in one State, under the Laws thereof, escaping into another, shall, in Consequence of any Law or Regulation therein, be discharged from such Service or Labour, but shall be delivered up on Claim of the Party to whom such Service or Labour may be due.

SECTION 3 *Admission of New States* New States may be admitted by the Congress into this Union; but no new State shall be formed or erected within the Jurisdiction of any other State; nor any State be formed by the Junction of two or more States, or Parts of States, without the Consent of the Legislatures of the States concerned as well as of the Congress.

The Congress shall have Power to dispose of and make all needful Rules and Regulations respecting the Territory or other Property belonging to the United States; and nothing in this Constitution shall be so construed as to Prejudice any Claims of the United States, or of any particular State.

SECTION 4 *Guarantee of Republican Government* The United States shall guarantee to every State in this Union a Republican Form of Government, and shall protect each of them against Invasion; and on Application of the Legislature, or of the Executive (when the Legislature cannot be convened) against domestic Violence.

ARTICLE V

Amendment of the Constitution The Congress, whenever two thirds of both Houses shall deem it necessary, shall propose Amendments to this Constitution, or, on the Application of the Legislatures of two thirds of the several States, shall call a Convention for proposing Amendments, which, in either Case, shall be valid to all Intents and Purposes, as Part of this Constitution, when ratified by the Legislatures of three fourths of the several States, or by Conventions in three fourths thereof, as the one or the other Mode of Ratification may be proposed by the Congress; Provided that no Amendment which may be made prior to the Year One thousand eight hundred and eight shall in any Manner affect the first and fourth Clauses in the Ninth Section of the first Article; and that no State, without its Consent, shall be deprived of its equal Suffrage in the Senate.

ARTICLE VI

Debts, Supremacy, Oath   All Debts contracted and Engagements entered into, before the Adoption of this Constitution, shall be as valid against the United States under this Constitution, as under the Confederation.

This Constitution, and the Laws of the United States which shall be made in Pursuance thereof; and all Treaties made, or which shall be made, under the Authority of the United States, shall be the supreme Law of the Land; and the Judges in every State shall be bound thereby, any Thing in the Constitution or Laws of any State to the Contrary notwithstanding.

The Senators and Representatives before mentioned, and the Members of the several State Legislatures, and all executive and judicial Officers, both of the United States and of the several States, shall be bound by Oath or Affirmation, to support this Constitution; but no religious Test shall ever be required as a Qualification to any Office or public Trust under the United States.

ARTICLE VII

Ratification and Establishment   The Ratification of the Conventions of nine States, shall be sufficient for the Establishment of this Constitution between the States so ratifying the Same.

Done in Convention by the Unanimous Consent of the States present the Seventeenth Day of September in the year of our Lord one thousand seven hundred and Eighty seven and of the Independence of the United States of America the Twelfth[6] *In witness whereof We have hereunto subscribed our Names,*

Presidt. and deputy from Virginia
G.° Washington—

NEW HAMPSHIRE	MASSACHUSETTS
John Langdon	Nathaniel Gorham
Nicholas Gilman	Rufus King

CONNECTICUT	PENNSYLVANIA
Wm. Saml. Johnson	B. Franklin
Roger Sherman	Thomas Mifflin
	Robt. Morris
NEW YORK	Geo. Clymer
	Thos. FitzSimons
Alexander Hamilton	Jared Ingersoll
	James Wilson
NEW JERSEY	Gouv. Morris

NEW JERSEY	
Wil. Livingston	DELAWARE
David Brearley	
Wm. Paterson	Geo. Read
Jona. Dayton	Gunning Bedford jun

[6]*The Constitution was submitted on September 17, 1787, by the Constitutional Convention, was ratified by the conventions of several states at various dates up to May 29, 1790, and became effective on March 4, 1789.*

John Dickinson
Richard Bassett
Jaco. Broom

MARYLAND

James McHenry
Dan of St. Thos.
   Jenifer
Danl. Carroll

VIRGINIA

John Blair
James Madison Jr.

NORTH CAROLINA

Wm. Blount
Richd. Dobbs Spaight
Hu. Williamson

SOUTH CAROLINA

J. Rutledge
Charles Cotesworth
   Pinckney
Charles Pinckney
Pierce Butler

GEORGIA
William Few
Abr. Baldwin

3 THE BILL OF RIGHTS (THE FIRST TEN AMENDMENTS TO THE CONSTITUTION)

AMENDMENT I

Freedom of Religion, of Speech, and of the Press   Congress shall make no law respecting an establishment of religion, or prohibiting the free exercise thereof; or abridging the freedom of speech, or of the press; or the right of the people peaceably to assemble, and to petition the Government for a redress of grievances.

AMENDMENT II

Right to Keep and Bear Arms   A well regulated Militia being necessary to the security of a free State, the right of the people to keep and bear Arms, shall not be infringed.

AMENDMENT III

Quartering of Soldiers   No Soldier shall, in time of peace be quartered in any house, without the consent of the Owner, nor in time of war, but in a manner to be prescribed by law.

AMENDMENT IV

Security from Unwarrantable Search and Seizure   The right
of the people to be secure in their persons, houses, papers,
and effects, against unreasonable searches and seizures, shall
not be violated, and no Warrants shall issue, but upon prob-
able cause, supported by Oath or affirmation, and particularly
describing the place to be searched, and the persons or things
to be seized.

AMENDMENT V

Rights of Accused in Criminal Proceedings   No person shall
be held to answer for a capital, or otherwise infamous crime,
unless on a presentment or indictment of a Grand Jury, except
in cases arising in the land or naval forces, or in the Militia,
when in actual service in time of War or public danger; nor
shall any person be subject for the same offense to be twice
put in jeopardy of life or limb, or shall be compelled in any
criminal case to be a witness against himself, nor be deprived
of life, liberty, or property, without due process of law; nor
shall private property be taken for public use, without just
compensation.

AMENDMENT VI

Right to Speedy Trial, Witnesses, etc.   In all criminal prose-
cutions, the accused shall enjoy the right to a speedy and public trial, by an impartial jury of the State and district wherein
the crime shall have been committed, which district shall have
been previously ascertained by law, and to be informed of the
nature and cause of the accusation; to be confronted with the
witnesses against him; to have compulsory process for obtaining Witnesses in his favor, and to have the Assistance of
Counsel for his defense.

AMENDMENT VII

Trial by Jury in Civil Cases   In Suits at common law, where
the value in controversy shall exceed twenty dollars, the right
of trial by jury shall be preserved, and no fact tried by a jury,

shall be otherwise re-examined in any Court of the United States, than according to the rules of the common law.

AMENDMENT VIII

Bails, Fines, Punishments   Excessive bail shall not be required, nor excessive fines imposed, nor cruel and unusual punishments inflicted.

AMENDMENT IX

Reservation of Rights of the People   The enumeration in the Constitution, of certain rights, shall not be construed to deny or disparage others retained by the people.

AMENDMENT X

Powers Reserved to States or People   The powers not delegated to the United States by the Constitution, nor prohibited by it to the States, are reserved to the States respectively, or to the people.[7]

4   THE FOLLOWING ARE AMENDMENTS ADDED SINCE THE BILL OF RIGHTS

AMENDMENT XI

Restriction of Judicial Power   The Judicial power of the United States shall not be construed to extend to any suit in law or equity, commenced or prosecuted against one of the United States by Citizens of another State, or by Citizens or Subjects of any Foreign State.[8]

[7]*The first ten amendments were all proposed by Congress on September 25, 1789, and were ratified and adoption certified on December 15, 1791.*
[8]*Proposed by Congress on March 4, 1794, and declared ratified on January 8, 1798.*

AMENDMENT XII

Election of President and Vice-President The Electors shall meet in their respective states, and vote by ballot for President and Vice-President, one of whom, at least, shall not be an inhabitant of the same state with themselves; they shall name in their ballots the person voted for as President, and in distinct ballots the person voted for as Vice-President, and they shall make distinct lists of all persons voted for as President, and of all persons voted for as Vice-President, and of the number of votes for each, which lists they shall sign and certify, and transmit sealed to the seat of the government of the United States, directed to the President of the Senate;—The President of the Senate shall, in the presence of the Senate and House of Representatives, open all the certificates and the votes shall then be counted;—The person having the greatest number of votes for President, shall be the President, if such number be a majority of the whole number of Electors appointed; and if no person have such majority, then from the persons having the highest numbers not exceeding three on the list of those voted for as President, the House of Representatives shall choose immediately, by ballot, the President. But in choosing the President, the votes shall be taken by states, the representation from each state having one vote; a quorum for this purpose shall consist of a member or members from two-thirds of the states, and a majority of all the states shall be necessary to a choice. And if the House of Representatives shall not choose a President whenever the right of choice shall devolve upon them, before the fourth day of March next following, then the Vice-President shall act as President, as in the case of the death or other constitutional disability of the President.—The person having the greatest number of votes as Vice-President, shall be the Vice-President, if such number be a majority of the whole number of Electors appointed, and if no person have a majority, then from the two highest numbers on the list, the Senate shall choose the Vice-President; a quorum for the purpose shall consist of two-thirds of the whole number of Senators, and a majority of the whole number shall be necessary to a choice. But no person constitutionally ineligible to the office of President shall be eligible to that of Vice-President of the United States.[9]

AMENDMENT XIII

SECTION 1 *Abolition of Slavery* Neither slavery nor involuntary servitude, except as a punishment for crime whereof the party shall have been duly convicted, shall exist within the United States, or any place subject to their jurisdiction.

SECTION 2 *Power to Enforce This Article* Congress shall have power to enforce this article by appropriate legislation.[10]

AMENDMENT XIV

SECTION 1 *Citizenship Rights Not to Be Abridged by States* All persons born or naturalized in the United States, and subject to the jurisdiction thereof, are citizens of the United States and of the State wherein they reside. No State shall make or enforce any law which shall abridge the privileges or immunities of citizens of the United States; nor shall any State deprive any person of life, liberty, or property, without due process of law; nor deny to any person within its jurisdiction the equal protection of the laws.

SECTION 2 *Apportionment of Representatives in Congress* Representatives shall be apportioned among the several States according to their respective numbers, counting the whole number of persons in each State, excluding Indians not taxed. But when the right to vote at any election for the choice of electors for President and Vice-President of the United States, Representatives in Congress, the Executive

[9]*Proposed by Congress on December 9, 1803; declared ratified on September 25, 1804; supplemented by Amendment XX.*
[10]*Proposed by Congress on January 31, 1865; declared ratified on December 18, 1865.*

and Judicial officers of a State, or the members of the Legislature thereof, is denied to any of the male inhabitants of such State, being twenty-one years of age, and citizens of the United States, or in any way abridged, except for participation in rebellion, or other crime, the basis of representation therein shall be reduced in the proportion which the number of such male citizens shall bear to the whole number of male citizens twenty-one years of age in such State.

SECTION 3 *Persons Disqualified from Holding Office* No person shall be a Senator or Representative in Congress, or elector of President and Vice-President, or hold any office, civil or military, under the United States, or under any State, who, having previously taken an oath, as a member of Congress, or as an officer of the United States, or as a member of any State legislature, or as an executive or judicial officer of any State, to support the Constitution of the United States, shall have engaged in insurrection or rebellion against the same, or given aid or comfort to the enemies thereof. But Congress may by a vote of two-thirds of each House, remove such disability.

SECTION 4 *What Public Debts Are Valid* The validity of the public debt of the United States, authorized by law, in cluding debts incurred for payment of pensions and bounties for services in suppressing insurrection or rebellion, shall not be questioned. But neither the United States nor any State shall assume or pay any debt or obligation incurred in aid of insurrection or rebellion against the United States, or any claim for the loss or emancipation of any slave; but all such debts, obligation and claims shall be held illegal and void.

SECTION 5 *Power to Enforce This Article* The Congress shall have power to enforce, by appropriate legislation, the provisions of this article.[11]

[11]*Proposed by Congress on June 13, 1866; declared ratified on July 28, 1868.*

AMENDMENT XV

SECTION 1 *Negro Suffrage* The right of citizens of the
United States to vote shall not be denied or abridged by the
United States or by any State on account of race, color, or
previous condition of servitude.——

SECTION 2 *Power to Enforce This Article* The Congress
shall have power to enforce this article by appropriate legislation.——[12]

AMENDMENT XVI

Authorizing Income Taxes The Congress shall have power
to lay and collect taxes on incomes, from whatever source
derived, without apportionment among the several States,
and without regard to any census or enumeration.[13]

AMENDMENT XVII

Popular Election of Senators The Senate of the United
States shall be composed of two Senators from each State,
elected by the people thereof, for six years; and each Senator
shall have one vote. The electors in each State shall have the
qualifications requisite for electors of the most numerous
branch of the state legislatures.

When vacancies happen in the representation of any State
in the Senate, the executive authority of such State shall issue
writs of election to fill such vacancies: *Provided,* That the
legislature of any State may empower the executive thereof
to make temporary appointments until the people fill the
vacancies by election as the legislature may direct.

This amendment shall not be so construed as to affect the
election or term of any Senator chosen before it becomes valid
as part of the Constitution.[14]

[12]*Proposed by Congress on February 26, 1869; declared ratified on
March 30, 1870.*
[13]*Proposed by Congress on July 12, 1909; declared ratified on February 25, 1913.*
[14]*Proposed by Congress on May 13, 1912; declared ratified on May
31, 1913.*

AMENDMENT XVIII

SECTION 1 *National Liquor Prohibition*   After one year
from the ratification of this article the manufacture, sale, or
transportation of intoxicating liquors within, the importation
thereof into, or the exportation thereof from the United States
and all territory subject to the jurisdiction thereof for beverage
purposes is hereby prohibited.

SECTION 2 *Power to Enforce This Article*   The Congress
and the several States shall have concurrent power to enforce
this article by appropriate legislation.

SECTION 3 *Ratification within Seven Years*   This article shall
be inoperative until it shall have been ratified as an amendment to the Constitution by the legislatures of the several
States, as provided in the Constitution, within seven years
from the date of the submission hereof to the States by the
Congress.[15]

AMENDMENT XIX

Woman Suffrage   The right of citizens of the United States
to vote shall not be denied or abridged by the United States
or by any State on account of sex.

Congress shall have power to enforce this article by appropriate legislation.[16]

AMENDMENT XX

SECTION 1 *Terms of Office*   The terms of the President and
Vice President shall end at noon on the 20th day of January,
and the terms of Senators and Representatives at noon on the
3d day of January, of the years in which such terms would

[15]*Proposed by Congress on December 18, 1917; declared ratified on
January 29, 1919. Repealed by Amendment XXI.*
[16]*Proposed by Congress on June 4, 1919; declared ratified on
August 26, 1920.*

have ended if this article had not been ratified; and the terms of their successors shall then begin.

SECTION 2 *Time of Convening Congress* The Congress shall assemble at least once in every year, and such meeting shall begin at noon on the 3d day of January, unless they shall by law appoint a different day.

SECTION 3 *Death of President Elect* If, at the time fixed for the beginning of the term of the President, the President elect shall have died, the Vice President elect shall become President. If a President shall not have been chosen before the time fixed for the beginning of his term, or if the President elect shall have failed to qualify, then the Vice President elect shall act as President until a President shall have qualified; and the Congress may by law provide for the case wherein neither a President elect nor a Vice President elect shall have qualified, declaring who shall then act as President, or the manner in which one who is to act shall be selected, and such person shall act accordingly until a President or Vice President shall have qualified.

SECTION 4 *Election of the President* The Congress may by law provide for the case of the death of any of the persons from whom the House of Representatives may choose a President whenever the right of choice shall have devolved upon them, and for the case of the death of any of the persons from whom the Senate may choose a Vice President whenever the right of choice shall have devolved upon them.

SECTION 5 Sections 1 and 2 shall take effect on the 15th day of October following the ratification of this article.

SECTION 6 This article shall be inoperative unless it shall have been ratified as an amendment to the Constitution by

the legislatures of three-fourths of the several states within
seven years from the date of its submission.[17]

AMENDMENT XXI

SECTION 1 *National Liquor Prohibition Repealed* The
eighteenth article of amendment to the Constitution of the
United States is hereby repealed.

SECTION 2 *Transportation of Liquor into "Dry" States* The
transportation or importation into any States, Territory, or
possession of the United States for delivery or use therein of
intoxicating liquors, in violation of the laws thereof, is hereby
prohibited.

SECTION 3 This article shall be inoperative unless it shall
have been ratified as an amendment to the Constitution by

conventions in the several States, as provided in the Constitution, within seven years from the date of the submission
hereof to the States by the Congress.[18]

[17]*Proposed by Congress on March 2, 1932; declared ratified on
February 6, 1933.*

[18]*Proposed by Congress on February 20, 1933; declared ratified on
December 5, 1933.*